A HISTORY OF CORNWALL

The Arms of the Borough of Penzance.

THE DARWEN COUNTY HISTORY SERIES

A History of Cornwall

IAN SOULSBY

Drawings by Michelle Richards

Cartography by Ian Soulsby

PHILLIMORE

1986

Published by
PHILLIMORE & CO. LTD.
Shopwyke Hall, Chichester, Sussex

ISBN 0 85033 612 0

Typeset in the United Kingdom by:
Fidelity Processes - Selsey - Sussex

Printed and bound in Great Britain by
Biddles Ltd, Guildford and King's Lynn

Contents

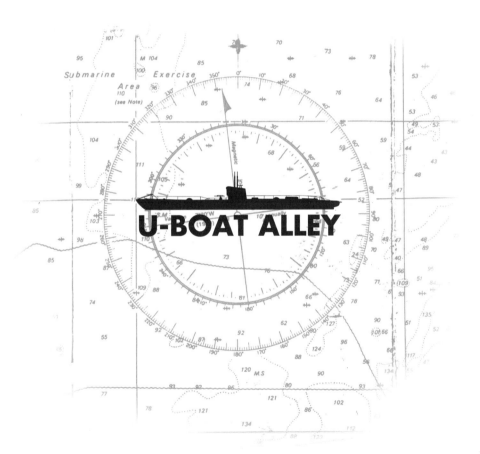

U-BOAT ALLEY

The U-boat War
in the Irish Channel
during World War 1

Roy Stokes

Compuwreck
Gorey,
County Wexford,
Ireland.

Front cover

The wreck of White Star Liner *Justicia*, sunk by German submarines *UB64* and *UB124* in the North Channel, on the 20th July 1918. Built as the *Statendam* (32,234 GRT) at Harland & Wolff Belfast in 1914, for the Holland-America Line.

The b/w photograph was taken at a depth of 70 metres in ambient light by Leigh Bishop

Justicia

Rear cover

Left to right
The Tedcastles flag, flag of the German Imperial Navy, and the house flag of A. Guinness.

Below
A concrete plaque situated on the wall of the Seaman's Mission at Eden Quay. The plaque commemorates the memory of merchant sailors who died in WW1. It is believed to be the only such public commemoration of this historical episode in the Irish shipping industry, erected in Dublin city.

Contents

Acknowledgements.

College of Physicians, Kildare Street, Dublin.
Dublin Port & Docks, Archives, Dublin.
Eircom Museum and Archives
(Tom Wall, Archivist).
Gilbert Library Pearse Street, Dublin.
International Court Of Justice, The Hague, Peace Palace, Netherlands.
Larne Borough Council Museum Service.-
(Joan Morris & Captain Willam Close's World War I photograph collection).
Military Archives, Cathal Bruagh Barracks.-
(Commanders Young and Lang, Archivists).
Maritime Museum Of Ireland.
(Technical assistance courtesy of Joe Varley).

Memorial University of Newfoundland.
National Archives Bishop Street, Dublin.
National Archives, Washington, USA.
National Library, Buenos Aires, Argentina.
National Library, Kildare Street, Dublin.
National Museums and Galleries, Merseyside.
The Imperial War Museum, London.
The Merseyside Maritime Museum.
The Public Records Office at Kew, London.
The Royal College of Physicians, Kildare Street, Dublin.
The Registrar's Office of the International Court of Justice at The Hague.
U-Boat Archives at Cuxhaven, Germany.

I would finally like to make special mention of several friends who have a passion for maritime research. Unlike those who are fortunate enough to domicile in countries that bestow generous research grants, collaboration and an unselfish exchange of material is often the only pragmatic approach to a discipline, which can be quite costly. These colleagues have been of invaluable assistance, not only for contributing material for this book but also by helping with its structure. I feel certain that the book could not have been completed without their generous help.

They are, Desmond Branigan of Marine Research, Dr. Edward Burke of Dublin,
Mr. Kevin Crothers, Dublin, Herbert Hasenbek of Hannover,
Philip Lecane of Monkstown, Cormac Lowth, Dublin, and Paddy O'Sullivan of Cork.

Treating me to a warm visit in his family home, Marcus Beresford was also very kind in providing me with a fascinating background and photographs of his late grandfather Lord Decies.

I would also like to take the opportunity of expressing special thanks to Richard McElwee, who wrote 'The last Voyages of the Waterford Steamers'. This excellent account of the loss of the two Waterford steamers in December 1917, is a marvellous insight into some of the dreadful attacks against shipping that occurred in the Alley. His book pointed the way to some very valuable research material.

The translation of 'Old German' in longhand was a continuing problem but was ably tackled by Aoife McKelvey.

Translation work was also carried out by members of the Goethe Institiute in Dublin, and by Stefan Graf in Frieburgh.

I am also grateful to Marlene from the Maritime Institute, Dun Laoghaire, who was a great help with the translations of Brazilian newspapers. And to Brian Graham of the Liverpool Pilots Association who was very helpful collating information on the loss of the pilots, crew & staff of the *Alfred H. Read*.

For his valuable and precise research at the Public Records in Kew, I would also like to thank researcher Brian Walker.

The Central Remedial Clinic

A special thanks to all the very professional and dedicated staff at the Central Remedial Clinic's Desk Top Publishing Training Unit, Clontarf, Dublin.

The C.R.C. provides training in Desk Top Publishing and In-Plant Printing, and this book production and others like it, are an outcome of the training provided.

General print production and finishing also gives employment to those at the C.R.C.

The Central Remedial Clinic is a Irish National Organisation for the care, treatment and development of children and adults with physical disabilities. Services are provided for people with physical conditions ranging from the very rare to the more familiar, such as cerebral palsy, spina bifida, muscular dystrophy and arthrogryposis.

Lastly, I would like to remember a diver buddy of over twenty years. A friend who has so enthusiastically shared so many searches for stories and shipwrecks around Ireland.

Philip Oglesby R.I.P.

Philip has left us with a space that will not fill, a wealth of treasured and humorous memories from our times together. His aprés dive, 'little devil', for example, being a favourite tipple with all aboard after a dive. Our deepest sympathies will always be with his wife Doreen and his daughters Lynn, Gina and Jen.

First published November 2004
by
Compuwreck
Gorey,
County Wexford,
Ireland.
© Roy Stokes 2004
ISBN: 0-9549186-0-6

This publication has received support from:
The Heritage Council
under the1998 Publication Grant Scheme.

British Library cataloguing publication data.
A CIP catalogue record for this book is available from The British Library.

Book Graphic Design & Layout, Print Reproduction Supervision:
David Lowe.

Photo Restoration:
Brian Duffy.

D.T.P:
John Donnelly.

Technical Assistance:
Donal O'Connor.

Print Production Liaison:
David Bolger.

Editorial Quality:
Sean Donnelly.

All of:
The Central Remedial Clinic
Desktop Publishing Training Unit,
Vernon Avenue,
Clontarf, Dublin 3.

Tel: (01) 805 7439 Fax: (01) 833 5496 email: workshop@crc.ie

Printed in Ireland.

Introduction

The crisis that the U-boats threatened during World War I did not recede until their operational strategies were overwhelmed in 1918. Their final offensive was of an intensity not previously witnessed in the Alley (the waters within a line drawn from Rathlin Island to Islay, and another drawn between Carnsore Point and Milford Haven). The effects of this campaign did not become significant nor apparent until December 1917, and its outcome remained in the balance until the following March.

Nowhere had U-boat operations been more critical than those in the waters to the north and south of Ireland, and later in the war when they began a new intensity in the channels that separate Ireland and England. These were the narrowest areas of the routes, through which the vast majority of Great Britain's food and material was conveyed and by which she could sustain her population and remain a great naval power.

It has been recorded by virtue of rumour and propaganda only, that some sections of the Irish population aided German submarines thus hindering their ultimate defeat.

The ultimate victory over the U-boats is generally only accredited to the efforts of Great Britain and the USA. There is almost no record of the crucial role that Ireland played, through her agriculture and industry, and the actions of her ordinary citizens and sailors, in helping to defeat Germany's attempt at isolating Britain in 1917-18.

Looking back now, it would seem that there were two reasons, which influenced me to write this book. The second of these was the persuasive efforts of Shay Wolfe. When the reader reaches the final chapter, 'A Christmas to Remember', the reasons behind Shay's persistent efforts will become clear. His wish for many years has been to record the story of his grandfather's final voyage on the Dublin steamer *Adela* (685 gross tons.) when he and twenty-three of his shipmates were killed after it was torpedoed in the Irish Sea during World War I.

Quite apart from remembering only his grandfather, Shay and I would like to think that this book might ensure that the thousands of other sailors who suffered a similar fate during World War I, will not be forgotten.

The other reason for this book sprang from a nagging curiosity in subjects which I began to discover were not sufficiently addressed in my previous book, *Death in the Irish Sea* (The Collins Press, 1998.). Amongst these was a need for further explanation as to why America finally abandoned her earlier determination to remain isolated from the war in Europe, and why she ultimately declared war against Germany at the precise moment that she did. Further detailed investigations into the extensive U-boat operations in Irish waters also revealed some startling statistics, and posed additional questions on a whole range of issues, including Germany's attempt at isolating Britain.

Germany had intended that her new U-boats would neutralise the threat posed by Britain's Grand Fleet. Even though she may have failed in this, the threat remained – and so did Britain's great fleet of surface warships. Instead, the U-boats directed their attacks against Britain's enormous fleet of merchant ships anywhere a U-boat could operate, and not least in the seas between Ireland and England.

The U-boat campaign in these channels could by no means be considered a simple attempt at tying up British naval resources with infrequent raids; but was in fact part of a deliberate plan to isolate Britain from a major source of food, material and military recruits in Ireland. The strategy culminated in hundreds of attacks by the U-boats against merchant and naval vessels just outside of many British and Irish channel ports. As well as the loss of hundreds of sailors, these attacks were also responsible for crippling and sinking numerous vessels in sight of the coasts of both countries.

In respect of Ireland, detailed facts concerning these operations have been difficult to assemble, and the history books have seldom mentioned the important part Ireland and its citizens played in this campaign. Nevertheless, an important amount of unpublished material was uncovered for this book, which reveals the actual role that Ireland and its merchant marine did play in home waters during this turbulent period.

Most casual students of the world wars will probably relate to German submarines, or U-boats as they came to be known (after the German description, 'Undersee Boot'), in terms of those represented in the memorable book and film, *Das Boot,* or by film scenes that have attempted to re-create submarine attacks against the Allied convoys in the North Atlantic or American ones in the Pacific. All of these depictions are representative of submarines and actions that occurred during World War II. Some film footage taken by a small number of German submarine commanders during World War I survives to this day, but is very rarely shown, and even when it is, the scenes are sometimes mistakenly represented as being from World War II. The U-boat war that occurred during World War I might thus seem to have retained no identity of its own, and somehow seems to have become blurred with the next world war.

Amongst other factors, this confusion has helped to disguise the fact that a significant amount of the most critical elements of the U-boat campaigns against merchant shipping during World War I occurred in Irish waters, during the winter and spring of 1917–18. It was in these seas, before America could muster and co-ordinate her enormous resources, that the key to a German victory over Britain lay.

To a large degree, the efficient Allied propaganda machine of World War II, which produced so many war movies with well-known Hollywood film stars, and the endless number of subsequent documentaries, has provided an awareness and record of that dark period. But in another sense, this propaganda introduced a certain commercial glamour to the recording of war, and until recent times, helped to draw a line of historic recollection that seldom reaches beyond tributes to those who suffered in the trench warfare of World War I.

Certainly, the inhuman excesses of World War II overshadowed those of the previous great conflict; and became the new benchmark for the horrors of global military engagements. But quite apart from black-and-white films being synonymous with World War I, and the advent of colour films with World War II, it is difficult, even today, to distinguish surviving footage of World War I U-boat operations from that of World War II.

The visual and sometimes historical confusion between the two submarine wars may be due in large part to the fact that the construction of submarines had changed relatively little between the wars. And to the casual observer, a silhouette of an Allied submarine became almost indistinguishable from that of a German one. It may also be difficult for some to believe that the large and heavily armed cruiser submarine, *U-155* (2100 tons), which appears in the illustrations under London's Tower Bridge, was only one of several advanced U-boats that operated off the east coast of America during World War I.

An interesting example of this confusion may be noticed, when one mentions German submarine operations off America during World War I. The listener will almost certainly offer the intervention, 'You mean during World War II', quite unaware of similar U-boat capabilities a quarter of a century earlier. It is estimated that during one six-month period of World War I, six U-boats made the 11,000-mile round trip to the east coast of America and destroyed 200,000 tons of shipping. (A patrol by the Deutchlander *U-151* to the western Atlantic in mid-1918 lasted three months and was responsible for the destruction of 61,000 tons of shipping.)

The advanced capabilities of these submarines were said to have originated in large part from the earlier and general adaptation by manufacturers of a design by the Irishman John Holland, who is credited with inventing the first practical submarine of war.

Holland was said to have sketched his first submarine design while training to be a teacher in Cork, Ireland, in 1859. He moved to the USA in 1872 where he continued with his teaching career and his keen interest in submarine design. Holland received commissions from the US navy for the design and construction of several submarines, and launched Holland II (The 'Fenian Ram') in 1881. This design could fire a torpedo with compressed air.

The Fenian Brotherhood was attracted to Holland's work, with whom they shared hopes of sinking Britain's great naval fleet. They never realised any possibility of such a contest, and the British navy actually purchased modified designs of the Holland submarine. James Dugan in *Man Explores The Sea* 1956, accredits the 'thin, weak-sighted Irish pedagogue' along with several other inventors of the period, with being the 'maker of the modern military submarine'. John Holland did not live to witness the full destructive power of his invention as he died at the outbreak of WW1.

Thousands of Allied merchant ships had either been crippled or destroyed, following the announcement of the first 'Unrestricted U-boat Campaign' in 1915. It became almost certain that if losses were to continue at such unsustainable rates, without some kind of respite or intervention by America, Britain faced defeat by the autumn of 1917. If the political and geographical boundaries of Europe, and elsewhere, were not to be drastically redefined in favour of Germany, some sort of a rescue plan was required. Such a plan was devised, but it was put into effect almost too late to save Britain. The plan involved persuading America to side with the Allies in the war against Germany.

Despite a widespread campaign of sabotage by German agents in America while the latter remained neutral, she for a long time refused to be drawn into the conflict. The timing of the seemingly inevitable intervention, which brought America into the war on the British side, has remained controversial ever since. And for the purposes of this book, some of the political and self-preservationist pressures that were exerted on President Wilson at the time will be discussed.

Some of these influences emanated within the USA from the industries that had much to gain by fuelling the requirements of both sides. Added to these were serious political and military threats emanating from Mexico, the growing restrictions on foreign trade, and a fear of exclusion from the high seas threatened by Germany's expanding – and superior – fleet of submarines. A popular reason often given for America's timely intervention has been Germany's impending victory over Britain. If America was not to have acted, this might have been construed as weakness or an unwillingness to challenge German expansionism. This in turn may have led to an increased German threat from within Mexico, and ultimately by threat already perceived from Japan.

If the threat to democracy by a 'new world order' was to be averted, the inevitable battle for control of the high seas was considered unavoidable. This battle, if delayed, might have presented the US with the possibility of being defeated by the combined fleets of Germany and those of a by then defeated Britain and France.

To enter the war too late might have meant the unthinkable defeat of European and American troops, which may have led to the same conclusion as not siding at all. The alternative was to go to war against Germany at a time when she was most vulnerable; in other words, at a time when victory for America was ensured. And where better to do battle against Germany than on someone else's doorstep, in Europe? The value of fighting a war that may prove in any event inevitable, with material only, on an allie's territory, possibly avoiding committing any of its troops into the fray, has always been considered strategically and politically desirable. A glorious rescue would also procure an American dominance in European affairs far into the future.

The reason for America entering the war at the precise moment that she did may also have simply been the result of prolonged and confused machinations by Wilson's complex mind, or even a simple opportunistic desire on his part to carve a place in history for himself. Any or all of these theories may be true, but could there have been another reason why President Wilson joined America with the Allies in the war against Germany at the precise time that he did? A relatively new theory involves the little known about biological warfare, waged by German saboteurs with anthrax and glanders against man and beasts in north and South America, and other parts of the world. The possibility of a global catastrophe resulting from the deployment of these 'new' and indiscriminate weapons by Germany, may have been only made known in timely revelations to President Wilson by the British secret service.

Although it might seem that biological attacks against man and beast in far-off continents are far removed from the U-boat campaign in the Irish channels, this is not so. They are in fact connected, and it is imperative to demonstrate just how critical the supply of food, materials, and servicemen to Britain had become. Some of the extraordinary lengths Germany went to, included the exploitation of long held Irish hatred for the English,

which is demonstrated in the following German transmission.

[German Foreign Office and General Staff, Berlin, to German Ambassador, Washington]
January 26, 1915.

For Military Attaché. You can obtain particulars as to persons suitable for carrying on sabotage in the U.S. and Canada from the following persons: (1) Joseph MacGarrity, Philadelphia, Pa.;   (2) John P. Keating, Michigan Avenue, Chicago; (3) Jeremiah O'Leary, 16 Park Row, New York.

One and two are absolutely reliable and discreet. Number three is reliable but not always discreet. These persons were indicated by Sir Roger Casement.

In the U.S. sabotage can be carried out in every kind of factory for supplying munitions of war. Railway embankments and bridges must not be touched. Embassy must under no circumstances be compromised. Similar precautions must be taken in regard to Irish pro-German propaganda.

Zimmermann.

In order to try to understand the elements that affected political, military and naval operations in Ireland during World War I, I have relied on additional material retrieved from various sources. Among some brilliant works are, *The Zimmermann Telegram* by Barbara W. Tuchman, *The Life and Letters of Walter Page* by Burton J. Hendrick 1924, *The Enemy Within* by Captain Landau of the British Secret Service, and *Three Wars With Germany* by Major A. Peaslee, who was a distinguished American lawyer and director of the American Courier Service. This last book was co-written with Sir W. Reginald Hall, the head of British Naval Intelligence during World War I. Their accounts of political and military intrigue during World War I are supported by other excellent publications that are listed in the bibliography. Despite researching a wealth of additional material, vital information on some topics remains elusive. This might lend weight to the suggestion that is often made, that history is more convincingly written by those who shape it.

The period was awash with political intrigue. Diplomats often doubled as spies, and 'gentlemen', who were somewhat reminiscent of characters from the television serial 'Riley Ace of Spies', or those from the tales of the mysterious Mata Hari, were to be found at the most respectable social and diplomatic functions. It all smacked of adventures with invisible ink, secret codes and clandestine escapades in exotic countries. The reality was that espionage was a serious business, and with the help of important officials with deep pockets, it was rife in America. Relative to this, the book will endeavour to explain the basis for the 'special relationship', which was developing at this time between England and America, in the form of a 'mutual interest' pact - one that remains in place to this day.

The politics of the period was extremely complex, particularly in America. On the other hand, Germany's reasons for courting Irish nationalism, and their U-boat strategy in the Irish channels, was simple: to isolate and defeat Britain by 'every means in her power'.

Some of the assumptions made in *Death in the Irish Sea* relating to the abilities of German wireless stations and U-boat transmitters, and Britain's ability to intercept and decode these transmissions, were based on material available at the time. These gave only a vague idea of a U-boats' capability to communicate with mainland bases from around the coast of Ireland. Despite further research, many of the facts surrounding the operations of British Naval Intelligence in Room 40, Old Admiralty Building, London, and its key role in intercepting German telegraph and radio messages, remains somewhat difficult to uncover. It will have to suffice for now, to state, that the maximum wireless transmitting range compiled by Royal Naval Intelligence in *German Warships of World War I* (1918) for the later U, UB and UC craft, was approximately 700 miles, with a one-kilowatt transmitter. This maximum range was unreliable, and was obtained by raising the larger hinged aerial masts that were situated fore and aft of the conning tower; an operation which could prove very tricky in rough seas. The range was doubled if the radio was operated during night-time hours, but it was halved by the use of its 'jump' aerial. These aerial wires are often prominently depicted, stretching from stem to stern across the conning tower. Some of the later cruiser U-boats had a two-kilowatt transmitter, which increased the range considerably, and were certainly capable of transmitting and receiving in favourable circumstances from as far as the Western Approaches to land bases.

On the balance of available information, it can be stated that U-boat commanders successfully transmitted to land-based stations in Belgium and Germany from positions around Ireland, particularly during the last eighteen months of the war, but hardly ever did so from the Alley.

Inter-submarine radio communication was routine but contrary to some popular opinion, there was not a great amount of unnecessary chatter between U-boats, particularly in the Alley. As the war progressed, the number of radio directional finding (RDF) stations established around the coasts of Britain and Ireland grew considerably, and resulted in a marked decrease in the number of U-boat transmissions in these areas. Stations on both sides of the Alley could pick up the familiar 'spark' of a U-boat radio transmission, and with the aid of additional 'fixes', could pinpoint the position of a submarine with more accuracy.

During operations, U-boats often waited until they had departed the Alley before making transmissions. If they transmitted within the Alley, making their presence known, they might have to run the gauntlet of the alerted patrols in the Irish channels. The approaches to the English and Fair Isle Channels were also significant areas of radio transmission by U-boats, where they communicated with one another, and with their bases. The main purposes of the transmissions were to relay operational and marine intelligence to another U-boat coming on or going off patrol and to receive 'coming in' instructions.

Even though U-boats were experimenting with underwater communication by 1918, the most significant point in respect of German communications during World War I, was that much of it was being intercepted by Britain and France, and decrypted by the Admiralty in Room 40. Indeed, when one examines British naval 'listening records' of individual U-boats on file in the PRO (Public Records Office, Kew, London.), and even

taking into account that many of the entries were made post operations, one can only come to the conclusion that British abilities in this regard were impressive.

This intelligence was invaluable, but destroying submarines on the basis of this information was not so easy. It must also be said that radio communication was a two-way street, and Allied communications were quite capable of being intercepted and decoded by German wireless stations and U-boat commanders. Unlike Germany's miscalculations of British intelligence in this respect, the British turned their weakness to an advantage, and sometimes purposely mislead the Germans with transmissions of erroneous information.

Although the battle for domination in the field of communications during World War I has received little attention, it is clear that Britain gained an early and vital lead in this area, and exploited it to the full. One particular record, indicating receipt only, by a U-boat in the Irish Sea, is evidenced in the log of *U-62* from her patrol during the night of 14 December 1917:

'Radio message received from Mediterranean station (Oran) for submarines. Submerged and steered east.'

It might seem that the message contained in this transmission was hardly intended for U-boats in the Irish Sea, as it had been transmitted from northern Algeria. An experienced radio operator has since suggested that its recording might only amount to what was known in the trade as 'floggin the log', that is, recording evidence of being on watch. If not, the transmission, or 'message', intended for U-boats in the Alley, might remain unusual. Alternatively, it may have had something to do with the coaling operations begun by the huge US transport ship *Leviathan* on 11 December, and her impending departure from New York for Liverpool with over 9,000 servicemen on 15 December.

Previously the pride of Germany's shipbuilding industry, the *Vaterland* was interred in New York at the beginning of the war and renamed *Leviathan* by the USN when a state of war between the two was declared. At the time of the above transmission she was setting out on her first transatlantic voyage to Liverpool as an American troop carrier, a role that was far from the one intended for the magnificent German liner. Later evidence will strongly suggest, that through the combined efforts of a number of U-boats, attempts were made to sink this liner when she reached the Irish Sea ten days later.

Directly after receiving the message, Commander Hashagen in *U-62* altered his area of intended operations from the Lizard and Land's End, to the Skerries off Anglesey. He stated that this was because 'here the guard was slack' and that there was 'plenty of scope for attack'.

Commander Hashagen, well remembered for the terrible loss of life he caused after he sank the two Waterford steamers, *Formby* and *Coninbeg,* in the St. George's Channel during the same month, also recalled in his memoirs, an interesting insight into why some U-boats might have been unfairly accused of attacking lightships and other 'innocent' vessels.

The value of telegraphic stations, situated in remote but geographically strategic outposts, such as lighthouses or lightships during World War I, is one that does not appear to have been explored or well known about. The part they played in defeating the U-boats is a fact little known about and never boasted. Their role in this regard would seem to be one of the war's best-kept secrets.

The engineering archives of Eircom (previously the Post Office Engineering Branch) clearly show, that far from British naval intelligence being totally reliant on wireless communication, there was a surprising and efficient network of telegraph and telephone installations situated in strategic locations right around the coast of Ireland. And maybe even more surprising, many of these installations existed well before the 20th century. The practical benefits afforded to the Allies by having such strategically - placed outposts connected by electrical communication to a central station proved invaluable. This aspect of communications in Ireland, and its value to the Allies during World War I, has been largely ignored. In an attempt to rectify this, the following chapters will explain how – and why – these installations came under the watchful eyes of the German and British navies.

With the help of files from the office of the Chief Censor in Ireland during 1916–19, I hope this book will also give a welcome airing to some of the issues of the U-boat war, insofar as they directly affected Ireland. Although Ireland and the Irish Sea were geographically and strategically of the utmost importance to the Allies during World War I, little has been written that explains why this was so. Until very recently, we have come to believe that the part Ireland played during this war was insignificant, despite the fact that so many of its young men fought and died in places so far away and of which they knew little. And in the majority of cases, no higher moral imperative has been suggested for this sacrifice, other than their aspirations to fend off hunger and unemployment. It has been suggested that nationalists, anti-conscriptionists, the barefooted poor from the cities, 'ignorant pig-breeders' from the countryside, and Irishmen in the trenches, by virtue of their nationality, position or domicile, could not have had any other part to play in the outcome of the Great War.

It was also claimed that the 'call to arms' was not taken sufficiently seriously by Ireland's otherwise insular population and that, as far as Britain, France and America were concerned, the numbers of 'Irish' volunteers was unsatisfactory. These assumptions will be shown not to have been accurate, and the contrary to have been true.

The available statistics indicate that, during the course of World War I, no fewer than 119 German submarines sank ships in the approaches to, and in the waters around, Ireland. Of these, approximately seventy sank ships in the vicinity of the Alley. In terms of all types of vessels destroyed, *UC-75, UC-65 U-96* and *U-91* represent the most successful U-boats that operated in the Alley. Other U-boats of note operating in all Irish waters were *U-57, U-24* and *U-61,* all of which were successful in other areas of operations. More detailed statistics are contained in chapter 7: 'U-boat and shipping casualty statistics for the Alley and around Ireland 1917-18 and 1939-45.'

The important target areas around Ireland, in terms of the number of ships sunk, were the Southwestern Approaches off Cork, the Alley, and the Northwestern Approaches off Donegal. In terms of the operating parameters of the coastal, smaller cruiser, and the mine-laying U-boats, the North-western and South-western Approaches extended to between 15 and 20 degrees longitude West.

These figures are computed from statistics which do not include repeat attacks by the same submarines, attacks on or the sinking of most vessels under 500 tons, failed attacks, or vessels which disappeared without known cause. Neither do they account for all non-British vessels. Although an appreciable number of casualties may have been overlooked, it is probably safe to assume that the U-boats already mentioned were also responsible for many of these.

The figures are exclusive to the waters mentioned, and other than the fact that the U-boats mentioned sank ships in these waters, at the times that they did, these have no bearing on U-boat activity in the other areas of conflict around the world. The persistent interest shown by the U-boats in the waters around Ireland was a direct result of its geographical and strategic proximity to Britain, and what she was capable of supplying her with. The entrances to the Alley are relatively well known and befit their description as 'danger zones', but almost nothing is known of the dangers that lurked between these zones during World War I.

Although attacks by U-boat at the extremities of the Approaches had been diminishing, the crisis that threatened shipping in the Alley during the winter of 1917–18 did not, even after the final Christmas of the war had passed, but continued to increase in severity until the end of spring. The number of U-boats being deployed in these areas was rising, and this escalation was mirrored in France by the masses of troops building on both sides for the massive engagement that would follow. After the first two indecisive years of the war, during which there was relatively little U-boat activity in the Alley, a steady increase in the number of U-boat operations began after April 1917. The escalation continued as the year progressed and peaked in an all-out offensive both on land and at sea during Germany's last great push in March 1918.

The areas to the south and south-west of Ireland were generally known as the Atlantic or Western Approaches. And because of the large numbers of ships sunk in these areas during the first half of World War I, these were also known to sailors as 'U-boat Alley'. I have borrowed this term in order to describe the similar dangers that erupted in the waters between Ireland and England during the latter years of the war.

The word 'alley' is sometimes used to describe a high-sided and out-of-the-way passage through which people or traffic may pass. With the exception of the North Channel, it might be said that this does not apply to these waters. The seas between Ireland and England are nevertheless considered in maritime terms to be a channel, which is exceptionally deep in areas, and through which highly sophisticated and heavily armed nuclear submarines make passage to this day. The word also conjures up a dark and sinister place where danger is always present. This too is an apt description for the Alley during this period of World War I.

It is more important however, to impress upon the reader just how significant U-boat commanders considered this narrow sea to be. These were men who could sail in their undersea boats from northern Europe to lay mines off the Irish coast, then surface and sink ships with their guns in mid-channel, and torpedo ships off Liverpool, all in the same day. By the time the reader reaches the end of the book, I hope he or she will come to appreciate, as did numerous skippers and victims of the small cross-channel steamers that fled from an unseen enemy, just how crammed with U-boats this channel became after April 1917.

In terms of greater Europe, Ireland's geographical position is one of isolation. A solitary outpost situated on its north-western extremity. And it might well be asked what Ireland might have accomplished in her home waters to affect the outcome of World War I? To address this and other related questions, I have included some previously undisclosed facts that surround the tragic loss of several otherwise small and insignificant Irish steamships. Two of these were Dublin vessels that had sailed back and forth across the Irish Sea as a matter of routine during World War I: the Tedcastles ship *SS Adela* and the Guinness-owned *SS W. M. Barkley*. Although both of these could be considered relatively minor vessels of the period, they are typical of the type of ships that made thousands of unprotected journeys in these waters, through sea-lanes which at one time during the war were mined and patrolled daily by German submarines. They delivered not only passengers but also large quantities of much-needed supplies and materials across the Alley to help the British war effort. These vessels were crewed by merchant sailors, many who lived in the immediate vicinity of port towns and some who were members of well known families with long traditions of seafaring. (The situation was none too different during WW2 when many more men with similar sounding names from these sea-faring communities were either lost serving on Royal Naval vessels or Irish merchant ships that were plying goods to a neutral Ireland in order to maintain her very existence.)

Lastly, I would like the reader to understand that my interest in World War I, and how it visited the shores of Ireland, began with my first scuba dive on the wreck of the *RMS Leinster*. Intrigued by the way propaganda had twisted the portrayal of this disaster, and the loss of 527 people – according to John Terraine, writing in *Business in Great Waters* – when she was torpedoed in 1918, I began to dig deeper

The result of this interest was *Death in the Irish Sea,* which represents my ambition to correct the memory of the details that surrounded that ship's final voyage. The research that uncovered the facts of this disaster also revealed that this episode was by no means the whole story of the death and carnage that occurred in the Irish Sea during World War I.

Having researched a wealth of new material and investigated many of the WW I shipping casualties resting on the seabed around the coast of Ireland, I hope my findings will demonstrate just how extensive was the U-boat campaign which took place on Ireland's doorstep during World War I, and help to explain the reasons for it.

Chapter 5

THE RELUCTANT

HERO

The Reluctant Hero

It was as a young boy, while watching Hollywood movies in the local cinema, that I first became aware of how great a country the United States of America must be. Before then, my understanding of that country extended no further than lessons in basic geography and the excited discoveries made in the eagerly awaited 'clothes parcels'. Our emigrant relatives, who had left Ireland in search of work and prosperity in a land of opportunity during the middle of the twentieth century, posted these back home, and occasionally the eagerly awaited parcel also contained a few dollars. Some time later, unbelievably small radios, called 'transistors', began to appear in the bundles. But the lightweight clothes, manufactured from strange new materials, were a wonder.

It wasn't until I had seen these movies that I formed a view of Americans, and their country's apparent wealth. Hollywood visited the children and adults of the world alike, and portrayed a comforting order to life, in terms of prosperity in return for hard work, 'good' to the rescue, and 'bad' being defeated. This righteous and comforting order was portrayed by its heroes, the Marines in Europe, the Navy in the Pacific, the Air Force in Korea, and its white cowboys and cavalry at home. It would never have occurred to me, that at one time, a president of America would not have wanted to rescue 'us' from our battles with Germany – or even worse, that he couldn't.

Many fine writers have described the horrible effects that World War I wrought on the populations of the countries that were sucked into its bloody vortex. Film producers have attempted – but not yet managed – to capture the grand scale of that era's intrigue and devastation, which almost hurled the world into a cataclysmic conclusion in 1917. Many brilliant historians and contemporary novelists who fought in the Great War recorded the battles which took place on land and at sea – battles that resulted in the disturbing and wasteful loss of millions of young military and civilian lives. The 'Peasant Pope', Pius X, died only days after the outbreak of the Great War, and despite frantic diplomatic efforts on his behalf, he had been unable to prevent the carnage that convulsed Europe during the next four years. His last words on the subject were reported to have been:-

'In ancient times the Pope with a word might have stayed slaughter. Now I am insignificant and forced to see the spectacle of my own children, even those who yesterday worked here with me, leaving for war and unrobing their cassocks and cowls for soldiers' uniforms. Yesterday, although belonging to different nationalities, we were here studying in sympathetic companionship, now we are in different fields; armed against each other, and ready to take each other's lives.'

Despite the fact that for some years prior to World War I, the Vatican had persistently meddled in the political affairs of Serbia and Austria, this 'Poor Pope' must surely

have been broken-hearted. And it may have been more kind that he departed the world when he did, never to have witnessed the full extent of the human carnage that followed, the scale of which he could not have imagined. Nor might he ever have imagined the abuses of drugs and alcohol, and the protracted effects of post-war starvation and sicknesses, which rampaged through the military and civilian populations around the world, on foot of demobilisation.

The great conflict reached a critical climax at sea during the spring of 1917, at a time when the Vatican was again involving itself in urgent but fruitless peace negotiations with Germany and the Allies. President Wilson's earlier hopes for 'Peace Without Victory', during a period when America was inextricably being drawn into the conflict, went unheeded. Further efforts for a peace by Pope Benedict XV, in August 1917, were also dashed. A total military victory, or Germany's surrender, became the only options for the new alliance. This period became a critical phase of the war, and with hindsight, we know it to have been the point of no return for Germany. It was at this point that she launched the full might of her powerful U-boat fleet in an unmerciful campaign against merchant shipping.

One of the most prolific writers on World War I was E.K. Chatterton. He wrote from the unenviable position of someone who had fought in it, and through his sheer volume of work, he became a 'biographer' of World War I. Chatterton served in the Royal Navy at Queenstown (which later became Cobh), county Cork, and during the height of the conflict he was transferred to the staff of the Historical Section Committee of Imperial Defence in 1917. An only son, with a classical education, he had been ideally placed to record a war which unfolded before his very eyes. He was also privy, during and after the war, to many confidential and first-hand anecdotal reports on wartime operations and actions from around the world, and included many of these in his brilliant accounts of naval operations throughout the Mediterranean and the Atlantic. But apart from his hefty volume *Danger Zone,* a detailed record of naval operations around Ireland during Admiral Bayly's command at Queenstown, little else has been written that fully describes the extent of the U-boat war that was waged in the waters that separate Ireland and England. Even in *Danger Zone*, very little is written about the naval operations in the Alley or the scale of the German submarine campaign waged against the cross-channel merchant fleet.

Neither does he dwell on the feeling of hopelessness expressed by senior Royal naval personnel or of the flagging morale within the navy's ranks, during the height of the U-boats' 'unrestricted' campaign in 1917. It must also be said that some naval officers expressed the view that at no time during the conflict did they expect to be overwhelmed by the U-boat campaign. Even though Chatterton is responsible for bringing an enormous amount of valuable material to the fore, he often – perhaps unwittingly – underplayed deficiencies on the Allied side. Much of his work was published between the two world wars, and some of his remarks might have been designed to conceal the real dangers that had threatened Britain at the time. He also failed to include certain facts, which may have resulted in a more sympathetic reflection on the chivalry of German naval personnel.

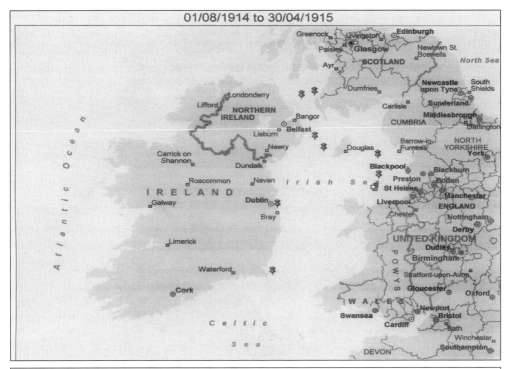

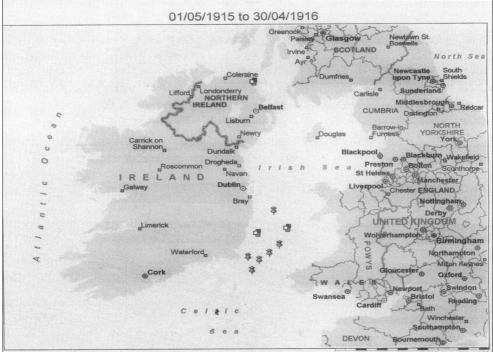

The above diagrams represent U-boat attacks and their shift in concentrations as the war progressed, in relation to the 'Irish Channel' ('The Alley') i.e. the North Channel, Irish Sea and George's Channel.

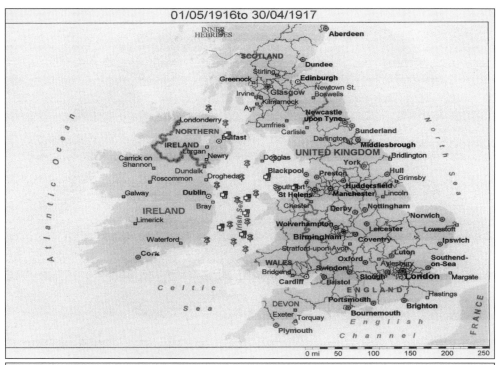

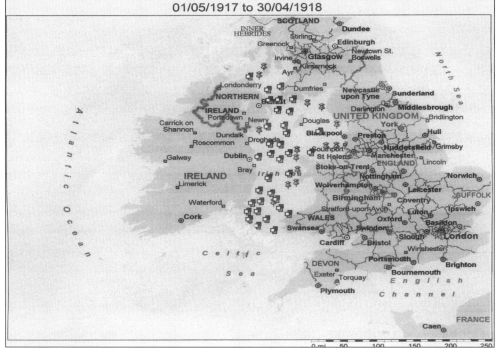

Attacks in other areas, such as The Approaches, continued (not shown) but decreased after April 1917.
Thumb pins = individual attacks. (one) Rectangles = Clusters of attacks (more than one)
Diagrams are courtesy of **COMPUWRECK**.

Some idea of the desperation that was felt at the time, was reportedly uttered by the First Sea Lord, Admiral Jellicoe to Admiral Sims USN, upon his arrival in London in April 1917: 'It is impossible for us to go on with the war if losses like this continue'.

Given the inevitable outcome implied in such stark admissions – which were only ever made out of public earshot, and nearly always absent from a strictly censored Press – the full extent of the devastation that was being caused by the U-boats was probably not widely understood, even to this day. Indeed, their campaign of destruction was not waged in the Alley alone but right around the coasts of Ireland and England. (For the purposes of this book, U-boat operations elsewhere will receive little mention.)

Certainly, as a boy growing up in Ireland, my formal education never alluded to the closeness with which the naval war of 1914–18 was brought to our shores, or to the scale of the destruction that occurred in the sea lanes between Ireland and England. In order to understand the crucial role played by Ireland's geography in the strategy of this naval war, we must examine the situation that existed between the principal belligerents at the time. Not least, we must consider the part that this geography continued to play after America declared its intentions and dispatched the first six destroyers to the Royal Naval base at Queenstown in 1917.

Britain had on the one hand used every method at its disposal to persuade this neutral to commit its fresh young blood and her industrial might on its side. Germany, on the other hand, used every trick in the book in an attempt to prevent such an alliance. The reluctant hero was of course the USA.

The almost unanimous decision by America's House of Representatives to enter World War I on 6 April 1917 did not come a moment too soon for Europe. The food situation had become grave, with people already dying from hunger in large cities. Britain was reported at the time to have only six weeks of food remaining. Even the British Royal family were said to have been restricted to 'meat only twice weekly'. Admiral Sims reported to the Secretary of the Navy on 14 April that a communication from the Food Ministry in Britain indicated that there was only 'sufficient grain supply' in Britain for three weeks. This may not seem to be so short a period as to warrant undue concern today. But if one considers that the United States was nearly two weeks away from Britain by a modern fast liner, and that grain carriers from South America could easily take at least twice that length of time, the danger becomes more apparent. Also remembering that successful crossings might largely depend on the vagaries of U-boat operations.

Ireland, by contrast, was Britain's nearest source of supplementary and even sometimes, essential food supplies. Less well-understood was the fact, that at a time when there were attempts by German agents to contaminate grain and meat in America, Ireland was totally free of such imports and was thus unaffected. Despite her small size, these supplies were of considerable proportions, and were less than one day's sailing away.

The shortage of nourishment was not the scourge of the Allies alone, as the German people also suffered death and widespread hardship from extreme food shortages, which continued long after the war had concluded.

This 'new spirit of togetherness' was portrayed in the Irish press. The propagation of this bonding was promoted in many ways after America entered WW1 in April 1917, and ever since.

The outbreak of World War I was precipitated by probably the most politically intriguing period of any conflict. If you read an Irish 'evening' paper from the period, you will discover that it was a war that was nervously proclaimed to have begun with a 'British Ultimatum to Germany', and that 'Germans Forced Passage through Belgium' *(Evening Herald,* 4 and 5 August). The *Evening Mail* of 5 August recorded that the public was 'Forced Into War' and ordered: 'Britons Hold Your Own'. Such headlines amounted to declarations and descriptions of an almost 'easing into' the war for Irish readers, and for some reason, seemed to be designed to almost cocoon its readers from the impact of an outbreak of hostilities, the likes of which had never been previously witnessed.

In contrast, this was a subject on which the 'dailies' did not see any necessity for vagueness. On 5 August, the *Irish Times* boldly announced: 'England Declares War on Germany'; on the same day the *Freeman's Journal* stated that: 'Britain and Germany, A State of War Exists'.

The differing emphasis between publications, might be perceived as its 'poorer' readership needing some kind of shielding from the knowledge of an impending global catastrophe, whilst the slightly better-off 'daily' reader, might be better prepared for, and might even avail of an opportunity in the new situation. Or, of course, it might simply have been the case that the earlier banner headlines in the 'dailies' had already exploited the news, leaving the 'evenings' to search for a slightly different angle. However the public considered the quality of their newspapers, it is known that many editors did actually consider the evening papers to be more influential than the morning ones.

Regardless of how news of the war erupted on to the front pages of newspapers, the politics of the period was confusing and complex, and continues to set historians some baffling questions. Although additional material relating to World War I held in the archives of the principal protagonists – with the exception of the Japanese intelligence services – continues to be unearthed, some 'secrets' still remain. Many historians have suggested the sinking of American ships, and the deaths of American passengers, as being the reason why the USA finally entered the war, the principal incident remembered being the sinking of the *Lusitania*. But America did not enter the war until two years almost to the day after this incident, and only after a further nineteen of its ships had been either attacked or sunk by German submarines. (US Navy statistics, 01/04/1923)

Political protests mounted by America were acknowledged by Germany, and had the effect of restricting U-boat operations to certain areas. The leash, however, did not remain on for long. Although large sections of the American public were appalled at the continuing loss of American civilians on ships attacked by U-boats, official protests often did not go beyond verbal criticisms and declarations of 'abhorrence'. The glaring weakness in some of America's diplomatic responses caused embarrassment amongst her diplomats but German responses sometimes cleverly made the protestations appear successful, for a time.

American Newspapers quite regularly lampooned President Wilson's inability or refusal to act against German sabotage and its blatant abuse of American neutrality during WW1. This one appeared in the New York Herald.

Another reason why America entered the war and one that is often overlooked, was The constant provocation caused by a substantial campaign of German sabotage waged on neutral American soil. (Germany countered this claim of neutrality by claiming, quite correctly, that America was supplying endless amounts of munitions to its enemies. If it had not been for Britain's blockade of Germany, American industrialists would just have easily taken German money for arms as it did for raw materials.) During the period that America had remained neutral, far more damage was done to life and property on American soil by German sabotage than the accumulated effects of U-boat attacks against her interests on the high seas. (Germany admitted to causing an estimated $150,000,000 worth of damage to American property by sabotage, during the period of the war that America remained neutral: Litigation of reparation claims by the Lehig Valley Railroad Co. and the Kingsland Assembly Plant against the German government, known as the 'Black Tom Case'. Tried at The Hague and Washington 1919-1939.)

The constant drip-drip effect of attacks against American vessels however, and increasing political pressure from several quarters, all became wedges, which when finally driven home, irrevocably split President Wilson and the USA from the strategy of neutrality, as early as 24 February 1917.

Daily life in neutral America, as it was reported during this period, appears to have been quite extraordinary. It was a veritable circus of spies, secret agents, provocateurs and a succession of diplomatic cocktail parties. These were frequented by representatives and diplomats from the countries whose armies were otherwise embroiled in wiping each other out. Whilst thousands were being killed daily in unbelievable conditions throughout the world, American newspapers were full of adverts for new houses and automobiles, designs for the development of submarines, ebullient stock-market reports, numerous pictures of grand houses for sale, and a very large dose of society gossip. All of this seemingly only outweighed by the almost unhealthy amount of interest expressed in the price and production levels of eggs.

Amid all of this, President Woodrow Wilson was coming under extreme pressure from two of the main protagonists. Britain was eagerly awaiting this 'fresh' giant of a country to come in on its side, and Germany was desperately trying to prevent it. As 1917 approached, it had become frighteningly obvious that Britain, by her own admission, was going to lose the war to Germany. The pot of gold that had been supplying the £5.5 million a day for war materials had run out. Britain was broke, and under the weight of US credit restrictions, she was being squeezed to make an embarrassing peace with an aggressor who seemed to have unlimited horizons on its expansionist policies.

Such a compromise would not have prevented Germany's redesign of the political and national boundaries of Europe, and would have left the remaining great warships of the German navy unscathed. This impressive fleet was almost the equal of Britain's but, given Germany's growing ship-building capacity, and the technological advances

that were being accomplished by her submarine industry, the outcome of a major naval conflict between the two great navies at some point in the future was not certain. (It has been conjectured by some historians that it was Germany's improving maritime capacity, both naval and merchant, described as 'expansionist', that had become the main threat to Britain's dominance in this regard, and that this was the real reason for the Great War. In addition, but not unlike the Allies, Germany had begun to export its superior U-boat technology to other countries.)

The prospect of the British fleet surrendering and being subsumed into a German one was unthinkable for America or any other nation depending on sea transport. It was reported in the editorial of the well-censored *Freeman's Journal,* as early as 13 December 1915, that:

'The whole question narrows itself down to the terms which Germany will now offer . . . the crossing of the Rhine, the smashing of the German Empire . . . the destruction of its militarism . . . are enterprises that look very much harder today than they did some time ago . . . Whether we shall spend Christmas in peace depends altogether on the terms which the enemy proposes.'

The early days and misplaced British optimism of a successful outcome to the conflict had ebbed away. Further proclamations of a quick victory were not to be heard, and were quickly replaced by a foreboding of the uncertainty that was beginning to loom. What would it benefit America if it had all of Britain's gold, if its customers in Europe lay hopelessly prostrate and in ruins under a bankrupt German dictatorship? Under some new political system and a subsequent rearrangement of European boundaries, rebuilding would have become a task of enormous proportions for a continent that had squandered all its commercial and civic wealth, together with the lives of its citizens.

The American ambassador to Britain, Walter H. Page, revealed in his correspondence of July 1917, just how close to bankruptcy Britain had already come:

'The whole Allied combination on this side of the ocean are very much nearer the end of their financial resources than anyone has guessed or imagined.'

From early 1915, Woodrow Wilson's unwillingness to enter the war had placed him in a desperately awkward position. He appeared on the one hand to be a generous benefactor to his country's war moguls and munitions industrialists, and on the other, found himself the butt of derision, heaped on him by politicians who wanted to come to the aid of Europe, for one reason or another. Many of these wise men did not appear to be in any doubt as to whose side they should send their armed forces to die for. Merchant seamen, who until then had borne the full brunt of the U-boat attacks, knew how the sea lay. They had seen their shipmates blown to smithereens on the high seas from the beginning of the war. A man who was there, Captain Bone, in his book *Merchant-Men-At-Arms,* recalls:

'The German submarine had grown to be a more complete and deadly warship. Sinkings had reached an alarming height: a spirit almost of fatalism was permeating the sea-actions of some of our Service. Our guns were of little avail against underwater attack. Notwithstanding the tricks of our zigzag, the torpedoes struck home.'

Although Britain retained a clear naval advantage in her surface vessels, Germany had methodically but simply calculated that a figure of 200 submarines unleashed in an unrestricted campaign against merchant and naval shipping would eliminate this lead. The calculated effect of this would be the severing of Britain's valuable lifelines of supplies and her isolation from the remainder of the world. It was the stated intention of the German generals to win the war by the end of the summer of 1917. This concept of victory, which was to be delivered by the U-boats alone, was in marked contrast to what was considered to be their role during World War II. During the next U-boat war, they would be regarded as just another arm of the fleet, another instrument with which to harry the Allies until the victory on land was accomplished.

Britain also made early and remarkable strides in code-breaking during World War I. These were greatly assisted by the installation of a large number of radio directional finding stations, and an increasing ability to intercept German radio transmissions. The secret advances made in this area were fiercely guarded, and to some degree, were not even revealed to Britain's allies. But being able to destroy U-boats or to provide protection from them with a diminishing fleet of suitable vessels was quite another matter.

It is well understood now that Britain had cracked German codes from the now famous but then very secret Room 40. It is also suggested by some authors – and this is a view that was probably never discouraged – that British Naval Intelligence was in receipt of intelligence from a sympathiser, placed as high as the German General Staff. Ian Wilson, in his *Shipwrecks of the Ulster Coast,* wrote that the First Sea Lord Admiral Fisher and Grand Admiral Tirpitz carried on secret correspondence during the conflict. The pair would seem to be very unlikely pen pals, but such a liaison is also alluded to in Robert Grant's book *U-boat Intelligence*. In it, he repeats this passage from the memoirs of Sir Bertram Hayes, commander of the *SS Olympic* during 1918:

'Our Naval Intelligence Service must have had trustworthy sources of information during the war, as they seemed to know where every submarine was located. I have heard it said by more or less responsible people that it was Admiral von Tirpitz himself who was giving us the information, and I have also heard speculations as to how much he was paid for doing so. Whether he was the source or not, the fact remains that the information was accurate.'

The authenticity of such stories is in some doubt, but it is a fact that even if secret information had been passed to British Intelligence, this did nothing to hinder the U-boats from entering and leaving the North Sea through the narrow Dover Channel until August 1918. (It is estimated that the last U-boat passed through the Dover Barrage at the end of August 1918).

Whether or not any member of the German Generals Staff was aware of intelligence leaks or of the advances made by British Naval Intelligence, they continued to remain optimistic. Admiral von Holtzendorff's assessment of the strategy adopted for the forthcoming unrestricted U-boat campaign of 1917 was clear: 'in the course of which every enemy and neutral ship found in the war zone is to be sunk without warning.' The possibility or the effectiveness of an American rescue was dismissed out of hand by Admiral von Capelle when he said: 'From the military point of view, the assistance which will result from the entrance of the United States into the war will amount to nothing.'

Albeit probably only as a result of being short of twenty to thirty additional submarines and experienced crews, Capelle's miscalculation of the 'sleeping lion' in the west proved to be his downfall. (The figure of 200 German submarines is commonly quoted as being necessary for a German victory. Germany never came near to having this number of submarines in service, and even if this figure had been attained, it would have to have been sustained and likely increased. It was also estimated in 1916 that over 300 submarines would have been required.)

President Wilson, elected on an anti-war ticket, had been unwavering in his determination to keep America out of the war. After America's adventurous debacles in Mexico, he had no wish to be responsible for further shipments of dead servicemen from a war on a different continent. At the very least, if peace could not be forced upon the combatants, America's entry into the war might be delayed until such time as the belligerents were exhausted. And in terms of American casualties, the scale of the intervention and losses might then be minimised. The strategy ultimately proved to be a success, and with some exceptions, it is a strategy which has remained a mainstay of American military campaigns.

After declaring war against Germany, America dictated the progress and direction of the war, to the point that relatively few US servicemen were lost in action whilst the victory was being achieved.

Arrogant in their notional ability to defeat Britain in 1917, German diplomats in Washington had continued to express the customary line of regret for the loss of American passengers and vessels on the high seas. But in effect, thumbing their noses at the inaction of the Wilson government. Nevertheless, Germany could never be certain of the US until it took out some additional insurance. Such an opportunity was identified and seized upon, in the form of America's soft underbelly, Mexico. And what if the Kaiser's age-old dream of an alliance between Japan, Russia and Germany could be realised? The idea had been abroad for some time and similar aspirations surfaced once again during the next 'great war' with the allied powers.

Japan was aligned with the Allies, providing arms and munitions, credit, and even warships for actions against the U-boats in the Mediterranean. She had also made territorial gains in the Pacific and was said to have kept an expansionist and opportunistic eye on the potential for naval facilities along the coast of Mexico. Never committing outright breaches of agreements with her Allies, she remained loyal but

canny. She was seemingly well aware of the importance of finding oneself on the right side of the fence when the smoke cleared.

Deeply annoyed by the introduction of legislation in Congress preventing Japanese nationals from owning property on America's Pacific Coast, and the increased restrictions that were placed on export of steel from the US, the Japanese probed along the Mexican coast. Their interest in this 'underbelly' created a reciprocal amount of agitation and nervousness for the US government. It must also be said that Japan nevertheless continued to remain a faithful ally for the duration of the war. And she behaved none too differently, and to a large extent less arbitrarily, than some of the other Allied powers during the geographical carve-up deals that were hammered out at the Paris Peace Conference in 1919.

The persistent whispers by Germany on the dangers of the 'Yellow Peril' in South America and Mexico began to take effect. After America's attempt at promoting 'honest and good men' to govern Mexico failed, and seeing off Diaz, Huerta at Vera Cruz, and Pancho Villa, she reluctantly settled on recognising General Carranza. The ousted General Huerta was having none of it, and with the aid of Germany, he plotted a comeback. Not to be caught without a foot in both camps, Germany was also seen to be capable of devious and simultaneous plotting with Carranza, when it was opportune to do so.

It should be remembered that Mexico supplied significant amounts of important commodities such as copper, and one quarter of the world's oil. Although large portions of the Royal Navy's requirements for fuel oil were being supplied from the Middle East, even greater amounts, were being supplied by Mexico. The Royal Navy remained heavily dependent on coal, but its move to, and reliance on oil, had increased considerably. The export of food from Mexico and South America had also become a strategic and more urgent importance to Britain.

Alarm bells rang in Whitehall in 1917 during the critical month of March, when reports were received from Mexico of Carranza's threat to impose embargoes one month earlier. The effects of such sanctions on these food shipments would have been bad enough, but equally or even more worrying, was the impact that similar actions might have had on British and American petroleum and mineral interests in regions such as Tampico.

Prior to April 1917, German intrigue and espionage activities throughout the US, Canada and South America had escalated considerably. Agents assisted in the supply of arms, military expertise, money, support for border raids, the destruction of oil wells, bridges and railways, interruptions of munitions production, the establishment of clandestine wireless communication facilities, and for officials to organise and threaten labour unrest. As the third year of the war began, the mounting pressure resulting from these activities in America had become intolerable.

Germany's strength in the US lay in the latter's fear of becoming inextricably absorbed into a conflict with Mexico and beyond, and her government's consistent

proclamations of a determined intention to remain neutral. US forces in Mexico under General Pershing had achieved little, and it was Germany's intention to push the US into a deeper conflict with Mexico, to the extent that she would be incapable of interfering in Europe.

Some of Germany's generals also supposedly drew comfort from the expectation that thousands of American-Germans domiciled in the US would rally to Germany's cause at the appropriate time. Although such confidence proved to be misplaced, a large number of arrests were made on America's border with Mexico after her declaration of war. Whether the greater part of this migration was prompted by a flush of German patriotism in a bid to defend their homeland or from the threat of internment in the US is not altogether clear.

There was also the 'Irish Question', and the ridiculous claims by some Irish-Americans that 75 per cent of Irish citizens 'at home' were in support of Germany. The part Irishmen and Irish-Americans played with the German generals in their subversive activities against America, or against British interests in America during World War I, remains a subject which some of today's Irishmen and women might feel is probably best forgotten, as it remains a delicate source of contention, and maybe even some shame.

After America had entered the war, this was not a subject on which the very popular ex-president Roosevelt was silent. By then, he was loudly proclaiming his government was behind the war effort and against all those who were not.

An important weakness of Germany's position in the US was its access to communications facilities. Conversely, this was one of Britain's greatest strengths. At the commencement of hostilities with Germany, Britain severed almost all of the transatlantic cables emanating from Germany. German communications with its interests in the US were thus carried on in several ways. There was 'clear' radio communication with Tuckerton, and Sayville at Long Island, both of which had been seized and put under naval censorship by the US authorities. To some degree, Germany was able to communicate via a high-powered transmitter at Nauen, with a new wireless installation established by its agents in Mexico City. The majority of Berlin's diplomatic communications with the US, however, were performed in code over normal telegraph facilities. The content of these communications was later found to be illegal, and the ruse became known as the 'Swedish Roundabout' (a method used by Germany to send its coded diplomatic messages through neutral Sweden's diplomatic and telegraph facilities). It had been Germany's misfortune that Sweden's unmolested transatlantic cable to the US also touched on the shores of Britain. Germany is also said to have communicated with America through a transatlantic cable from Holland.

An alternative method of communication was the much slower surface mail, also directed through South America. Either way, and unbeknownst to the Germans, each of these methods of communication was being monitored by the British, and their secret messages were successfully intercepted and decoded by the men in Room 40,

under the watchful eye of Admiral Hall, head of British Naval Intelligence.

Impatient with failed attempts at provoking Wilson into premature and irreversible reactions in Mexico, German diplomacy sank to new levels of skulduggery. The fat was most certainly in the fire when the famous 'Zimmermann Telegram' of 16 January 1917 was discovered.

Arthur Zimmermann had become Germany's Foreign Secretary in November 1916, and was immediately seen as a man who might be more amenable to America's difficulties than the outgoing Gottlieb von Jagow. This view was a mistaken one, and almost immediately, Zimmermann donned two hats: a diplomatic and apparently caring one for the difficulties of the US State Department, and another signalling an ambition to share with Germany's U-boat commanders a glorious victory born out of the 'unrestricted' campaign of aggression against merchant shipping.

Almost at once, he helped to devise a plan with the German General Staff that was thought certain to win the war. It was intended that the estimated two hundred submarines considered necessary to win the war, would be available by mid-1917, and it was planned to unleash their vanguard on 1 February 1917, in unrestricted aggression against all 'enemy' ships. It is probably due in large part to these arrogant miscalculations that the Allies evaded complete isolation in the spring of 1917, thus preventing the possibility of a European civilisation being forever influenced by a Teutonic dogma.

After the announcement of the 'unrestricted campaign', there were never more than between 130 and 150 submarines available for all operations at any one time. This figure fell well short of the number that had been predicted as necessary in order to achieve a victory. Once again during World War II, it was this same over-optimistic miscalculation that contributed in great part to Germany's inability to achieve naval dominance in the North Atlantic.

The intention of the 'unrestricted' U-boat strategy was to starve Britain and force it to surrender. The 'unrestricted' declaration was not to be revealed to America or other neutrals until the last possible hour, thus reducing any possibility of altering the odds for a successful outcome. It was predicted that this could be achieved by September.

The daring plan also included prior approaches that were to be made to President Carranza of Mexico. These contained a promise of assistance in the retaking of Mexican lands lost to America, and urged approaches to be made by him to the Japanese, for their assistance in the proposed invasion of America.

The first part of this elaborate scheme was sprung at the last moment on the last day of January 1917. Washington was informed by the German Ambassador, Count von Bernstorff, that some of the growing number of U-boats that were already at sea for some time, were being reported off the east coast of America, and that unrestricted attacks on shipping would commence the following day. If the second part of the plan could be implemented, America's interest would certainly have been diverted from Europe, leaving the U-boats to have it almost all their own way in the Atlantic, and around Britain and Ireland.

A copy of the message to the overseas German Delagations, which was intercepted by British Naval Intelligence. It contained the instruction to announce the unrestricted U-boat campaign, which began on February 1st, 1917.

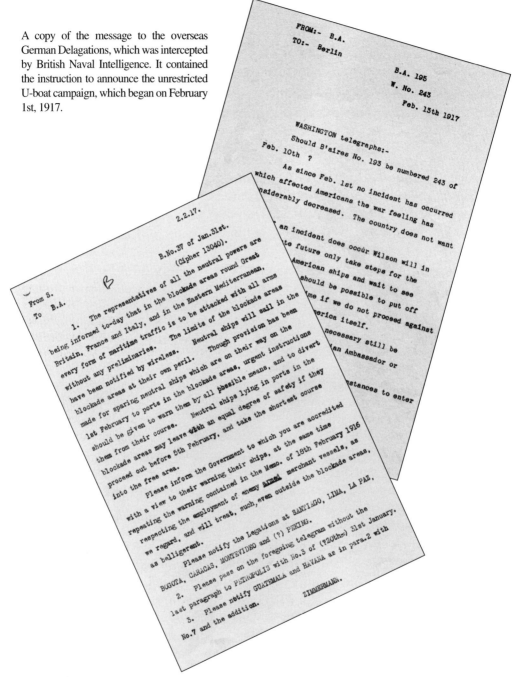

A copy of a German message intercepted by British Naval Intelligence, describing President Wilson's or his country's reluctance to enter the war. This post dated the famous 'Zimmerman Telegram', which proposed an alliance of Germany, Mexico and Japan, and threatened invasion of the USA.
It is especially interesting to note Ambassador Bernstorff's mention of putting off the 'real war' which he expected would follow.

This second part entailed the sending of a message to the German ambassador in Washington in three different ways. He in turn was to see that this message was relayed through the German ambassador Heinrich von Eckhardt in Mexico, to Carranza. The message was to travel via the Swedish Roundabout to Mexico, and then by radio to Long Island and Bernstorff in Washington. Lastly, and most surprisingly, it was to be sent over the American State Department's own direct cable or 'channels', also to Washington. This final and most extraordinary route was one that had been in restricted use, after Wilson's closest foreign-policy adviser, Colonel House, had recommended it.

Apparently having fallen under the spell of Zimmermann's civility, House recommended access to this cable for diplomatic exchanges between Germany and its embassy in Washington. The concession was intended to facilitate the sending of urgent messages during peace negotiations between the US and Germany. Going against advice from several other high-ranking State Department officials, who had strenuously objected to this most dubious and precarious arrangement, Wilson continued to allow Germany use the cable. President Wilson's ongoing search for peace was such that, in order to explore every conceivable avenue, he trusted the Germans to use the cable honourably. His judgement was misplaced, and German communications were subsequently found to have included hidden messages in their transmissions, which were unintelligible to the Americans. Their daring plot was not so unintelligible to the British, however!

This sub-sea cable ran from the State Department in Washington, across the Atlantic to Copenhagen, and then overland to Berlin. But it, too, touched on the shores of Britain. British intelligence had been monitoring and decrypting traffic in the new German 0075 code, not only on this cable but also on the other routes mentioned. German arrogance prevailed, and believing that interception and deciphering of their communications was not possible by lesser British minds, the now famous 'Zimmermann Telegram' was sent from Berlin via the 'State Department's cable' to Count von Bernstorff on 16 January.

It read:

WE INTEND TO BEGIN UNRESTRICTED SUBMARINE WARFARE ON THE FIRST OF FEBRUARY. WE SHALL ENDEAVOUR IN SPITE OF THIS TO KEEP THE UNITED STATES NEUTRAL. IN THE EVENT OF THIS NOT SUCCEEDING, WE MAKE MEXICO A PROPOSAL OF ALLIANCE ON THE FOLLOWING BASIS: MAKE WAR TOGETHER MAKE PEACE TOGETHER, GENEROUS FINANCIAL SUPPORT, AND AN UNDERSTANDING ON OUR PART THAT MEXICO IS TO RECONQUER THE LOST TERRITORY IN TEXAS, NEW MEXICO, AND ARIZONA. THE SETTLEMENT IN DETAIL IS LEFT TO YOU.

YOU WILL INFORM THE PRESIDENT [OF MEXICO] OF THE ABOVE MOST SECRETLY AS SOON AS THE OUTBREAK OF WAR WITH THE UNITED STATES IS CERTAIN AND ADD THE SUGGESTION THAT HE SHOULD, ON HIS OWN INITIATIVE, INVITE JAPAN TO IMMEDIATE ADHERENCE AND AT THE SAME TIME MEDIATE BETWEEN JAPAN AND OURSELVES.

PLEASE CALL THE PRESIDENT'S ATTENTION TO THE FACT THAT THE UNRESTRICTED EMPLOYMENT OF OUR SUBMARINES NOW OFFERS THE PROSPECT OF COMPELLING ENGLAND TO MAKE PEACE WITHIN A FEW MONTHS. ACKNOWLEDGE RECEIPT.
ZIMMERMANN.

The message was accompanied by instructions for onward delivery to the German Imperial Minister von Eckhardt in Mexico. It was duly relayed to Mexico on 19 January, and it was reported that the message was sent in the older 13040 code. This communication was also successfully intercepted and decoded by British agents. British intelligence is credited with having plucked this explosive message from both the wires and the air.

After extended British deliberation on how best to inform the US authorities about the secret message and the plot that it contained, without revealing their source, the text of the message was delivered to the American ambassador, Walter Page. The full text, place and time that this message was intercepted, whether in Britain, Berlin, Copenhagen, the American State Department or in Mexico, remains a contentious issue. (It is understood that only partial deciphering of the message using the later 0075 code took place at the British end but that this was added to by the interception and deciphering of the relayed message in the older 13040 code at the Mexico end.) In any event, the long wait for an opportunity finally to kick his old comrade, Wilson, into the war and at the same time regain some respect amongst his British friends had ended. Ambassador Page immediately went to work, relaying the contents of the incriminating message to Washington on the 23 February.

To the astonishment of many of his associates, and with the U-boats already sinking ships as per their 'unrestricted' instructions, President Wilson remained unmoveable and would not declare against Germany. The New York Herald printed the following large, bold banner on 1 March, which was believed to be the headline that would clinch every American's support for involvement in the war:

INVASION OF US BY MEXICO A PART OF GERMAN SCHEME TO CONQUER THE WORLD: JAPAN AND MEXICO ASKED BY PRUSSIA TO JOIN THEM AND MAKE WAR ON AMERICA: DARING PLOT LONG KNOWN TO MR. WILSON.

It appeared that even the most obstinate of Wilson's reservations could not but crumble under the tremendous pressure generated by this German declaration of aggression. As a result of the telegram and the obvious implications it contained for American business, American-Germans and some of America's primary citizens and industrialists who had remained comfortably nailed on the fence, finally got the wind up. They quickly realised that the war was not one in which Germany was about to halt its army and warships at the western shores of Europe, but instead, was one that was quickly shaping up to represent a threat of invasion to the US itself.

Not convinced, several congressmen cried 'foul' – a British foul. Suspecting dirty tricks by British Intelligence, they wanted to know how the knowledge of this

astonishing message was obtained, and whether it could be believed. Britain was certainly not going to reveal this information, and those few Americans who knew were sworn to secrecy. President Wilson was fast finding himself in a position with very little room left for manoeuvre.

American military intelligence had suffered badly from consistent under-funding due to the fact that its agencies were historically considered to be a 'poor relation' within the services. This fact was reflected in the ease with which espionage and sabotage had been carried out in the US until 1917. Despite this underachievement, and aided by some valuable assistance from British intelligence, their reports of German acts of sabotage on American and Canadian soil eventually reached embarrassing proportions. This happened to coincide with a time when Wilson was running out of reasons why he should not declare war against Germany. And if he committed to war, would America's southern borders be so weakened as to invite invasion? These were questions that might not have remained unanswered if German intentions had been kept secret.

On 3 March, said by many to be inexplicably too soon after the famous Zimmermann telegram had been sent, an event took place, which still defies a rational explanation. At a hastily convened press conference, Arthur Zimmermann quite astonishingly admitted to the authenticity of the published telegram. Why Zimmermann responded so quickly or why he admitted so readily to his subversive handiwork, or why he did not just issue a denial or even have said nothing for a while longer, are all questions that have never been satisfactorily answered. The whole episode, including Zimmermann's admissions, remain a most extraordinary series of actions by a man who was supposedly trying so desperately to keep Wilson from entering the war. Whatever his intentions, the effect of this confession achieved quite the opposite effect and immediately began to force Wilson's hand.

If Zimmermann's first message had not been sufficiently explicit, and a period remained in which Wilson might still be forgiven for not declaring against Germany, it proved to be brief. After Admiral Hall revealed the contents of yet another message sent on 5 February, directly to Mexico by Zimmermann, a wind of change immediately swept through the White House. After the 'unrestricted' U-boat offensive had been officially announced by Germany, during a time when the US was still neutral, Zimmermann's second message was urging soundings to be made to Japan on the proposed invasion of the US, 'even now'. These utterances, which amounted to an act of war against the US, are said to have almost certainly heralded the end of American neutrality.

Decoding and revealing this second and even more serious message of intent against American neutrality, might seem to have been a well-calculated move on the part of Admiral Hall. Especially when you consider the contents of another interception between Bernstorff and Zimmermann dated 13 February, immediately preceding

Bernstorff's departure from the US for Germany. Its contents, set out below, would indicate that despite its naked aggression, German officials continued to harbour the view that America might yet be dissuaded from entering the war:

. . . AS SINCE FEB. 1 NO INCIDENT HAS OCCURRED WHICH AFFECTED AMERICANS. THE WAR FEELING HAS CONSIDERABLY DECREASED. THE COUNTRY DOES NOT WANT WAR.

IF AN INCIDENT DOES OCCUR WILSON WILL IN THE IMMEDIATE FUTURE ONLY TAKE STEPS FOR THE PROTECTION OF AMERICAN SHIPS AND WAIT TO SEE WHAT WE DO: IT SHOULD BE POSSIBLE TO PUT OFF REAL WAR FOR SOME TIME IF WE DO NOT PROCEED AGAINST THE UNITED STATES OF AMERICA ITSELF.

NEGOTIATIONS CAN IF NECESSARY STILL BE CARRIED ON THROUGH THE AUSTRIAN AMBASSADOR OR THE SWISS MINISTER.

WILSON WISHES UNDER NO CIRCUMSTANCES TO ENTER UPON AN ALLIANCE WITH OUR ENEMIES.

(It is unclear how and at what precise moment Admiral Hall made known the contents of the second telegram, if at all, as it was never made public at the time. Indeed, precious little of these intercepts were ever made public, and even then, not until many years later. This cable's existence was not discovered or made known until well after the end of the war.)

The signals emanating from the German General Staff seemed confused. German political intrigue in the US appeared geared at concentrating the mind of America's military and political strategists on Mexico, and on its own interests in South America. But simultaneously, there was a sudden rise in the number of attacks and the sinking of American ships by U-boats, between February and April 1917, despite the fact there had been only a few previously. These actions would seem to suggest a contradiction, one of almost goading the US into retaliation. A partial explanation may be found in the increased number of U-boat patrols, and in the continual cry by their commanders, of being unable to determine whether their targets were a belligerent or not.

President Wilson was inaugurated for his second term on 5 March and fell sick for two weeks from the seventh. This began Wilson's slow drift towards the decision from which 'he had no alternative'. Almost magically, events, which would whittle away at President Wilson's last hopes of remaining out of the war, began to unfold. Further loans for Britain and France were approved, merchant ships were armed, and General Pershing, sent earlier to squash the exploits of marauding 'bandits' in Mexico, had returned, leaving President Carranza with a loss of appetite for further intrigue. Carranza declared on 16 March that Mexico would remain neutral. The Russian Revolution had also erupted, and early indications of seeking peace with the revolutionaries created the possible threat of additional German forces being diverted from the Eastern to the Western Front. The dream of a German–Japanese–Russian alliance vanished.

Wilson finally grasped his sense of place in the world, and four days prior to entering the war he acknowledged the embarrassing mountain of sabotage reports that had been

accruing against his neutral country over a protracted and lengthy period, when he declared:

'They have formed plots to destroy property, they have entered into conspiracies against the neutrality of the Government, they have sought to pry into every confidential transaction of the Government in order to serve interests alien to our own.'

The saboteurs in the cities were rounded up first, followed by a rush to the borders, where numerous spies and undesirable activists were also arrested. Commercial radio stations were closed, and quickly followed by the deployment of US army detachments that rounded up and impounded thousands of privately- held wireless sets throughout the country. A wave of threatened labour disputes faded and the country got down to the business of war.

During the clampdown on labour activists, what might at first seem to be an unrelated event took place. Jim Larkin, the leader of Dublin's great labour revolt, the 'lockout' of 1913, had left Ireland three years previously, was arrested in America. Such arrests were widespread, and culminated in show trials, which led to the imprisonment of many labour dissidents then and in subsequent years. The programme was directed by the office of the US Attorney General, where the rising J. Edgar Hoover was whetting his appetite for a career in anti-communism. Larkin was arrested a second time in 1919, and was imprisoned in Sing-Sing in 1920. Larkin's activities during this period of his life, and his memory of them later, became crucial to American lawyers when they were collecting evidence during the 'Black Tom' reparation case, taken against Germany's earlier sabotage campaign in America. In 1934 Larkin testified in an affidavit given to the American Lawyer J.J. McCloy in Dublin, that he had been approached and had several meetings with German representatives in Mexico, where:

'He [Franz von Bopp] asked him whether I would engage in a sabotage of munitions plants, that there was no danger to human life since the means they had were safe. He also wanted me to become concerned with the stoppage of mules and horses, especially mules, where the concentration shipping point was St Louis. He said they had plenty of Germans living and around St. Louis but they would not take any risks. It was necessary he said to inject disease cultures into animals, which would bring on fever in a space of time and make utterly incapable of working. It was a slow developing culture, which was to affect the animals during their voyage. I told him I would have nothing to do with such methods.'

Larkin would not seem to have countenanced complicity in this type of subversive activity but his voluntary statement does confirm the extent to which Germany was prepared to go in order to achieve a victory. The activity by German agents during this period of the war in this respect remains vague to this day.

Hopes of victory on both sides lay in the battle that ensued between the might of the American industrial war machine and the German U-boats, and freedom of speech was relegated to second place.

The naked threat to sink American ships was a bid to control access to the high seas. Long after the telegrams were sent, Wilson had continually confounded his advisers and friends with his entrenched position of neutrality. In particular, his old friends, such as Ambassador Walter Page in London, and his adviser Robert Lansing, were beside themselves with anger and embarrassment. Notwithstanding the political ignominy he suffered at home, the casualties across Europe had been mounting at an alarming rate, and the threat to democracy appeared imminent. Despite Ambassador Page's pleas to Washington, Wilson would not concede to the squandering of American lives in a European conflict, one which he considered to be of its own making. Until the very last moment, he clung to such hopeless suggestions as 'armed neutrality'. The concept behind this approach was to arm American ships in defence, and to fire on German submarines when they were sighted. So, were there other more compelling reasons that might have persuaded Wilson to go to war when he did?

Despite a wide variety of accounts detailing the international political climate prior to and during World War I, no new theories have been advanced to explain why President Woodrow Wilson abandoned neutrality and declared war against Germany at the precise moment that he did: that is, many months after he became aware of Germany's extensive regime of sabotage in his country, and a full two months after the declaration of the 'unrestricted' U-boat campaign. The seemingly self-preservationist idea of fighting the growing threat of 'the Hun' in Europe, and a preferably exhausted one, rather than on American soil, is not a popular one. Nevertheless, it is often fact, that the truth is even more startling.

Whatever circumstances finally separated Wilson from neutrality, they appear to have developed during the period of his illness, 9 March to 2 April, a period during which he saw very few people. On 9 March he paid no mind to an urgent message from his ambassador in Britain, which alarmingly claimed that failing America's approval of a war loan to Britain, she would be unable to buy another gun or crate of goods from America. Events had been escalating rapidly, and after the overthrow of the Russian tsar on 19 March and the deliberation by Wilson's Cabinet on 20 March in favour of war, Wilson confided to a friend on 1 April, that there was no way to avoid war. So on 6 April, four days after President Wilson's memorable speech in which he declared that 'The world must be made safe for democracy', democratic Americans voted by an overwhelming majority to go to war. Was there no other way to save democracy, or was Wilson politically boxed into a corner?

Not unlike the continuing practice within intelligence-gathering organisations today, it was imperative for Admiral Hall to prevent his opposite number in German intelligence from discovering how their communications were been compromised. To this end, he had waited until Count von Bernstorff relayed the contents of Zimmermann's telegram to Ambassador Eckhardt in Mexico. Hall's agents intercepted the message again; as anticipated, it contained subtle differences to the original one sent by Zimmermann. With these subtle differences, the message was revealed, and it was gambled, that during the inevitable investigation of its leak by German intelligence,

FOOD WILL WIN THE WAR
You came here seeking Freedom
You must now help to preserve it

There was a strong emphasis on the shortage of food in Britain during 1917, and both sides did all in their power to deprive the other of it. Germany went a step further and waged a secret biological war against animals and food supplies.

that there would be no evidence that the Americans had not broken the code themselves. The ruse worked, but the revelation of British intelligence's ability to intercept and decipher secret German messages had the inevitable effect:. American authorities developed a sudden interest in the activities of British Intelligence.

Soon after, Hall supposedly revealed additional information from further intercepts, particularly in relation to German subversive activities in South America. Included in these was the basis of damning evidence relating to Germany's biological warfare activities in South America, Mexico, and in America itself. And when revealed, did these leave President Wilson under no illusion about the lengths to which Germany was prepared to go in order to win the war? Barbara Tuchman in her book-

The Zimmermann Telegram put it this way:

'What made him change his mind? Just when and how did the President come to see the true nature of the Germans?'

It was forcefully proclaimed in 1917 that 'Food would win the war'. Even so, very little attention has ever been given to the campaign of biological warfare waged by German saboteurs against food and beasts during World War I. Despite the fact that there were unusual outbreaks of strange sicknesses amongst the pig population, mules and horses, in the USA and France during 1917-1918, and that the numbers of animals available for service, were seriously depleted that year. Alfred Crosby for example, in-

America's Forgotten Pandemic, stated:

'In April 1918 doctors at a veterinary hospital of the French army began noticing an influx of horses with a respiratory illness, called *gourme*, that had symptoms like flu. Coincidentally, there seemed to be a disproportionate number of very early cases of flu among the personnel at the French veterinary centres. Veterinarians of the American army also saw what must have been *gourme* at Bordeaux that Spring and simply called it horse influenza. Several eminent bacteriologists concluded that *gourme* and human flu where the same, caused by a filterable virus.'

How this campaign affected humans is not clear but senior American and British intelligence sources did suspect that there was a possible link between it and the millions who died in 1918 from the disease know as the flu.

During correspondence between Admiral Hall and US Major Amos Peaslee in 1925, recorded in *Three Wars with Germany* (written by both men), Peaslee states.

'...There were grave indications in the cables [British intercepts of German communications.] that the Germans were responsible for the terrible epidemic of disease which occurred amongst the soldiers in America and on shipboard in the Spring of 1918. I note that the disease cultures were sent to Arnold [German saboteur.] in South America, and that he forwarded them by a secret agent to the United States in January 1918. Do you know whether that theory has ever been developed and whether any study was made by medical authorities to determine whether the disease among cattle and mules which Arnold was "treating" bore any resemblance to the disease among our soldiers? It seems significant that the dates coincide. Of course, we were exporting men, not mules, as they were from South America.'

Admiral Hall replied.

'….I do not think that any study has been made on the lines you suggest. It did occur to me at the time that there might be a connection between the disease in animals and the disease in men. The two types of "treatment" used by Arnold were anthrax and fungus in wheat - these two were known for certain but there may have been more.'

Did Wilson discover the true nature of instructions given by the German High Command. Instructions that ordered, 'all measures necessary to be taken' in order to achieve victory?

America was at first reluctant, but bound by similar philosophies and 'interests', she finally yielded to a destiny alongside that of Britain. The long-awaited end to the titanic struggle, the outcome of which had remained so elusive, seemed to be at hand. After repeated offensives and counter-offensives, and having laid waste the lives of millions of young serviceman across a devastated Europe, the final act had arrived.

It took American serviceman another twelve months to reach Europe in numbers that would prove to be of any consequence. And just then, all over the world, millions of servicemen and civilians began to drop like flies from the flu. Twice as many died in just a few months than had fallen in combat at sea, in the air, and in the trenches during the previous four years of war. Despite this, the Yanks were not for turning, and the Allied victory became unstoppable.

Although germ warfare in one way or another may have contributed to the 1918 pandemic of flu and the millions who died from it, it must also be pointed out that there does not seem to be any evidence that food was contaminated in Ireland during this period. (It is an interesting fact, that very similar attacks using the same type of germs, were plotted against the British occupational forces in Ireland by the Irish Republican Army during 1920. The discovery of this threat would seem to have very quickly concentrated minds on all sides.) Neither were there any references to it amongst the surviving files from the censor's office or at the P.R.O. in Kew. In fact, the complete absence of comment on the subject would almost lead one to conclude that this global catastrophe hadn't occurred at all. There was only one mention of the flu amongst the thousands of documents contained in the twelve large boxes from the Irish censor's office, now held in the National Archives. This referred to an employee from the censor's office in Cork, who was unable to attend for work due to influenza.

Admiralty House Cork.
The command centre at Queenstown, now Cobh, which directed naval operations around Ireland.

Cross channel steamer of the period leaving Kingstown, now Dun Laoghaire.

Chapter 2

IRELAND S
'UNRESTRICTED WAR'

Ireland s Unrestricted War

World War I was a period, which remained unspoken of in my grandfather's family. It was a period in his life from which he emerged with a lifelong nervous disorder known as 'shell-shock'. As a young boy, I sometimes accompanied his daughter when we made the unusual but exciting journey by train on the old Harcourt Line to see him in the veterans' hospital at Leopardstown, .

The recurring bouts of the sickness that remained with him until he died were incomprehensible to me then. The polished brass shell-case memento in the family's glass-cabinet, fashioned into a caddy for tobacco, always captured my imagination, but he related practically nothing of his experiences from a land and a great conflict which were seen only by men who 'went away'.

There were essentially only two important areas of battle during the First World War: the one which took place at sea, and the other which resulted in the loss of millions of lives across the battlefields of Europe and beyond. Although the fledgling aeroplane did not play a major part in determining the course or outcome of the war, its development at the time was quite rightly seen as being of great importance, and huge resources were allocated by the Allies to its improvement and production. These efforts did not bring results until very late in the war, when the Allied forces finally achieved superiority in the air. The advantages of aeronautical mastery of the battlefields, which had become both apparent and probably only possible for the Allies, dramatically influenced their ambitions to continue with a rapid-development program for the aeroplane after the war had ended. Improvements to that 'new weapon' continue to the present day.

Not nearly as bloody as the land war, but far more strategically important, was the battle to dominate the oceans. It was recognised early in the conflict by each of the belligerents that the sea was the main highway on which finance, raw materials, agricultural produce, machinery and personnel could be transported to and from their countries. For some countries, the oceans were lifelines and the only means of accessing areas of strategic interests. Ireland, self-sufficient in food, occupied what was probably the most strategically important area of the northern Atlantic. Less critical now, she was Europe's most westerly and remote sentry, guarding the only maritime thoroughfares to and from northern Europe. Victory in Europe was the prize for whoever controlled these waters.

From the time of the ancients, the importance of Ireland's geographical position had not been lost on maritime nations, and its occupiers have played a significant role in the development of trade routes across the Atlantic and to Europe. This belief was also shared by the Secretary of the German Navy, Admiral von Capelle during World War I, when he said that he regarded the entrances to the Irish Sea and the western approaches to the English Channel, as the 'decisive U-boat theatres', because they were 'the highways of the world's traffic.'

Vice-Admiral Sims also reiterated a similar view in his report to the Secretary of the US Navy on 16 July 1917:-

'The most effective field for enemy activity is, of course, close into the Irish Sea and Channel approaches, where all lines must focus.' And during World War II Winston Churchill is reported to have said that: 'The Mersey, the Clyde were the lungs through which we breathed.'

Breaths taken by the Mersey's lungs during World War II were aided considerably at one time by an almost complete closure of the southern entrance to the Alley. This was accomplished by a barrage of anti-submarine mines laid between Pembroke and the south-east coast of Ireland, which for the time being, meant that Britain had only the entrance via the North Channel to worry about. Coastal traffic in Ireland and England and some traffic to Portugal continued but in the main convoys operated north about Ireland into the Atlantic and south to Gibraltar or west to the USA.

Ireland might seem to be a small and insignificant place when compared to the remainder of Europe. However, if one compares the complexities of launching naval operations from England's most westerly ports with others further west in Ireland, such as Queenstown, Berehaven or Lough Swilly, then the value of the increased range for naval patrols becomes obvious. These distances were described with concern during the negotiations on Ireland's Treaty Ports as being '400 miles' in the south, and '200 miles' in the north.

During a time when operations by scarce destroyers were already seriously hampered by limitations on their range, the large and secure naval base at Queenstown proved invaluable in the fight against the U-boats during World War I. If one considers the prospect of having to patrol the Western Approaches with coal-burning warships entirely from say, Plymouth or Pembroke Dock, then the importance of the Queenstown facility 250 miles further westward, immediately becomes apparent.

This fact was of considerable importance not only during World War I but once again during World War II. Said to have been the continuation of the inconclusive first world war, when the second broke out, Winston Churchill found it very difficult to come to terms with the Empire's decision to cede control of Ireland's major Atlantic ports to the new Free State government of Ireland, in 1938. Access to these ports was of such urgency to the British during World War II that secret plans were laid to occupy them by force. Churchill was not alone in his wish to seize this valuable piece of geography, as the German invasion plan for Britain, 'Operation Sealion', also envisaged the invasion of Ireland under 'Operation Green'. Some historians consider Hitler's plans to have been a bluff and Churchill's threats as amounting to nothing more than feigning concern, or a counter to the insult perceived in Irish stubbornness by not relinquishing the ports to the operational control of the Royal Navy. And nothing more than a performance made purely for public and political appearances.

At one point the threat of a possible German invasion would seem to have been real enough but if Churchill's antics amounted to nothing more than politics, then these ideas were totally separate from some suggestions he made in a historic telegram to

A drawing by Douglas MacPherson depicting *U-21* and commander Hersing sinking ships on the first foray by a U-boat into the Irish Sea in January 1915. Placing bombs aboard captured ships or sinking them with its deck gun was a frequent practise by U-boats during the first half of WW1. This was discouraged when merchant ships were armed with a defensive gun.

President Roosevelt in May 1940. The suggestions included: 'The visit of a United States squadron to Irish ports, which might be prolonged.'

This suggestion fell on deaf ears in Washington. Although equally upset by Ireland's outward adherence to neutrality early on in World War II, Roosevelt knew full well the potential the scheme held for unfavourable electoral fallout amongst the Irish-American lobby, some of whom were still rabidly anti-British.

The Americans also saw the value of the ports and Ireland's geography, but approached the problem more subtly than had been suggested by the British. The destroyers came, the first five of the 'fifty that saved the world' to Belfast in September, and were followed by many more US naval craft that berthed in Londonderry, a port almost the equal of Lough Swilly, and only a short bus ride away. Other ships loaded with fuel, guns and radio transmitters also arrived for Ireland's defence. It would appear to have been a period of frustration for Churchill, during which he seemed to be almost obsessed with establishing British naval bases in Ireland, emphasising once more the importance given to the strategic locations of some Irish harbours. Churchill did not achieve occupation of the ports, as the Irish government had become inextricably attached to a policy of neutrality, but neither did Hitler.

The topic, which saw a new country stretching its sovereign limbs, was a daily item of censored debate at the time. Some questioned who might Ireland 'declare itself neutral against?' Some declared her as being 'nervously neutral', and others almost equally, as 'destructively neutral'. Her actual position was only revealed many years later. It is well known that thousands of Irish citizens died while fighting on the side of the Allies. But at home also established 'air corridors' for Allied aircraft, and provided the occasional safe passage and haven for Allied naval vessels. They also showed preferential treatment for downed Allied troops and equipment, deployed hundreds of coast-watching personnel around Ireland, agreed an Anglo-Irish plan to counteract a German invasion, and did not hinder British eavesdropping into Coast-watch radio transmissions that were reporting enemy shipping movements. Did providing these facilitate to the Allies mean that Ireland was something other than neutral? It appears that this question will continue to require answers.

In addition, it was reported sometime later that subsequent commendations from the government of the United States for members of the Irish Defence Forces, in respect of services rendered by them during the war, had to be put aside. This action was supposedly taken to prevent the embarrassment, which might have resulted over the actual pro-Allied position adopted by Ireland during World War II.

There is now a growing amount of material, almost reluctantly being revealed, which strengthens the opinion that Ireland has had little to regret over maintaining its position as a 'neutral' during World War II. And despite appearing to have been antagonistic towards Britain during this crisis, quite the reverse might now seem to have been the case. This being so, the stance adopted by the Irish government can be viewed as one which made a very valuable contribution to the overall strategy of security in the British Isles. For the moment, 'coming out', on this topic would seem to be another matter altogether.

The strands of the story which surround the apparently stubborn but extremely nimble political tightrope performance by Éamon de Valera and his government during this period continue to unfold. Instructed in the art of political dexterity, by a neighbour who had accomplished unsurpassed mastery of it for generations, it appears that de Valera adopted a very clever 'Irish solution' to an extremely difficult British problem. On the one hand, Ireland had fought and won a blood-soaked independence, a newly won pride, which could not appear to be relinquished easily. On the other hand, de Valera recognised the threats, not only from within, but from both Germany and the Allies. He must also have been well aware of the similar but dangerous promises on land restoration made by Germany to Mexico during World War I. Northern Ireland, a part of Ireland still under British rule, presented a valuable bargaining chip.

The arrangement that appears to have appeased both sides was that certain facilities would be made quietly available to the Allies, but strict neutrality was Ireland's declared national policy. On the face of it, the strategy appears to have mollified Churchill and Roosevelt, and kept those who might have hurled the Irish population into the abyss once more, just to spite Britain, off de Valera's back. The alternative to this strategy was to align. There was only one realistic possibility of alignment, and that was with the Allies. This would have removed any protection from attack neutrality might have provided, if not from the sea, then certainly from the air. Ireland might remain safe from invasion because of where Britain was situated, and Britain needed to feel safe because of where Ireland stood. History and further releases of important records may reveal the true extent to which Ireland helped to defeat Germany with its 'neutrality' during World War II.

It is difficult to obtain a clear impression of what the common feelings were within the Irish armed forces towards Britain at the time or of the real part Ireland should have played during World War II. But these few words, which were expressed to me by a champion conservationist of the Shannon river, the retired Irish Army officer Colonel Michael Gill, may reveal a more general and clear understanding of the mood which existed amongst the ranks during that period: 'We never felt neutral.'

The preceding few paragraphs have been included to demonstrate, that, despite the progress that had been made in transport at sea, in the air and on land, Ireland's geographical position had remained critical for many years. The passage of time has led to the general belief that the importance of this position has now been eradicated by technology. Notwithstanding this, some Europeans still feel it necessary to place far-seeing radar and radio masts on the most remote mountaintops of Ireland's western seaboard. More recently, refuelling facilities for American military transports at Shannon have also become contentious.

Accusations that the population in certain parts of Ireland was sympathetic towards the German U-boats and their crews persisted during World War I, and surfaced once again during World War II. The folklore of exchanging food with U-boat crews was probably founded on some facts, and memory of it from both world wars remains to this day. However, folklore of similar food exchanges that occurred between the crews of US naval vessels during World War I does not. Reports of sympathy and trade with the U-boats were stretched to the point that clandestine bases for U-boats were supposedly established in Ireland during World War I.

Reporting restrictions have long since been lifted but the extent to which U-boats were capable of carrying out raids from Germany to any part of the Irish coastline during World War I, without the need for any such bases, continues to be misrepresented and misunderstood. If there were ever a possibility that 'secret bases' existed in remote parts of Ireland for say, refuelling, it is unlikely that such arrangements would have had any strategic value by extending the range or period of a U-boat's patrol in the Atlantic. A U-boat's crew had a very definable length of time at sea in which they might remain efficient, healthy, and of sufficiently high morale. Even if fuel, provisions and heavy stores could somehow be shipped, off-loaded ashore and stored on remote parts of the Irish coast without being detected, it was even misunderstood by some sections of the public what type of fuel these submarines required.

Not exceptional by any means, but equally inaccurate, were the following comments by Lady Clodagh Anson Blackshaw in her memoirs, relating to the U-boats and Ireland:

'Though there were no food restrictions in Ireland during the war, we had plenty of submarines to make up. They were swarming thickly round the South coast, and made their base in all sorts of wild coves along there, as they could always get any amount of petrol and food from the people who were anti-English to a man. Sometimes we could see their periscopes from the cliffs, but they never shelled us at Ardmore (County Waterford), as they did not want to annoy their friends, and might have hit them by mistake. Of course everyone knew about this, and we spent our time telling the authorities in London, but oh no, they knew better, and refused to pay any attention or do anything about it. I don't suppose there would have been one quarter of the ships sunk without this naval base of theirs, for they could not possibly have stayed out for months as they did without supplies, and the English Channel was not so easy to pass through.'

The quote is typically anti-Irish, and demonstrates a complete misunderstanding of the U-boats and their capabilities, and the protection presumed to be afforded from them by the English Channel at the time. Their fuel requirements were quite wrongly, but often stated as being petrol or gasoline (which was rationed), when it was in fact diesel oil. There may have been no food restrictions for some people in Ardmore (this is a view held by many of Lady Clodagh Anson Blackshaw's class at the time, which tends to be confused with quite the opposite situation existing amongst the working class in the cities) but there certainly were in Dublin.

It is more likely that these stories were rather like many of the U-boat sightings from around Ireland, which were 'always good for a pint'.

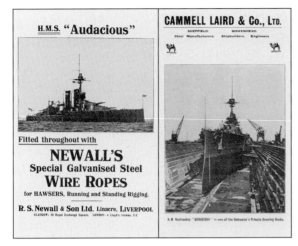

The pictures on the top left are from 'Jane's Fighting Ships 1914'. The advertisements represent the proud construction of the new battleship. HMS *Audacious*, by Lairds at Birkenhead. So much was depending on her rapid completion and how she might affect the balance of sea power. A German mine laid by the liner *Berlin* changed all of that, when it sank the great ship shortly after being lauched on October 27th, 1914.

The photograph on the bottom left was taken on board the liner *Olympic*. She had attempted to tow the stricken *Audacious* to safety before she sank off Lough Swilly in Northern Ireland. In order to conceal this loss and create confusion amongst the enemy as to the condition and disposition of the Grand Fleet, a fleet of 'Dummy Battleships' was conceived by converting fourteen merchant vessels. This was carried by Harland and Wolff shipyard at Belfast.

The top right photograph show the 'resurrection' of the HMS *Audacious* in the form of a 'dummy battleship'. Converted from the *SS Mentcolm* and steaming in Belfast Lough, the silhouette might appear quite convincing to an enemy submarine.(Courtesy of the Ulster Folk & Transport Museum Cultra Co. Down.)

'Dummy' vessels were again used for the same purpose during WW2, and sailors in the photograph on the bottom right can be seen carrying the lightweight timber guns on the converted battleship *Royal Sovereign* (ex. Pakeha).

The reprint in the illustrations of the censored newspaper article from October 1917 contains a somewhat unusual reference to the discovery of a 'submarine base' at Tory Island. The article submitted by the *Freeman's Journal* is a typical example of a proof submitted to the Chief Censor, Lord Decies, for consideration, the content of which was then hurriedly dispatched by telegram to Admiralty Intelligence for an opinion. In this case, the article was subsequently issued with a 'D notice' and publication was refused. The suggestion that such bases existed in the likes of Kerry and Donegal was so persistent throughout the war that these comments were thoroughly investigated by the Admiralty, who consistently denied the possibility of this being the case.

In this connection, but less well known, are the adventures of the steam yacht *Sayonara*, which Admiral Hall sent cruising along the west coast of Ireland in order to check up on these stories and some others relating to the activities of spies. The yacht was commanded by her new captain, Lieutenant F. M. Simon R.N.R., and was supposedly on a winter cruise with her new sham owner, Major Wilfred Howell. Admiral Hall had borrowed the yacht from her real owner, the wealthy American Anthony Drexel. Major Howell had an extremely interesting and thorough education, and among his many talents were his abilities as a soldier of fortune. These had been exercised in several countries before he went to work for British Intelligence. The major reportedly spoke excellent German, and adopted the name of McBride.

On its way to the west coast of Ireland in December 1915, the *Sayonara* docked in Queenstown, where Major Howell appeared as a wealthy German-American brandishing his adopted name of Colonel McBride. Another equally false McBride visited Queenstown quite soon afterwards. This was none other than 'Captain William McBride', or more accurately, Commander Godfrey Herbert R.N., of the infamous *Baralong* incident.

The *Sayonara* was fitted with a hidden aerial and radio, and had a German-speaking owner and fifty marines capable of being armed at a moment's notice from a well-hidden cache of arms. Their purpose seems to have been mixed but included the hunt for the mysterious U-boat fuel depots, arms dumps, intelligence-gathering on Sinn Féin activists, and setting a trap for Roger Casement and his plot to land arms on the Irish coast. The trap to catch Casement in the act was premature in this instance. The areas where this spy vessel operated seem to have been between Shannon and Achill, with some emphasis on north Galway and Mayo. The ruse was said by the Admiral to have been successful and to have yielded results, and it was supposedly of great benefit during the uprising in 1916.

Notwithstanding the Admiral's claims, the yacht and its owner aroused the suspicions of local inhabitants during its unusual cruise on the west coast of Ireland during winter. The reported suspicions of a strange vessel apparently provoked boardings by British patrols, which might alternatively indicate that the actual successes of the operation must remain in some doubt. In respect of the 'U-boat bases', the Admiral concluded that such bases would have been almost impossible to establish. But then again, our friend Admiral Hall is reported to have laid many a false trail.

An interesting aside to these claims is the fact that similar operations were carried out

by British Intelligence around the coast of Crete during World War I, and were designed to ensnare similar would-be German collaborators. These took the form of a British submarine posing as a German one, and manning it with German-speaking personnel. These were put ashore at places around the island in an attempt to make contacts with supposed German sympathisers.

One of Britain's main strategies during World War I was to maintain complete control of the maritime commerce to and from Germany, thus starving her of the raw materials which were essential for the execution of the war. Almost to the point of hostility, American interests, north and south, that had been enjoying the commercial opportunities presented by the war, became extremely unhappy with the restrictive practises of the British navy. American's sense of fair play was further upset when the blockade was also used to censor the mails, and to enforce the blacklisting of some American companies. In the longer term, however, America eventually supported the idea, and even adopted the policy in her own sphere of influence.

Almost immediately after the outbreak of the war, Britain deployed a fleet of armed auxiliary merchant vessels and began her blockade of Germany. Their operations are extensively outlined in *The Big Blockade* by E.K. Chatterton. It was a round-the-clock, seven-days-a-week, and all-year-round operation, and was carried out in all weathers for the duration of the war. This division of the navy was known as the Tenth Cruiser Squadron, and mainly consisted of armed and converted merchantmen. There task was to prevent 'contraband', 'blacklisted' goods and 'undesirables' from entering Europe – or more precisely, from reaching Germany.

The blockade had three objectives, although maybe not all three were thought of at once. Firstly, to help prevent elements of the High Seas Fleet breaking out into the Atlantic, thus preventing the second, which would have been the resulting threat posed to British shipping by the 'escapees'. The third was an attempt to starve Germany. Britain did not at first consider it possible for Germany to leapfrog their blockade and threaten England and its approaches with submarines from the Atlantic.

Patrols by the blockaders extended as far north as Iceland and beyond, and eastward to Norway. The operation was as thorough as weather and machinery permitted, but many of the goods, which were falsely manifested as being bound for neutral Scandinavian and European countries, and subsequently allowed to pass and reach their destination, were ultimately finding their way overland to Germany. Searching and seizing ships in this manner antagonised other neutrals, including South Americian countries. Many of these nations were quite happy to do business with any of the European countries during the early years of the war, including Germany. Although Britain's blockade created endless diplomatic wrangling and squeezed Germany's economy to a considerable degree, it was not a complete success until America entered the conflict and subscribed its industrial, political, military and naval influence to the operation. It might also be pointed out that, despite America's earlier and persistent objections to the principle of blockading 'legitimate' exports to 'neutral' countries, it wholeheartedly embraced just such a practice on South American countries after she declared war on Germany. This demonstrates how serious the business of winning a war can become, once the mind is concentrated on the alternative. The eventual acquiescence of the Scandinavian countries was another principal factor in what became an almost complete cessation of Germany's imports.

The seas around Ireland and its Atlantic approaches to the north and south were patrolled by naval vessels from a number of auxiliary bases established by the Royal Navy around Ireland. These were in turn controlled by a command centre at Admiralty House, in Queenstown Harbour, Cork. In command there was a man who seems to have made every effort to steer clear of publicity, and one who favoured action over words, Admiral Bayly had overall control of these operations from the end of July 1915 until the war concluded.

With precious few resources to throw against the growing number of U-boats until the US destroyers arrived in May 1917, it was this man's leadership, and the duty, bravery and endurance displayed by the young officers and crews under his command, which were largely responsible for the final victory. Captain Dorling Taffrail in his book *Endless Story* (1931), summed up the enormity of the task that faced Admiral Bayly during the earlier years of the war:

'In an area of about 25,000 square miles . . . there were sometimes as few as four British destroyers available for patrol work. Never were there more than fifteen.'

It should also be pointed out that a shortage of suitable vessels was not peculiar to the Royal Navy, as it was reported in Washington in May 1917 that France had only five destroyers available for duty on her west coast.

Germany for her part attempted to achieve the same result by imposing a similar blockade on Britain, but by a totally different method. She had developed a significant advantage in submarine technology, and by deploying a fleet of modern submarines had intended to sink enough ships in an attempt to sever the flow of war materials and the critical life-sustaining food supplies that were being shipped to and from Britain. Britain is essentially an island, albeit a very large one, and although she is also a very powerful nation, she remains far smaller than the European family of nations as a whole. However, she was then an island dependent on others, and unable to supply all of the necessary produce in order to sustain herself. In this respect, Ireland played a significant role in Britain's survival before and more critically during the war. Apart from the 50,000 who left Ireland and never returned from the battlefields, Ireland also made a significant agricultural and industrial contribution to the welfare of Britain. Extremely fertile, and considered to be an offshore British farm, Ireland's agricultural and industrial potential during the war also presented significant opportunities to those engaged in cross-channel commerce.

Although considered at the time to be vital to Britain's survival, history has neglected to record the important contribution made by Ireland during World War I. This consisted of a whole range of agricultural products, and many unlikely industrial ones.

The importance of these lifelines meant that considerable efforts, albeit too late for many, were made protecting shipping in the approaches to the north and south coasts of Ireland, and particularly in the 'channels' within the Alley. Ireland's richness as a source of food had grown since the 'Famine', and it is not overstating the case to suggest that it played a crucial role in Britain's successful prosecution of the war.

The situation was somewhat comparable during World War II, but, not having the same access to the offshore Irish farm, Britain's position was not as favourable. And although treaties had been signed between the two countries, Britain took stern measures in order to insure that Ireland's ships and exports could not go too far afield. Britain's food shortages during this period necessitated the introduction of an austere regime at home in order to increase the production of basic foodstuffs. The measures were seen as imperative and were reinforced to the point that farms and holdings were seized from farmers and tenants who did not comply with the new instructions for achieving higher food-production targets.

During World War I, the amount of foodstuffs shipped from Ireland to Britain also helped the Allies to hold out until such time as America entered with relief. Food, America had in plenty, but the impressive industrial might of this giant was nowhere more evident than when it established a marine equivalent of the Ford assembly methods. This was the very efficient prefabrication procedure introduced into shipbuilding and elsewhere under the 'Liberty' flag. By November 1918, she boasted that from the time of 'laying down', American shipyards could produce and commission a destroyer in 'seventy days', whereas the pre war completion time might have taken as long as two years. A record time of forty-six days was achieved for the commissioning of the USS Reid.

One could produce a long list of engineering items, such as ships, munitions and machinery, which flowed across the Atlantic in a torrent after US industrialists had tooled up. Once the full potential of US industrial might was unleashed, there was no way that Germany could have attained a victory with her dwindling resources in any 'ordinary' way.

Nineteen seventeen was the second time Germany initiated an all-out and 'unrestricted' campaign of submarine attacks against shipping. For allied shipping and German U-boats, it was the most critical period of World War I, and brought the Allies face to face with defeat. It was the year when Britain nearly starved because cargoes of food, and all manner of supplies, were confined within the holds of merchant ships in America, unable or unwilling to sail. The submarine was just the instrument, but the war became centred on preventing the movement of troops, supplies and food.

At the outbreak of the war, Ireland was capable of exporting vast quantities of agricultural produce to Britain, and because no live animals were imported, she was in the unique position of having almost totally disease-free livestock. (This was stated to be the case at the time, even though it had been reported only a few years earlier that, due to the deplorable conditions in which pigs were kept in Dublin, the city was riddled with swine fever.) Stock breeders and herd managers were quick to recognise

Courtesy of Dublin Port & Docks Museum, this picture depicts German warships on a visit to
Kingstown (Dun Laoghaire) prior to the outbreak of WW1.
(Courtesy visits are not always what they seem).

British torpedo boat No. 87 at Kingstown (Dun Laoghaire) after the end of WW1.
Note the hinged door near the waterline in the bow for launching a torpedo.
(MaritimeMuseum, Dun Laoghaire).

the new opportunities. At a specially convened meeting of the Council of Agriculture in the Concert Hall of the Civic Exhibition in Dublin, Mr. T. Russell from the Department of Agriculture and Technical Instruction stated that:

'There were articles which were bound to increase in price, and these were precisely those articles which the Irish farmer produced or was in a position to produce.' He also stated that there would be: 'An improved market for Irish cattle [on which the then current animal health restrictions were about to be lifted] and that there would be a further abnormal demand for horses . . . and Irish bacon threatened to become even more of a luxury than it was at the present time.'

The virtues of the Government War Risks Insurance Scheme were also extolled, to the point of being thought to have become nearly obsolescent. He stated that protection for shippers might be considered almost 'unnecessary', because the policing of the seas by the Fleet had secured such a freedom on the seas that 'The truth was that the German flag was not now to be seen on any of the great waterways.'(Applause)

This address was reported in the *Evening Herald* on 28 August 1914. Those were early days, and such jingoistic optimism was in for a rude awakening before the last of the summer's harvest appeared in the stores. The German flag was not going to be seen so much above the water, as it was going to be felt from below it.

By the spring of 1917, at the peak of the massive U-boat offensive, the level of food stocks in Britain reached crisis proportions, and all manner of 'food orders' were introduced, in England and Ireland. Despite considerable increases in food production, and the growing exports of beef, pork and sheep meat from Ireland to Britain, shortages were beginning to emerge. President Wilson's statement that 'the fate of the nation depends upon farmers' shows how important this weapon had become. Due to financial reasons, and the shortage of valuable space in ships, the distribution of certain commodities was restricted, and even banned in many instances.

A plethora of restrictions governing the maximum prices on certain foods had already been introduced before the *Freeman's Journal* announced it on 4 April. Under 'The Public Meals Order', premises serving meals 'in excess of a charge of one shilling and threepence' should not serve 'meat, poultry or game on the meatless day, which shall be Wednesday'. A similar order stated that 'no potatoes shall be served except on meatless days and Friday.' By 10 April, the *Freeman's* stated that 'The *Times* Reports that the Food Question Was Serious.' It continued with criticism of the authorities, stating that they should be 'completely frank about the food scarcity' and that 'the country is very much shorter of wheaten flour than anything else.'

Sometime later, the availability of adequate amounts of cereals in Ireland became the exception to the Irish farmers' good fortune, and they eventually became sorely dependent on the importation of grain and animal feedstuffs. Unfortunately for Ireland, the bulk of cereals from South America were being shipped to Britain; Ireland depended on these being reshipped from there.

By 1918, the growing number of ships being lost was having a severe effect on the availability of food, and the *Freeman's Journal* on January 3 critically but naively appealed to the Admiralty in respect of its policy of divulging only minimum amounts of information on shipping losses. Hoping that official frankness might promote more tolerance and understanding amongst the public, more accurate and plain announcements as to the extent of the casualties were demanded. The *Evening Herald* on the same day included this CHAIRMAN RYME. No.63, (Form of advert.) which helps to give some perception of the difficult food situation, and the benefits which were perceived to be had from tobacco:

> When Smith consumed his wife's mince-pie,
> He looked around and said "Goodbye!"
> For he had bought the candied peel,
> The flour and war potato-meal,
> The currants bearded, dry and hard.
> The suet, and the dubious lard.
> "Alas!" he cried, "for my inside,
> Poor Johnson tried one, and he died."
> And all the comfort Smith could get
> Was from his CHAIRMAN cigarette.
> 4¹/₂d for 10.

An adjacent column contained a lively criticism of the high prices of food in Ireland, resulting from the large amounts being sold to unscrupulous 'English buyers'. Despite a vigilant censor, the criticism continued:

'The Food Controller does not seem to care a thraneen (Irish for something small) how the Irish people are affected by the smuggling away of our food so long as the people of England, and especially the families of the English workingman, are served. An Order is made. Why is it not observed? If this illegal traffic is not stopped at once then Irish people must act for themselves.'

If the situation hadn't already been bad enough, some greedy distributors of milk were watering down the precious liquid, at a time when poorer countries were distributing it free of charge. Frequent prosecution notices of well-known distributors, such as Lady Arnott, appeared in the daily newspapers.

As in all wars, extraordinary contrasts existed side by side during the Great War. Not unlike the well-documented accounts of the relative wealth displayed by US servicemen on leave in Britain during World War II, Commander Taussig of *USS Wadsworth* made somewhat similar observations in September 1917.

After prolonged and arduous patrol duties, the commander, who had been based at Queenstown since his arrival there in May, was given orders to proceed with his

British Cruiser *HMS Foreward* in Kingstown (Dun Laoghaire) 1914
She was despatched to that harbour to discourage gun running.

The photograph depicts different types of British submarines that operated around Ireland during WW1. Third out from the depot vessel is *E-54*, which took part in one of those rare, submarine against submarine, engagements. On May 1st, 1917, the German submarine *U-81* was in the act of sinking the *SS San Urbano* 180 miles off the Fastnet. It was surprised by the British submarine *E-54*, which fired two torpedoes, scored a direct hit, and sank it.

The German commander and seven of her crew were saved by the British submarine.

destroyer to Liverpool for a refit. After landing in Britain, he recorded a sense of surprise in his diary at the relaxed attitude of the population, amongst whom there were 'many men in uniform. Except for this, one would not know that a war is on.' Similar observations were not uncommon amongst visiting non-nationals, and many senior US naval personnel made similar ones. More to the point, the commander found no difficulty in obtaining a first-class dinner at the Savoy Hotel, and recalled the sumptuous menu as follows: 'it was a very good dinner – oysters, soup, lobster, broiled chicken, etc.'

In view of all the food orders that had been made, the menu could only be considered as extravagant, and maybe this luxury was only available to a few. Why a plentiful supply of fine food might exist for some, while others were dying of hunger, was explained in the commander's own observations of the age-old privileges attached to one's position in society: 'Although there may be some scarcity of food it has not reached the point where one cannot get anything they want as long as they have the prices.'

Commander Taussig had thought the meal to be expensive at ten shillings and sixpence, and did not repeat the banana he consumed after the following day's breakfast, at a price he thought to be prohibitive, two shillings. This was the equivalent of one day's pay for a manual labourer in Dublin. His observations are an interesting reflection on difficult times but only confirm once again that 'some things never change'.

By the last months of the war it was clear just how important Irish food production had become. Whilst on a visit to the Belfast harbour works, the Lord Lieutenant of Ireland addressed the Harbour Board on 5 August 1918. Amongst his obvious anti-Irish sentiments, he expressed these concerns on the subject:

'Now we know very well what a prosperous and flourishing city Belfast has been for a long time past, and we know the reason for that prosperity. But why is it that we are unable now, only perhaps within the last few years, to apply such a description to the whole of Ireland? It is because everything has been done by the Imperial Parliament that could possibly have been done to enhance the prosperity and well-being of the Irish farmer, but in the last four years there has been a greater and more remarkable reason. The war has created a great demand for what Ireland can most easily supply, viz. foodstuffs. And why can Ireland so easily supply this want when war is raging round her all over the world? Because the efficiency of the Imperial Army on land, and the protection of the Imperial Navy on the sea, has kept Ireland safe and secure, and has enabled her to grow and her abundant harvest to be gathered in peace and quiet when other nations are over-run and devastated by fire and sword.'

A speech laced with some emotion, and no doubt the times would allow for this, but the Lord Lieutenant forgot to mention the age-old and singularly successful incentive of profit. Neither could it be said that Ireland was 'peaceful and quiet' during those four years. He continued to extol the virtues and qualities of rural farming:

'But rural Ireland has begun to share in this wonderful prosperity. She has supplied Great Britain during the last year with nearly one million head of cattle. The value of food and drink stuffs exported from Ireland to Great Britain has increased in the last four years from thirty millions to fifty millions.'

I'm sure the Lord Lieutenant would have received lively argument from the farm labouring population of 'rural Ireland' about who was benefiting most from the booming exports across the Channel. His last few paragraphs placed particular emphasis on how important Ireland's position as a major contributor to the Great British 'bread basket' was, and how difficult it was going to be for Ireland to escape this destiny alongside Britain:

'Here is peace, prosperity and plenty for all within our grasp if we will only cease to follow will o' the wisps, and settle down to hard earnest endeavour.'

Many British landlords and businessmen in Ireland had become wealthy because of their position and influence – and at the expense of their tenants and labourers. The strategic offshore 'Ireland farm' was considered to be secure within the Dominion. The Lord Lieutenant's next words show how it was intended that this should continue to be the case:

'Industrial effort and agricultural effort, the great co-partners of success in any country, will then gradually transform this country into the Denmark of the United Kingdom.'

These sentiments might appear to be totally unrelated to Ireland's position today, but are they really? Although belonging to, and having access to the enlarged European marketplace, Ireland has remained dependent to a significant degree for a major portion of its total exports on the British market. And as Ireland has now no national merchant fleet, a considerable amount of Ireland's exports must be shipped by foreign vessels or pass by road through Britain in order to access Europe. For instance, might Britain reintroduce tariffs on Irish imports and exports, but only this time on goods that are being transported on its motorways to or from foreign markets? Tolls and tunnels may yet exact a high price from such dependence. (At the time of writing, some British parliamentarians are promoting the idea of introducing such taxes.)

Although activities of the war-related industries in Ireland have not been well recorded in the past, this has been rectified recently by J. F. Kelleher (RIP) in his book *Ireland's War Industries 1361–1987*. World War I was no exception, and other than the obvious benefits accruing from, and to, a considerable number of Irish engineering works, shipyard repairers, clothing and medical suppliers, there was also a considerable amount of aeroplane and munitions parts manufactured throughout Ireland.

The Kynoch works at Arklow employed between 3,500 and 4,000 people during the height of the war, and was at one time considered to be 'one of the largest and most complete explosives factories in the world.' It was said that the quality of munitions produced at Kynochs during World War I was so high that it was used as a benchmark for munitions production throughout Britain.

Despite improvements in the quantity and quality of munitions produced in Britain and Ireland at this time, it was nevertheless necessary to import vast quantities from America and Russia. (Sabotage had badly affected munitions production in America prior to April 1917.) Shortages became critical by 1917, and after severe public criticism of the shortcomings in supply and production qualities, which were often discovered too late by the troops at the front, a general shake-up followed what was described as the 'shell scandal'.

Despite begrudging opposition by some British industrialists, it was decided to establish National Munitions (Shell) factories at Belfast, Dublin, Waterford, Cork and Galway. In addition to these, there were at least 'fifty other subcontractors' (Censor's files, National Archives) employed in munitions manufacture in the south of Ireland. A prominent and well-remembered name in this regard is Pierce of Wexford. Indeed, the prospect of having a munitions factory in one's own county was thought so desirable that it led to a flood of petitions from local businessmen and public representatives throughout the country.

Munitions productions from a number of these factories were railed to an inspection depot adjoining the Royal Hospital in Kilmainham, which later became a manufacture and training depot for the Post Office Engineering Department (Eircom). The existing rail system was extended to these stores from the adjacent Heuston Station railway sheds at Kingsbridge, consignments, which were railed to and from these sheds on Guinness locomotives, were operated by the company free of charge.

One of the earliest companies to get permission for establishing munitions production facilities during the war was the Dublin Dockyard Munitions Company, which was situated at the North Wall in Dublin Port. This factory manufactured artillery shells to a very high standard, and for its brief life span the enterprise was said to have been a resounding success.

The war required more than shells, however, and the Ministry of Munitions maintained requirements for a wide variety of products from Irish industrialists, north and south, for the duration of the war. These covered items ranging from high-grade optical lenses for periscopes and military ranging equipment, to margarine and special oil products (the export of margarine products from Ireland more than quadrupled during the war years) and chemicals, to 'artificial human eyes'. Extensive contracts were also awarded for the supply of woollen and linen-based articles such as military uniforms.

Many of the companies involved were already prominent and many remain household names today. These included names like Roadstone, Ford (only beginning then), Inchicore Railway Works (G.S.&W.R.), Dunlop, Hammond Lane, Booth Brothers & Ashenhurst Williams, Brooks Thomas, Philip Pierce & Co., county Wexford.

The British depot vessel, *HMS Vulcan*, which was commanded by Captain Nasmith, and operated around the Irish coast out of Queenstown under the overall command of Admiral Bayly. Many of the earlier British submarines had short cruise capability and required a high degree of maintenance. The depot or 'mother' ships provided much of these needs and often travelled to remote places in support of its submarines. Anti-U-boat operations with Allied submarines were often quite limited, sometimes only cruising one at a time in an area in order to prevent mistaken attacks.

British submarine *E-56* leaving Queenstown during WW1.
Photograph courtesy of Offen Collection.

Hundreds of fishing boats such as drifters were 'hired in' and built for the Royal Navy during WW1, and were used to hunt and patrol for U-boats. Some were fitted with wireless, and most were fitted with a deck gun as shown on the port side in this picture. Note the resting position of the gun in the picture, fore/aft, at the same level as the boom in a lowered position. This made recognition of the gun very difficult from a distance. Second depiction right, shows the crewman of an armed drifter signalling with flags (Semaphore).

A rare photograph depicting a large fleet of armed trawlers, mine-sweepers and fishing vessels, in Larne Bay. These were patrolled by the Admiralty during WW1 in the North Channel for submarine detection. The silhouettes give no clue as to which were armed.
The photgraph is courtesy of the Larn Borough Council Museum Services and the Captain Close collection. (Neg. S/H 53).

The majority of workers employed in these industries were women; in the case of munitions, this was due in large part to the stipulation by the Ministry of Munitions that not more than 5 per cent of the total workforce could be men.

The large optical works in Rathmines, Dublin, was owned by the well-known Howard Grubb, and his works had a permanent armed guard placed on it, as it figured prominently in the manufacture of a whole range of goods for the British Army and Navy during the war. Not least of the important work carried out there was the fitting out of periscopes with high-grade lenses for British submarines.

What might now seem to be a most unusual practice, was the production of special machine parts and fuses at the Belfast Municipal Technical Institute and at the Royal College of Science in Dublin, now UCD, for the munitions industries. The staff who carried out the work at these institutions, were mostly volunteers from the professional classes.

The shipbuilding and repair facilities at Queenstown were considerable, and were kept extremely busy. Those at the Dublin Dockyard facility were also very important, and were noted for the pioneering methods adopted in the construction of the 'Standard Ship' for the Ministry of Shipping. This was a specially designed vessel built to a 'standard specification of 2,450 tons' (there were several different 'standard' designs constructed throughout Britain and Ireland), and the Dublin yard built twelve of these during the war. The central position of Dublin Port to the Alley also meant that it was especially well located to handle construction and repair work for the cross-channel trade, and even for some of the transatlantic convoy work. Agreements entered into with the Admiralty for this work during the war kept the yards extremely busy, and the workforce in the ports wholeheartedly embraced the operations.

This ever-present commercial evidence only goes to support the belief that for many, the opportunity to work and make profits during war is often a welcome one. However, in respect of employment opportunities that developed in Ireland during the war, the following question must be asked: just who benefited from them? And no matter who they were, it is a sad fact that a very large part of this manufacturing capacity in Ireland was dismantled and disappeared – along with its wages – almost immediately after an armistice was announced.

To what degree these industries became significant targets of the German submarine campaign, is not altogether known. However, there was an increase in the number of attacks in the Alley as 1917 progressed, and these coincided with an increase in munitions output from the newly constructed National Shell Factories, particularly in Waterford. Even though the sum of these industries was in no way comparable to the industrial might of Great Britain's large industrial cities, they played their part. Many of these were subsequently dismantled, and their machinery shipped to Britain when the war ended.

This policy of dismantling Ireland's industries did nothing to help the employment prospects of those returning to Ireland from the battlefields, and even worsened when the exodus of British businessmen and landowners accelerated after 1922.

Whilst the poor in Ireland, and probably those in most of Europe, were paying high prices for food, many others became wealthy from the land during the war. Food production was given an extra high level of priority, as were those who harvested and shipped it. Spared from conscription, Irish croppers in Britain were occasionally run off the land for taking up such work. The action was regrettable but taken because their employment was considered by English farmers to be freeing-up their sons for conscription. Some of the work taken up by Irishmen in England was actually exempt from conscription, and in certain cases, English workers refused to work alongside Irish ones.

Ironically, this was a very similar idea to the one proposed by the French in 1918. The French suggested that Irish labourers might salve their awkward dilemma, between being anti British and anti German, by travelling to France to replace Frenchmen destined or at war, in order to free them up for farm work.

Preventing food getting from Ireland to England was a priority for Germany, and she dispatched increasing numbers of U-boats to the Alley in order to accomplish the task. Even though it is generally acknowledged that Germany could not have forced Britain's surrender once 1918 had arrived, this did nothing to deter the efforts of the German army. Neither did it weaken the resolve of the U-boat commanders or dispel a belief that, at some point, the High Seas Fleet might 'break out' in a decisive action with the British fleet.

Germany's interest in Ireland's exports of food and materials to Britain remained a focus for submarine attacks until the summer of 1918. This strategy, and Germany's willingness to continue offering arms to Sinn Féin, is clearly outlined in the following telegram sent from Berlin to a German agent in Spain, during March 1918. The reference to 'he', concerns a man known as Herr Arnold, who was said to be 'Germany's most successful agent in South America'.

'He must try to keep the Sinn Féin Movement continually going, and set on foot propaganda to prevent the export of provisions to England. The Leaders of the Irish Movement should try to dispatch via neutral countries a thoroughly reliable Irish-man to initiate and maintain communications from Germany to Ireland and vice versa.

It is important to know what arms the Sinn Féiners would like from Germany and when and where they could be safely landed in Ireland and safely received by the Sinn Féiners.'

Although this book primarily concerns itself with the effects the U-boat war had on shipping in the Alley and its strategy of isolating Britain, there is another vital aspect to the shift of U-boat attacks into the Alley. There were, in fact, right through the war, significant amounts of material and troops outward bound from the same areas to the theatres of conflict in the Mediterranean. These, too, were capable of being interrupted by U-boat patrols in the Alley.

Britain was totally unprepared for the extent to which the German U-boat campaign overtook them during the early part of the war. She had underestimated each of the important elements of the new U-boat designs: their speed, diving capabilities, armour and artillery, and the improvements Germany had made with mines. The Admiralty had also miscalculated the power and range of German torpedoes. Crucially, she had not kept abreast of the advances that were being made with the diesel engines developed for the U-boats, and the profound effect that these would have on their range and role during the approaching war. There was a distinct difficulty at first, even on both sides, in understanding the full implications of what was truly a new and deadly weapon.

As early as August 1914, Britain began what can only be described as a haemorrhaging of its capital vessels. It began in the North Sea with the loss of two light cruisers in August and September, by torpedo and mine, and continued with four submarines, an aircraft carrier and two battleships in October and November. One of these battleships, the brand-new *HMS Audacious,* was lost off Lough Swilly on 27 October 1914. By far the most devastating blow to the morale of ordinary sailors occurred when five cruisers were lost during the period 22 September to 1 November. The much feared and hated submarine commander Otto Weddigen sank three of these in quick succession. In the relatively crude early design, *U-9,* he torpedoed and consigned to the depths *HMS Aboukir* (12,000 tons), *HMS Cressy* (12,000 tons) and *HMS Hogue* (12,000 tons). These three large and ageing war vessels were sunk with the loss of 1,460 servicemen, in a matter of hours off the Hook of Holland; their loss changed everything. (Otto Weddigen and his 31 crewmates were lost when their submarine *U-29* were rammed by British vessels off the west coast of Scotland on 10 March 1915.) The value of these old cruisers was questionable, but nonetheless, the multiple loss of the vessels, and the large number of their crew, at the hands of Germany's new underwater weapon, came as a great shock to everyone and created a mountain of recriminations. The full dimension of the threat posed by Germany's emerging fleet of U-boats was slow in being appreciated at the Admiralty. At the same time, it was clear to others that the Admiralty had dragged its feet in the development of a British equivalent, and until almost the outbreak of the war, many within its lofty halls had harboured such short sighted sentiments as. 'The idea of submarine navigation is a morbid one', and that 'the submarine was the arm of weaker powers'.

The growing number of reported U-boat sightings began to worry the Admiralty to the point that, in early October, it was considered that those elements of the fleet based at Scapa presented an unacceptable risk of attack, due to the inadequate defences there. The decision was made to move them to Lough Swilly in Northern Ireland, and Mull in the west of Scotland. Amongst these elements of the fleet, was the First Battle Squadron, commanded by Vice-Admiral Lewis Bayly. The Admiral would ultimately play a pivotal role in the defeat of the U-boats in the waters around Ireland, but not before a second battleship under his command was dealt a mortal blow by one of them. During manoeuvres and target practice off Malin Head on 27 October, the *Audacious* was rocked by a huge explosion and immediately began to list. Not believing that the German navy was capable of laying mines so far west as Lough Swilly, it was first suspected that the battleship had been struck by a torpedo. However, the spanking-new battleship had sunk after striking a mine, which was only one of many that had been laid by the liner *Berlin* off the entrance to Swilly on 22 October. The same nest of 'black eggs' also sank the merchant steamer *Manchester Commerce* (5363 tons), with the loss of her fourteen crew. In addition, it was reported (according to Admiral Jellicoe, in *The Grand Fleet*) that the four-masted sailing vessel *Caldaff* had struck a mine off Malin Head the previous day. As late as the following February, these mines were being blamed for the loss of several more vessels in the waters opposite the entrance to the North Channel.

Not long after the loss of the *Audacious*, Admiral Bayly was ordered to take command of the Fifth Battle Squadron, where he lost a second battleship, *HMS Formidable* (15,000 tons). Commander Schneider in *U-24* torpedoed and sank this battleship while she was taking part in firing practice off Portland on 1 January 1915. Once more, the British had miscalculated the capabilities of the German submarines.

Compounding the large number of losses at the time, several capital vessels were also out of service due to repairs and maintenance. Probably as a result of being equally unprepared at the time, the German navy did not exploit this real but temporary weakness of the British navy. It had also been a period when the U-boats were politically restrained in their attacks against merchant ships; if this had not been the case, they might have made a serious dent in the amount of troops and supplies that were able to cross the Channel.

Having at first suspected that the mines which sunk the *Audacious,* were planted by a U-boat, the admirals at Whitehall began to detect a chill wind. An audit of the Fleet at the time showed that its margin of superiority over Germany's 'was unpleasantly small'. This opinion was based on a number of facts, not least of which was that a number of British capital ships were unavailable for service due to their being laid up for repairs, leaving the Fleet relatively equal to the German one but having only half as many destroyers.

Even though British submarines were three times more plentiful than German ones at the beginning of the war, their qualities were considered to be nowhere near equal to those of the German boats. The main operational difference between the two was tactics. Even if they could locate them, British submarines were generally not sinking German ships, whereas the situation became quite the opposite with the U-boats.

On 8 February 1918, during a period of particularly severe losses in the Alley, Admiral Jellicoe, who had only recently been relieved of his position as First Sea Lord, was asked why the submarines were so active. Despite the censor, he was reported to have made an unusually frank reply. He began by stating that he had 'little difficulty about speaking on naval matters', for he 'had nothing to do with the business', and further believed that:

Another rare photograph courtesy of the Larne Borough Museum Services and the Captain Close collection (Neg. S/H 54). It depicts a 'captured' U-boat being brought into Larne Lough'. As there is no record yet of a 'captured' U-boat' being brought into Larne Lough, this submarine mey be one of the many 'surrrendered' ones, which toured British and Irish harbours after the war. One visited Kngstown in the Spring of 1919, where the public could board for sixpence. This U-boat, with the British ensign flying above the Gernan one, appears to be later UBIII class, and its number is only barely visible.

This unusual photograph of a considerable number of RN vessels based at Lough Swilly was reportedly taken in October 1918. The view depicts armed trawlers, destroyers, submarines and at least one cruiser. The photgraph is said to have appeared on a postcard. It is very unlikely that permission for such a photograph was given to an individual in the first place.For it to appear on a postcard would seem under ordinary circumstances to have been very unlikely.

A rare photograph taken by Commander Hashagen while on patrol in his submarine *U-62* in the Irish Sea during 1917. This U-boat torpedoed and sunk the Waterford steamers *Formby* and *Conninbeg* in December 1917. All of the eighty-three aboard the two ships were lost.

'The methods of the submarine were sprung upon the British Navy in the way of a surprise....and that there was no one in a responsible position who agreed that the German Navy would really do such a thing as Lord Fisher expected.'(In reference to the unexpected use of the submarine against merchant ships.)

The situation with the U-boats had certainly become difficult but the Admiral's opinion was tinged with acrimony, and he may only have being permitted to continue to dig the proverbial hole for himself.

Such was the alarm in the Admiralty following the news of the loss of *HMS Audacious* that the Lords hurriedly set about creating a fleet of 'Dummy Dreadnoughts'. This was a fleet of fourteen commercial vessels, which were bought in and converted by the use of steel, canvas and timber at Belfast under Admiralty instructions, so as to resemble the existing fleet of dreadnought warships. The notion was conceived out of a wish to hide from Germany the embarrassing loss of the *Audacious*, and to confuse the enemy wherever possible as to the real strength and position of Britain's great fleet of warships. Viewed through a periscope in poor light conditions, or from some distance away, these dummies might have appeared convincing. Their big disadvantage was speed, or more the lack of it, and the vessels were said to have only resembled a 'crippled' warship.

The overall result of employing the 'Dummy Plot' was considered to be a gross underestimation of German Intelligence, and a failure. The failure of the ruse was almost assured, when a reference to the construction of 'Dummy Dreadnoughts' at Harland & Wolff appeared in some Irish newspapers as early as mid-December 1914, before the censor could prevent it.

Compounding the problem of secrecy, photographs of the sinking *Audacious* by passengers travelling on the out-going *Olympic*, which by virtue of coincidence, was bound for America at the time, and had attempted to tow the stricken warship to safety. Despite the subsequent and enforced delay of the *Olympic* at Lough Swilly, and the efforts that were made to round up the embarrassing snap-shots, these were later published when the liner docked in America.

The 'dummy' experiment reflected a sense of desperation within the Admiralty, and it was reported, not only to have been an embarrassing failure but an expensive one also. In the light of the vulnerable position that the British Fleet had found itself at the time, and if the ruse had the effect of persuading the German High Seas Fleet to postpone a foray into the North Sea, then it might alternatively have been considered a success. The experiment did not deter a more extensive and probably more successful use of 'dummy' military and naval equipment during World War II.

The first occasion on which a U-boat patrolled in the Irish Sea was January 1915. Commander Hersing's attacks in the more modern and larger *U-21* against totally unsuspecting merchant ships, were treated with the same incredulity as his earlier romp up to the Forth Bridge. That his patrol outside the entrance to one of Britain's most important ports, Liverpool, appeared to have been unstoppable, was also a reflection of Britain's miscalculations in respect of the U-boats' capabilities. After shelling petrochemical works and an air base at Walney Island, where the armaments factory of Vickers was also situated, Hersing sank the *Ben Cruachan* (3092 tons) near *Morecambe Bay* light-vessel. He then continued to the entrance of the Mersey, where on the same day, 30 January 1915, he sank the *SS Linda Blanche* (369 tons) and the *SS Kilcoan* (456 tons).

Each of these vessels was sunk in a similar manner. By first arresting the vessel with the threat of gunfire, and then calmly boarding it in daylight and placing bombs in the ship's hold. This was a daring and economic use of a U-boat's armaments far from its base, and on the doorstep of the enemy. And although the vessels in question were sunk, this particular method of attack was of some comfort to the poor crews. They were allowed to board the lifeboats, after which they were summoned to the U-boat for questioning. None of the crew were reported to have been injured during the attacks.

The actions of Commander Hersing in *U-21* were those of a lone U-boat, but the ease with which he accomplished his assaults, at once focused the minds of both sides on the possibility of Britain becoming encircled by them. It was a strategy that Germany thought possible since 1912, and was proposed by the German Naval Staff in 1916, when they clearly stated their intention in item No.2 of a memorandum to the Kaiser in January 1916:

'The shutting-off of the British isles from all incoming and outgoing passengers and mail supplies in such a way that the British Isles are encircled by blockade and forbidden to neutral shipping; any ship attempting to breach the blockade will be destroyed. The blockade will be enforced in the inner waters, as far as our resources allow, by mine-laying from mine-carrying U-boats.'

Three weeks later, the Admiralty closed the wider and more northern approach to the North Channel, between Rathlin Island and the Mull of Kintyre, leaving Rathlin Sound as the only official route for all shipping passing in and out from Liverpool. The measure was an instinctive reaction but it did not prevent the U-boats from gaining access to the Alley.

The following two years of the war were relatively quite in the Alley. *U27* followed up *U21's* earlier attacks by sinking two merchantmen in February 1915. The first was the *AMC Bayano* (5948 tons) (An Elder and Fyffes Ltd. merchantman converted for the Admiralty to an armed merchant cruiser.) in the North Channel. *U27* then torpedoed and sank the *SS Hartdale* (3839 tons) two days later off South Rock in the Irish Sea. A total of two lives were lost during both attacks.

Although there were relatively few attacks made by U-boats within the Alley during 1915-1916, one particular U-boat made somewhat of a name for itself in the George's Channel during March 1915.

After sinking several vessels off Lundy Island, Lt. Commander Freiherr von Forstner in *U-28,* stopped and sank the first passenger ship of the war, west of The Smalls, on 28 March. Despite allowing the passengers to disembark the *Falaba* (4806 tons), Forstner torpedoed the vessel during disembarkation, and 104 were killed. The passengers were bound for West Africa, and the action became significant in so far as it was said to have broken the Prize Rules, and was later seemingly insensitively defended in the German Press. The incident was later coupled with the *Lusitania* one shortly after, in order to put pressure on US neutrality.

The relative quietness of the Alley was again interrupted in June after the most successful U-boat of both world wars travelled north about. Its famous Commander however, Lothar von Arnauld De Perier, was not aboard on this occasion, as he did not assume command of *U-35* until November. During her rare patrol to Irish waters, *U-35* proceeded down the west coast of Ireland and sank the sailing vessel *George And Mary* (100 tons) off Eagle Island on the 4th. She reached the Alley on the 6th, and began to sink ships off Wexford and further north into the George's Channel before turning her attentions southward to the Scillies on the 13th. *U-34* and *U-20* were also in this area sinking ships at this time.

It was not until *U-80* sank at least three steamers in the Irish Sea during November-December 1916, that a wind of change was detected. Any prospect of quiet returning to the Alley was further upset when two U-boats attacked the Admiralty transport vessel *SS Van Stirrum* (3284 tons) on Christmas Day, also off The Smalls. One of these was *U-24,* and despite being torpedoed and shelled, the steamer refused to sink right away. The trawler *Nadine* came to the rescue of the crew and took the vessel in tow for two days. Despite her efforts, she finally sank four miles off the *South Arklow* light-vessel.

Nineteen seventeen arrived, the crisis presented by the new U-boat campaign became stark, and the Alley was rocked by a wave of U-boat attacks, the likes of which had not been seen before.

Left: A rare view of the large Aeroplane base established by the U.S.N. during WW1
at Ferrybank, Wexford .
Right: Another bird's-eye view of the British Airship Base at Anglesey, Wales .
Aircraft based at both were used to patrol the 'Alley'.

Airships could regularly be seen patrolling the 'Alley' in search of U-boats. Their effectiveness in destroying U-boats was limited but they did have the effect of keeping them submerged when in the area. They were also used to accompany convoys through the 'danger zones'.

This photograph shows *SSZ 33*, which was a common visitor to the airship base at Malahide on the outskirts of Dublin, over its base at Anglesey.

(Courtesy of the Royal Air Force Museum).

During the early years of the war, Britain was in utter want of fast and suitable anti-submarine warships and destroyers, and a good many of what they had were occupied babysitting the Grand Fleet. Both navies were effectively deprived of valuable ships by being tied up in port, each attempting to anticipate and counter possible action by the other. Despite indecisive engagements in the North Sea, and off South America, neither side was willing to risk 'coming out' in total, for fear of loss, or of being in the wrong place at the wrong time, and ultimately giving a free hand to the other side. The effects of being unable to deploy enough of these vessels were no more painfully felt than between the decks of Britain's merchant fleet.

Despite the belated fitting of wireless sets in merchant vessels, during an attack these were at first only of direct benefit to others. Given enough time, they could issue warnings to other vessels and inform patrols of the position of the attacking submarine. The apparatus was also useful when accurate intelligence on U-boat positions was made available to the Admiralty, which could then be relayed to other vessels afloat. But it was hardly ever as simple as that.

Deck guns were also fitted on the poop deck of many merchant vessels – but on too few, and too late for many others. The fitting of deck guns had been actively pursued with the Admiralty by the merchant marine, and when fitted, they had the effect of keeping many submarines submerged. Conversely, the fitting of these guns also provided the compelling argument why U-boat skippers should shoot first. When manned by a well-trained gunnery crew, the enterprise was also somewhat of a morale boost for all aboard the merchant vessel.

However successful this measure was perceived to have been, it was nevertheless pooh-poohed by some of the more efficient U-boat commanders, who said that they could outgun the merchantmen from a greater distance than it could effectively return fire from. There remained a marked difference between being able to sink a merchantman with a naval gun on a U-boat in the more favourable conditions of the Mediterranean, and attempting a similar feat in the predominantly more turbulent Atlantic. The practical consequences for the unfortunate ships was the elimination of what at best might have been an early but dubious warning of a screaming shell fired from a distant submarine. Or perhaps, the chance of sighting the periscope of a U-boat that might have ventured closer in order to fire his torpedo.

Another method of keeping U-boats submerged was the introduction of the 'mystery ship', otherwise known as the 'special services vessel' or 'Q-ship'. (These vessels were allotted a 'Q' number.) The concept is well known now, and consisted of fitting out an ordinary-looking steamer with concealed heavy-calibre guns, and adopting an innocent and sometimes neutral merchant role. Where in fact, the disguised vessel was manned by highly trained naval personnel.

The ruse was acted out as follows. During the earlier years of the war, the U-boats were in the habit of attacking isolated vessels with their deck guns while on the surface. The 'innocent mystery merchantman' would meander about in a designated area, inviting attack. When a surfaced submarine ended its distant bombardment of the vessel, it then closed the distance with its prey. At just the right moment, the helpless steamer and her crew would drop their cleverly designed disguises and fire on the surprised U-boat. Many of the more notable losses and operations by these decoy vessels occurred in the waters around Ireland, and despite the higher rates of pay in this branch of the service, the duty played havoc with servicemen's nerves. The ruse was considered to be successful until a submarine escaped the trap and exposed the operation. The use of this particular type of decoy produced a nasty side effect, just as with the 'innocent' fishing boats. The U-boats remained afar or submerged; they shot first and sometimes talked later.

The merchant fleet was more or less left to its own devices until late 1916. Ships were requisitioned and so were men. There was no such thing as a convoy system or any structured method for the protection of merchantmen while they were at sea. Ships were going to sea with inadequate crews, and although sailors' wages had risen in common with many other jobs from the beginning of the war, sailors jumped ship in America for even higher rewards. The shortages lead to embarrassing accusations in respect of the subsequent use of black seamen. If a black soldier was expected to give his seat to a white one on a bus in Belfast during World War II, one might imagine the discrimination that existed more than twenty years earlier.

The Ministry of Shipping issued numerous instructions to shipping companies during the war, and ships' captains had to complete additional burdensome layers of bureaucratic paperwork before facing the deadly U-boats that often lurked just outside the ports. All of these new shipping procedures had to be completed before permission to sail was given to masters of liners or coasters. It was not until the paperwork in triplicate was complete, and with little more than their patriotism and gallant seamanship to protect them, that the darkened vessels were finally permitted to sail from the safe confines of a harbour into the teeth of an unseen enemy.

The Allies were slow to come to terms with the ease with which Germany transgressed the 'international law of the seas' in their bid to master them. In this regard, Germany was continually criticised in the use of her 'new weapon' - the U-boat and its 'attacks without warning'. The condemnation continued throughout the remainder of the war but did little to save the lives of merchant sailors. It might appear that it was more the embarrassment of Germany's near-mastery of the oceans with their advanced U-boats that vexed tender pride within the Admiralty.

As to the revulsion that was often expressed on the use of the 'new' weapons, which was sometimes described as 'ungentlemanly', there was no hesitation by the Allies in using the same weapons, then and later. The heavy-calibre long-range cannon, gas weapons, tanks, aerial bombardment of cities, and submarine, were employed by both sides, and were all new weapons.

In the meantime, Britain was forced to deploy every type of ship that it could muster in order to keep her sea routes open and to protect her coastline. A huge variety of retired naval and private vessels were pressed into service. These included large numbers from Britain's extensive fleet of fishing drifters. Although these were

seemingly unsuitable vessels with which to tackle a submarine, the courage that the crews of these vessels – often the original fishing crews – showed during the war, against a hidden and menacing foe, could only be described as remarkable. Their bravery has gone almost unrecorded, but it was well known that, during the war, Admiral Bayly had the highest regard for the men who manned these vessels. After the loss of one such vessel off Cork harbour on 19 November 1917, he issued this memorandum to the fleet:

'It is with very great regret that I have learned of the loss of HM Trawler *Morococala* with all hands, blown up by a mine. During the two and a half years that I have held this command I have never failed to respect and admire the devotion to duty and seamanlike ability of the trawlers attached to the coast of Ireland. In spite of tempestuous weather, fogs, mists, etc., although usually out-gunned and out-ranged by the submarines they have engaged with, with few comforts on board and the knowledge they have no watertight compartments to keep them afloat, yet they are seen day after day to go out to their duties with the one idea – to destroy their country's enemies who ruthlessly prey on helpless ships, showing neither honour, manliness, nor self-respect in their cruel and brutal attacks.'

It was never the intention that these wonderful crews would exactly 'do battle' with the U-boats, but they were to patrol and deploy special nets in which it was hoped to damage or ensnare the underwater menace. Although these small craft and their crews were considered by many to be unsuitable to make the long journeys to reach the conflict in the eastern Mediterranean, they demonstrated the same raw bravery when they sailed in small convoys to reach such far away places. During actions with superior enemy vessels both in home waters and abroad they displayed a brave and dogged seamanship.

Of those deployed around Ireland, the vast majority came from Britain. At Rosslare in County Wexford, for instance, there were twenty-eight Scottish vessels, with no apparent history of local vessels being employed. This would seem to reflect either the lack of suitable vessels in Ireland or a distrust of Irish seamen and their vessels in home waters, for what were probably well-founded security reasons. In support of the former opinion on the lack of suitable vessels, figures show that in 1914, there were over 4,800 fishing vessels operating out of Irish harbours, and by 1916, there were only nineteen exceeding 25 tons.

American submarine *L-3* approaching Berehaven harbour, County Cork. Note the small size of the vessel and the painted white stripe across its foredeck. This stripe may have been for recognition and to prevent attack from Allied aircraft, which were based there. (U-boats sometimes had a circle painted on their decks to give similar protection).

The surrendered converted mercantile cruiser submarine *Deutchland (U-155)* under Tower Bridge after the war's end. She too sank ships off southern Ireland. It can be readily seen from this partial view, how large these submarines were. They had a double hull and a cargo carrying capacity in excess of 800 tons. These submarines had eighty crew members and were later fitted with two 5.9" calibre guns.

While the *Deutchland* was in America as a mercantile submarine in 1916 she was apparently unarmed. The small number of these submarines were in effect no greater benefit in European waters than the much smaller and less expensive to build UB class, which had become very popular with U-boat crews.

(Courtesy of National Archives, Washington).

Two cross-channel ferry routes mark the entrances to the Irish Sea. The shortest of these, the Larne-to-Stranraer route to the north, straddles the well-known waters of the North Channel. To the south there is the much wider Rosslare-to-Pembroke route, which crosses an area that is sometimes referred to as the South Irish Sea but is in fact the George's Channel. It was from these ports, and to a lesser extent from some other minor ones that hundreds of these fishing vessels patrolled, day in and day out. They often had to put to sea in the most unfavourable weather conditions in a bid to prevent submarines operating in the 'danger zones'.

Although sometimes patrolling in pairs, these drifters appeared to be hopelessly outmatched by the modern U-boats. Having been overcome by a U-boat, the crews of fishing boats were sometimes taken aboard the submarine for interrogation, and even joined by others captured from a second or third. Mostly, they were subsequently released without harm. Occasionally, however, they were released in conditions that were described as uncivilised and criminal. In extreme weather conditions, far from shore, and sometimes injured, they struggled for safety in unsuitable lifeboats. Naval personnel or masters of merchant vessels, who had been captured in these circumstances, were sometimes taken back to Germany for interrogation, and remained prisoners for the duration of the war. There are some accounts of U-boats submerging their craft and leaving survivors stranded on the deck but there are seemingly almost no cases of physical abuse by their crews.

On the other hand, some U-boat commanders were known to be compassionate beyond ordinary expectations. Such an instance occurred on 6 December 1917, when the American destroyer *Jacob Jones* was torpedoed off the south-east coast of Ireland, with the loss of sixty of her crew. Her attacker, *U-53,* subsequently radioed a message in plain English, giving the position of survivors on three rafts. This was received at Queenstown and at Land's End, from where rescue was effected. The commander of the U-boat, Hans Rose, also took two prisoners, from whom the first details of the earlier loss of *UC-42* off Cork were learned.

Rose was one German U-boat commander that many American naval officers had little difficulty remembering, and some even came to admire him. At the beginning of October 1916, Admiral Gleaves, Rear-Admiral Knight, and several other American officers were attending a luncheon party aboard the *USS Birmingham* in Newport harbour. Much to everyone's surprise, Commander Rose suddenly appeared alongside in *U-53* flying the man-of-war flag. After Commander Rose had handed over some important dispatches for the German embassy, and the customary formalities had been observed, some of the US naval officers were shown around the 'smart-looking sub' (*The Admiral* by Albert Gleaves, USN. 1985.) During the tour of the submarine, Commander Rose showed Admiral Gleaves a loaded forward torpedo tube and remarked that it was 'All ready for firing but nothing to shoot at.' Rose's tongue must have been firmly embedded in his cheek when he made this remark.

The British, on the other hand, had no cause for such admiration, and were furious with the Americans after subsequent actions by this U-boat. Shortly after leaving the safety of the American harbour, Commander Rose sank four British steamers off the

Nantucket LV on 8 October, by capturing them first, and then firing his previously made 'ready' torpedoes into them. Some accounts put the total of ships sunk at five. The actual total may have become confused by the inclusion of two Dutch vessels, the *SS Bloomersdijk* and *SS Chr. Kmudsen*. Although another report puts the toll as high as nine vessels, there was no reported loss of life as a result of Commander Rose's action. Matters were not helped when the British discovered that there were several US naval vessels in the area, which could not intervene. They did, however, pick up the survivors from the sunken vessels.

These attacks were similar in effect to many of those carried out by another commander, a man said to be the most successful submarine commander ever, Commander de la Periere of *U-35*. This particular commander has become legendary, not least for the precise gunnery abilities of his submarine but also for the repeated compassion shown by him to the survivors of his handiwork in the Mediterranean.

It might be said that just like today's wars, we sometimes attribute war crimes on the participants of only one side, the real misfits often avoiding any recrimination, and even subsequently rising to high office once again.

Amongst some of the specially prepared stories about U-boats released to the press, such as the ones containing details about the mistreatment of 'helpless vessels' and their crews, there were also reports of unusual instructions given by German crews to some of the survivors. After a U-boat attacked a vessel, and the survivors were being released into lifeboats by the submariners, some U-boat commanders were reported to have instructed them: 'If you pull hard you'll make the train for Wexford' or, depending on the place of the attack, for 'Queenstown'. If these reports were not true, it is difficult to understand what was intended by them, except that some kind of attempt was being made to establish some kind of fictitious relationship between U-boat personnel and local knowledge, or local Irish people.

Attacks on small fishing vessels in the waters around Ireland were almost non existent during World War II. Instances of boarding and sinking of vessels by placing bombs in them, or the shelling of vessels by surfaced U-boats, were negligible by comparison to similar events in the same waters during World War I, and were non-existent in the Alley.

Even though there were thousands of patrols by these fishing drifters, and numerous acts of heroism by their crews, accounts of their encounters with the U-boats have by comparison been neglected by our history books. As they were considered to have been minor vessels, the records kept of their activities are not as comprehensive as those of the larger warships. Many of these smaller craft and their enlisted fishermen crews were lost only a short distance from the coasts of Ireland and England. The following brief details describe the loss of two drifters in Dublin Bay, and only came to light during the research for this book.

The *Deliverer* (97 tons) disappeared off Howth Head on 3 November 1917, and the *Guide Me II* (100 tons) was rammed by the Cork steamer *Glengarrif* and sank off Dalkey Island on 29 August 1918.

The *Deliverer* lies in less than 20 metres of water, and there is little of her remaining forward of the wheelhouse, where there are clear signs of an extremely violent end. The radio station at Kingstown entered the following report, which it received from patrols at 11.30 pm on Sunday the 4th:

'Regret to report feared loss of HMS Drifter 2561 *Deliverer* which was detailed on Thursday to patrol outside Dublin Bay. As submarine was seen in Bay yesterday, Saturday, it is thought the loss is due thereto. Armed Drifter *Amity* reported today Sunday that she passed some wreckage on Saturday. As boat belonging to *Deliverer* has been picked up one mile E.S.E of Bailey's Light undamaged with cork fender and two oars inside, it is possible that some of the crew have been taken prisoners by submarine in order that her presence may not become known (and thus frustrate possible attacks on the troopship due to sail at midnight tonight Sunday). Names of crew with addresses will be telegraphed.'

The report attributes the loss to a submarine but it was not clear how the loss occurred. This mystery however is cleared up to some extent later by entries extracted from the log of *UC-75*.

The hull of the *Guide Me II* remains relatively intact and upright on the seabed in 35 metres. She is badly holed, with a vertical gash amidships on the starboard side, indicating the violent collision it suffered when it was struck by the *SS Glengarrif* about one and a half miles south east of the Muglins, off Dalkey. There appears to have been only one life lost on this occasion. Given the number of times these vessels operated without lights in Dublin Bay, such a collision might well have been expected. Some months prior to her loss, she only barely avoided what might have resulted in a similar calamity, but on that occasion the incident was a near collision with a U-boat. The message log at Kingstown recorded the following on 3 November 1917:

'My 2145* [Reference to previous message number.] Drifter *Guide Me II* reports submarine, fired Verys Light over her off Burford Buoys at 7.30 PM. 3rd Submarine passed drifter 50–100 yards on port side steering N.E. at 12 knots and disappeared in darkness immediately. 11.20.

* Mail steamer not sailing tonight. Submarine sighted in Bay.'

The contents of these two messages, although revealing little as to the ultimate fate of the vessels and their crews, give an idea as to how daringly close to the coast U-boats would often venture, even into such well-patrolled areas as Liverpool and Dublin Bay. (The Burford Buoy is only four miles off the entrance to Dublin Port, and less than two miles outside what was the Auxiliary Naval Base at Kingstown.) The U-boats had only to wait outside of these ports, and had patiently done so on many nights, before they sank the *W. M. Barkley*. Along with many others, they would also sink the *Adela*. Returning to the *Deliverer*, recent researches have since revealed that *UC-75* laid ten mines between Wicklow town and the *Kish LV* on 2 November. The last four in this series of ten were laid as illustrated in Commander Lohs' sketch of the operation, which appears in this book. These were: two just to the south of the *Kish* light-vessel on the Dublin- to -Holyhead track, and the remaining two just to the north of it, close to the Bennet Bank on the Dublin -to- Liverpool track. The latter two were let go in the immediate vicinity of where the wreck of the *Deliverer* now lies.

It is almost certain then that the mines laid by *UC-75* were responsible for the loss of the *Deliverer,* one of which could easily have accomplished the massive damage, which is apparent in the wreck today. It is also likely that this was the same submarine, which gave the crew of the *Guide Me II* a surprise off the Burford Bank, just before the loss of the *Deliverer*. I say 'likely', because even though the log of *UC-75* indicates she had departed the area a little before this time, it is unlikely to have been another U-boat, given that she had instructions to lay mines, where and when she did. The *Deliverer* was assigned to this specific patrol area, and the cause of her ultimate fate is now almost certainly resolved.

One of the men lost on the *Deliverer* was the trimmer, Henry Maher R.N.R., who lived at 16 Wellington Street, Kingstown. The names 'Maher' and 'Kingstown' also figured prominently in the events following the torpedoing of the *RMS Leinster,* when the stoker, Thomas Maher, was awarded a medal award for saving several passengers and crew. The other nine R.N.R. seamen killed on the *Deliverer* were mainly from west Scotland. Their names appear at the end of this chapter.

There is another aspect to this naval episode, which merits some additional observations. The message log at the Kingstown Naval Base records that 'possible attacks' were expected during the disappearance of the *Deliverer*, and links this statement to the departure of a 'troopship' on the night of the 4th. This entry helps demonstrate the interminable problem Admiral Bayly and the Admiralty claimed they were having with the activities of spies. The departure of the troopship could of course have been coincidental, but these minelayers never laid their valuable mines at random, and acted almost always on predetermined orders based on intelligence reports.

It might seem completely improbable today that German spies could have operated undetected in Ireland, and that they could have presented an appreciable problem during World War I. The fact that they did operate to varying degrees of success is a matter of record. They were captured, interned and sometimes executed, and their activities assisted in a number of successful operations by German minelayers around the coast of Ireland. One might also consider the extraordinary circumstances surrounding the operations of *UC-75* in the Alley during the period of Christmas 1917, when Commander Lohs narrowly missed sinking the largest ship afloat, the *Leviathan,* during mine laying operations in Liverpool Bay,

One should also take into account the recurring references by Admiral Bayly to spies in Cork, and his belief that their actions were directly connected with the mines laid by German submarines in the entrance to Queenstown harbour. These activities quite often anticipated the arrival of US destroyers, and the Admiral believed that Allied merchant shipping and naval intelligence was getting into German hands. Vice-Admiral Sims also suspected leaks, and remarked on the need for secure communications, and of his informed suspicions of communications being intercepted by some 'neutrals'. His fears were contained in a lengthy report to the Secretary of the Navy on 16 July 1917, in which he concluded item sixteen with:

'The enemy secret service has proved itself to be of extraordinary efficiency.'

Despite persistent claims that Irishmen spied on the British forces during WW1 and relayed intelligence to the German side, no evidence has ever been produced to substantiate that such an organised network of Irish spies ever existed in Ireland at the time.

It is to the eternal credit of the Admiralty that they recognised the useful role that these fishing boats and their stout-hearted crews could play in warding off the U-boats, and that they were able to keep so many of them operational until events became more favourable. Although these were only ex-fishing trawlers and drifters, sometimes operated by their original crews, their role became one of more than just 'passive patrol', and without any great drain on service personnel or presenting any unacceptable logistical strain.

The strategy of their deployment was a very clever one but could also be viewed as a somewhat dangerous use of fishing vessels. Sometimes remaining in their original paint work, and even carrying their fishing registration numbers, they did confuse the enemy, but the practice also placed the crews of these – and genuine fishing vessels – at great risk. It was a strategy, which made life difficult on occasions for German submariners.

It could be said, and indeed should be said more often, that the brave crews of these drifters and their like, bore a disproportionate brunt of the U-boat war until more suitable vessels were either built or made available.

A U-boat patrol to Irish waters often lasted a month and covered as much as 5,500 nautical miles. The large majority of this was completed on the surface during the day and at night. This fact might at first appear to depict a U-boat commander as being brazen or brave, but it was in fact a necessity. The reality was that it was impossible to achieve the complete journey continually submerged. A U-boat's batteries had an endurance of only about two hours when delivering top speeds of 7 to 8 knots when submerged. This duration could be dramatically increased to twenty-three hours by halving that speed. However, the reduced distances travelled militated against maintaining such a slow speed. It was always the practice of U-boat commanders to operate well within the limits of their batteries and fuel. Hygiene, health, general onboard living conditions in cramped quarters and the morale of submariners were also daily considerations for U-boat commanders.

Mass production techniques used in the construction of the later UB class of German submarine. 1918.

A painting by Bernard Gribble depicting the arrival of the first six American destroyers at Queenstown in April 1917.

The *SS Breynton* undergoing repairs at Dublin Dockyard after being badly damaged by a U-boat attack in the 'Alley' during November 1917. Her cargo of empty oil drums saved her from sinking.

Despite the technological advances made in submarine design between the world wars, having to travel long distances on the surface in these boats was a worrying consideration once more during World War II. The situation might have been altered considerably by the development of the 'snorkel'-type submarine, if it hadn't come so late. By then the ability to attack from the air had considerably advanced on both sides, and ultimately made life for a surfaced U-boat intolerable. (By comparison to their activities during World War I, U-boats were scarcely seen in the Irish Sea until the final six months of World War II.)

Such extensive cruising on the surface by U-boats during World War I meant that the more eyes you had on the water, the more likely it was that a patrolling U-boat might be spotted. These ever-vigilant eyes presented a difficulty for U-boat commanders while approaching the silhouette of what might seem to be an innocent fishing boat. That is not to say, that at a distance, U-boat commanders could not differentiate between the smaller fishing smack, of which they sank so many, and the larger and possibly more lethal drifter or steam trawler.

To encourage a sharp lookout by those abroad on the seas, a reward or bounty of £100 was offered by the Admiralty for a confirmed U-boat sighting. A ready willingness to claim this reward persuaded some U-boat commanders to be less discriminating when trying to determine whether a vessel was a genuine fishing vessel or one that might radio his position, or even one that might attack him. Statistics relating to the cause of U-boat losses show that the likes of drifters figured prominently, and supported the Admiralty's decision to use as many of these vessels as possible.

Although many of the drifters were commanded by Royal Navy personnel or by officers from the Royal Naval Reserve, many were also manned by gutsy fishermen or ex-merchant sailors who were hurriedly enlisted as RNR personnel. These were 'part-time' seamen who not only did their duty but often saved the day. There are more than a few recorded instances where these sometimes only wooden-hulled and lightly armed fishing boats took on and defeated, in a seemingly hopeless mismatch, a more heavily built and armed U-boat.

The following encounter, which involved a whole fleet of fishing boats in the Irish Sea being faced down by a powerful U-boat, was somewhat untypical in respect of the sheer numbers involved on this occasion.

On 30 May 1918, a mixed fleet of eleven (also reported to have numbered thirteen) fishing boats from Kilkeel in County Down were challenged by a U-boat off Ardglass. The U-boat surfaced unexpectedly, and after its commander queried the crews of the vessels as to whether they were armed or not, he subsequently allowed their small lifeboats to be launched and their crews to disembark. He then calmly motored from one vessel to another and sank ten of the fishing boats, including two from Ardglass, with bombs. The *Moss Rose* was spared and allowed to accompany the lifeboats back to shore. All the surviving boats were eventually met and taken in tow by the *Queen Bee* back to Kilkeel.

One of the unusual aspects of reporting such losses became evident in this instance. The loss of these fishing boats was reported in *British Vessels Lost Sea* as being 26 miles WNW of the Calf of Man. Although this is correct it is probably more correct or clearer, to have reported that this position was only 5 miles off Ardglass in county Down.

Once again the German skipper seems to have had no difficulty communicating orders to the fishing vessels in perfect English, and some members of the U-boat's crew were even reported to have reminisced about an earlier visit to the county. The operation took over three hours to complete, during which there were no allied patrol vessels sighted.

This was not the senseless act that it might appear to have been – that is, one of violence against fishermen, none of whom were injured, for its own sake. Neither was it one perpetrated on insignificant or 'innocent' vessels. It was simply an act of striking terror into fishermen and an attack on 'food', albeit a little too late.

Some opportunity was nevertheless salvaged from the attack. The Royal Naval Reserve, ever-anxious to maintain the strength of its fleet of armed trawlers, used this occasion to post the following advert, with which it was hoped to stir the passions and perhaps the injured pride of the coastal communities:

'German submarine sinks County Down fishing boats.
Men of County Down! Are you going to permit this?
Be revenged by joining the Trawler Section, Royal Naval Reserve!
Age 18 to 50. Pay 3s 8d per day with 1s 8d extra for food allowance when serving afloat.'

Deprived of a livelihood by German sailors, they and their families might also have benefited from the steady pay and conditions that could be had in the Royal Navy.

The culprit on this occasion has not yet come to light, but Commander Hess in *U-96* had begun a patrol on the 25th, and was known to be in the area at the time.

Another similar incident involving Irish fishing boats and this particular U-boat, occurred two months earlier, and demonstrates how fatal an encounter with Commander Hess could be.

The Kilkeel crews may not have known it but they were far more fortunate than those of the FVs *Geraldine and St Michan* out from Howth, on 30 March 1918. Commander Hess had left Helgoland on 14 March and was having varying degrees of success after reaching the Irish Sea six days later. On the 20th he was patrolling off the Isle of Man when he gave chase to, and without success, shelled the *SS Dunaff Head* (5877 tons). He also torpedoed but failed to sink the *SS Custodian* (9214 tons) on the same day. His mixed fortunes improved when he torpedoed and sank the *SS Destro* (859 tons) and the *SS Inkosi* (3661 tons) on the 25th and 28th. Two days later it was the turn of the fishing boats from Howth.

After *U-96* surfaced undetected off Lambay Island, Commander Hess fired on the unsuspecting *Geraldine* (23 tons), and sank her with his second shot. It wasn't long after when the *Saint Michan* (43 tons) was dispatched in the same fashion. The crew of the *Saint Michan* were fortunate to escape in a small boat but five of the nine crew from the *Geraldine,* all of whom resided in Howth were killed. The *Geraldine* was not equipped with an engine but the *St. Michan* was. Commander Hess and *U-96* both survived the war. Joseph Rickard, Joseph Gaphney, Patrick O'Rourke, Christopher Farren and Patrick Harford, were all from Howth, and lost their lives when the *Geraldine* was sunk.

As has already been stated, U-boat commanders sometimes showed a good deal of compassion towards their victims. Another commendable example occurred around the same time as one of the most controversial U-boat attacks, the sinking of the *Lusitania.* The attack on this great liner, which resulted in the loss of a large number of its passengers, many of whom were American citizens, occurred without warning, during what is described as the U-boats' 'first unrestricted campaign', which began in February 1915. This campaign is said to have been a direct result of Britain's sea blockade of Germany.

In contrast with accusations of callousness made against the U-boat skipper on this occasion and the regrettable loss of life during the attack, another commander's behaviour during the sinking of the Harrison Line steamer *Centurion* (9,000 tons) off Tuskar Rock the following day, was described somewhat differently,

During this attack, the commander of *U-21* ordered the crew from the ship before he torpedoed it. The ship failed to sink, and thinking that the U-boat had gone away, the crew returned to the vessel. Once more Commander Hersing ordered them from the ship, before he sank it with another torpedo.

Another incident, which warrants mention in this regard, was the U-boat attack off Ardmore, Waterford, on 11 March 1917. The Cunarder, *SS Folia* (6705 tons), was torpedoed without warning early in the morning, killing seven of the crew. The attacking U-boat, *U-53*, surfaced and fired on the sinking ship with its deck gun, before firing a second torpedo at the crippled steamer.

The *Ardmore Journal* No.5, 1988, includes an interesting letter, apparently written by an eyewitness or a close associate of someone who was saved from the *Folia*. It concludes an account of the incident with the following remarks, which one might not ordinarily have expected to read in a newspaper at the time:

Also in Dublin port, the vessel on the right (Bottom) is the '*Dunaff Head*'.
She was attacked twice by a submarine in the 'Alley', during March, and again in June 1918.

The Head Line steamers made a major contribution to the commerce of Dublin port during WW1, and the company lost several of its vessels during the war. Commissioned as a replacement vessel the '*Orloch Head*' (Top), was built to the 'Standard' design at the Dublin Dockyard.

'The Captain of the ship disguised himself as they usually take the Captains prisoner. Seven of the crew went down with the ship. They were in the part of the ship that the torpedo struck. When they had taken to the boats the Captain of the submarine, who was very courteous, came up to them and told them. 'They were all right and to row to Ardmore four and a half miles away'.

The actions of Commander Rose in *U-53* continued to figure prominently throughout the war and his actions are referred to again further on. He was a man who gained the respect of many on both sides of the conflict. Despite the many abuses of widely acceptable and internationally agreed codes of behaviour at sea during war, there remains to this day a code of conduct amongst those who travel on the seas, a bond, which is almost unexplainable. This can be witnessed on so many occasions, not least by lifeboat crews, or by ocean-going yachtsmen who selflessly sacrifice their prospects and lives during races, when they rush to the aid of another in distress.

Two submarines operating off southern Ireland at this time, were *U-20* and *U-21*, commanded by Lieutenant Commanders Schwieger and Hersing respectively. The transport of arms by passenger liner was always intended to be a no-win situation for U-boat commanders. The need for arms and munitions was desperate, and it was clearly the intention that such a ship carrying munitions might be insured from attack by virtue of its civilian passengers. That is to say, even if a U-boat commander could determine whether or not a ship was armed, it was unrealistic for him to attempt to halt and search it, and for him to wait until all of the passengers – as many as 2,000 – had disembarked, before sinking it with gunfire or bombs. In no time at all, radio calls would be made, and the nearest destroyer despatched to deal with the attack. So unless the U-boat had prior intelligence on the cargo carried, he must either attack it without warning, or not at all. (Schwieger had also become known for his adherence to the rules during the taking of war prizes.)

One month later, another pair of U-boats was operating in the same waters. These later became the scourge of the Mediterranean, where they were responsible for destroying an enormous amount of merchant shipping. The U-boats were *U-34* and *U-35*, commanded at this time by Rucker and Kophamel, and were the latest ocean-going submarines of nearly 900 tons. They were armed with four torpedo tubes and had two deck guns rated as 10 cm or 4.1 inch. This class of U-boat was sometimes fitted with a heavier-calibre gun to improve surface attacks from a greater distance. This was the preferred and very effective practise of *U-35*'s subsequent commander, Captain von Periere. Sinking ships by gunfire was also the preferred method of sinking ships by many of the U-boats' commanders early in the war.

Having left Germany in May, these two aggressive commanders went north about until they reached the south coast of Ireland. Early in the patrol, and already refered to, *U-35* stopped and sank the sailing vessel *George and Mary* (100 tons) off County Mayo on 4 June. Just a week earlier, an armed Admiralty trawler had an unusual encounter with one of these big submarines.

Munitions workers in a production facility at Dublin port during WW1. A number of shell factories were established throughout Ireland under a National scheme to supply munitions for the war. Kynochs at Arklow was a private enterprise and maintained some of the highest standards for munitions production in the British Isles.

The incident occurred when the *Ina Williams* (337 tons) encountered what was believed to have been *U-34* about twelve miles southwest of Mizen Head. The lethally armed U-boat, measuring three times the size of the trawler, surfaced three miles off her port bow. The *Ina Williams* immediately made in her direction, firing on the U-boat but without success. The U-boat refused to do battle and disappeared without further incident. The action might appear cowardly but one has to consider who had more to gain or lose.

Two days later, on 1 June, the steam trawler *Victoria* was sank southeast of Cape Clear. She was engaged by a U-boat, which apprehended and sunk her by placing bombs in the hold. Details of the action are unclear but some initial firing by the U-boat is likely to have taken place, as six of the fishing boat's crew are recorded as having been lost, before four others were taken prisoner into the submarine. The saga continued the next day, when this U-boat surfaced again and fired on the unsuspecting Cardiff steam trawler *Hirose* (274 tons). Skipper Francis Ward was making his way to their fishing grounds, and suspected nothing until water began to erupt in great plumes around his boat from the shells being fired at him by the U-boat. The attack was discontinued, and the U-boat commander gave orders for the boats to be lowered and the crew to disembark the doomed trawler. The crew of the *Hirose* were forced to board *U-34,* where they were astonished to meet the four surviving crew of the *Victoria.* The men were questioned, and all fourteen were released into an overcrowded little lifeboat in rough weather, well south of the Irish coast, and safety.

After attempts at making a sail, the small boat was picked up twenty-four hours later by the *SS Ballater.* The survivors were found to be alive but in a 'pitiful condition'. No excuses were ever offered for such uncivilised conduct, but it can be seen how difficult it must have been for some U-boat commanders to safely determine what type of 'fishing' these trawlers were engaged in. Having had their vessel sunk so far from land, the sailors were extremely fortunate to have survived in such difficult circumstances.

Fishermen hadn't only to contend with the menacing warships from below, as their difficulties with the Admiralty were none too infrequent either. Unable to reach some of their fishing grounds, their situation was further compounded by a deep mistrust by the Admiralty of independently - minded Irish fishermen, and special instructions were issued through the Department of Agriculture and Technical Instruction for Ireland in respect of their operations. Essentially, these amounted to a designation of the waters around Ireland into security zones of varying importance. These were areas in which fishing was either restricted by special permit or forbidden altogether. The latter, for example, was the case within fifteen miles of Kingstown harbour. These confidential instructions were distributed to all harbourmasters, with orders to prevent any publication of them in the press or, in the event of any risk of them falling into enemy hands, to destroy them. It was imperative for the Admiralty to know exactly who was on the water, in what, and at what time. Where doubt or disagreement occurred, either in harbour or at sea, this additional overriding addendum to the instructions prevailed:

The map shows the areas in which fishing was restricted around Ireland during WW1. Permission was granted by permit with a variety of attached conditions. There were more stringent restrictions in the more sensitive areas such as the North Channel, Kingstown, Arklow, Queenstown and Bere Island. In some of these, fishing was forbidden altogether. These orders were issued by the Admiralty through the Dept. of Agriculture and Tachnical Instruction of Ireland in circular G./20/5 of April 1918. This instruction did not refer to the waters west of Ireland or the central Irish Sea.

'The permission to fish given by these orders is in all cases subject to any verbal or other orders which may be given by the Naval Authorities. The orders given by the Naval Authorities are in all cases to be obeyed, even when they conflict with these orders.'

If any doubt had existed in the mind of a skipper of a fishing boat as to the consequences of disobeying such an order, he was reminded in his instructions that 'they risk being suspected as hostile vessels, and will probably be fired on by patrol vessels.' This might seem fair enough during time of war, but fishing permits in certain areas at certain times were issued with additional qualifications. One being that permission was given only on the 'understanding that fishermen would do all in their power to assist the Naval Authorities in the defence of the country.' This was not a request but an order, and it did not sit well with some Irish fishermen.

Like so many regulations at the time, it is not clear how the rules were actually enforced on the ground around Ireland but it is important to remember that, later on, fishing, and maintaining large catches, was extremely important to the overall food supply.

Despite the important contribution which was being made to the national breadbasket by fish catches, the value of fish and fishermen was not always fully appreciated. The constant calling for the population to produce more food at times rang hollow with fishermen, and expressions of their anger sometimes reached the newspapers. They claimed that transport for their catches to markets was often non-existent, and resulted in tons of fish going to rot on quaysides. This situation was exasperated even further when fishermen got wind of deals being done for the purchase of fish from Norway, whilst Irish catches were being left rotting. Despite this, the amount of fresh fish exported from Ireland to Britain during the war actually doubled, and at times even trebled when compared with pre-war figures. The amounts of rocky inshore shellfish declined during the same period. This decline might have been a reflection of the operating restrictions ordered by the Admiralty in these areas. It seems unlikely that it was a result of an increase in its distribution on the home market.

Government policy is seldom so clear and transparently even-handed that it never invokes misinterpretation or requires amending, especially during wartime. By introducing armed fishing vessels during World War I, the Admiralty, probably out of sheer necessity, put at risk the innocent and lawful pursuit of fishermen, in favour of the greater good. The world was at war, and many citizens might have sympathetically compromised, and taken the view that this was a rather minor inconvenience, and a situation well worth breaking some rules for.

Despite the counter-measures taken by Britain, the advanced U-boats had brought the prospect of encirclement and confinement of the British Isles a significant step closer. They flagged their intentions early in the war, and almost completely strangled the approaches to Great Britain and Ireland in 1917.

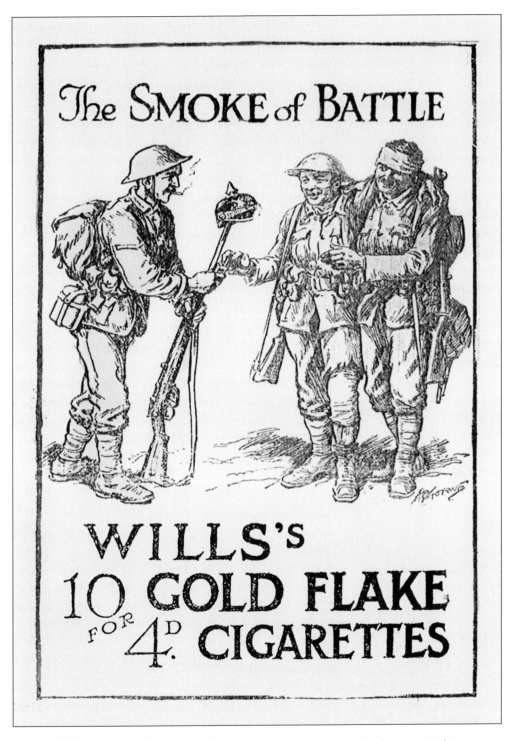

WW1 advert for tobacco. Advertisers of cigarettes have never missed an opportunity, and their products have probably killed more people than many wars.

It was to have been no later than late summer, in the waters around Ireland, that Germany had mistakenly calculated the outcome of the war would be determined in their favour. America had entered the war in April, but Germany had optimistically presumed they would strangle the movement of shipping around Ireland and Britain before this industrial giant could make a difference.

It may seem curious now that Germany did not at this point, probe to a greater degree, the jagged expanse of largely unprotected coastline on the west of Ireland. It can be deduced from a number of accounts, such as the saga of the gun-running *Aud*, that Germany's submarines, and some of her surface ships, could approach Ireland's western seaboard almost at will. It is convincingly argued that the *Aud* did not approach at will, nor undetected, but was allowed to proceed on its mission, and was being shadowed by the Royal Navy in order to ensnare 'bigger fish'. Nonetheless, the *Aud* eluded patrols for some time and was said to have even fooled boarding parties. And like many other cases, she remained free from detection for an undesirable period of time during her journey. Although eventually apprehended by the Royal Navy, that she failed in her mission at all was due in large part to her having no wireless set, and not having completed the rendezvous at the appointed time with the Irish rebels in county Kerry.

There is still controversy over what was ultimately intended for the endgame in this episode. The *Aud* was previously the British steamer *Castro* (1228 tons) before she was captured by the German navy and renamed *Libau*. She was given the name *Aud* to disguise her as the Norweigan ship of the same name. The Admiralty seemed to be aware of the *Aud's* intentions but they were also worried by reports of other disguised vessels that were said to have been operating with U-boats off the west coast of Ireland at the time.

There are also some references in the Irish Censor's files to 'special operations' or strange naval activity and 'landings' somewhere on the coast of Clare in June 1918. After which the county was declared a 'special military area' and a large number of troops and artillery rushed to the area. The *Clare Champion* suffered some enforced disruption of publication during this period, and several articles on the urgent manoeuvres were suppressed. Reward notices seeking information on the landing of arms were posted. The authorities subsequently declared that they had seized a number of arms caches on the 'Atlantic seaboard', and all further comment on the incident faded from the files of the censor.

These references may refer to the same incident as the one alluded to by Robert M. Grant in *U-Boat Intelligence 1914–1918* where he tells of *U-19* making a radio transmission off the coast of Clare on 12 April 1918. The submarine supposedly communicated that it had successfully accomplished the task of landing an Irish agent on Crab Island during the night of the 11th–12th. The transmissions from *U-19* were intercepted, and it was reported that the agent was subsequently arrested.

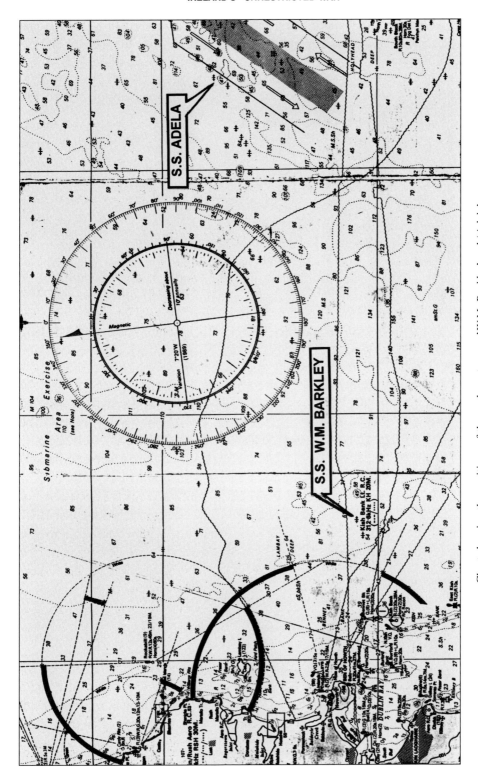

Chart showing the positions of the sunken steamers *'W.M. Barkley'* and *'Adela'*.
Note the number of other shipwrecks maked by the official symbol (+++). These are largely the result of U-boat attacks during WW1.

The most interesting of two additional references in the censor's files relating to this subject, refer to a supposed naval engagement off Donegal. Although there appears to be no official record of such an encounter, the files refer to an alleged encounter between elements of the 'German Fleet' and British destroyers off Horn Head in Donegal. This supposedly took place after a failed German invasion, sometime shortly before 3 October 1918.

The second of these references, which has proven to be more credible, is of yet another 'landing'. This event was said to have taken place in May of the same year, when a friend of Roger Casement, and two German officers, were put ashore from a U-boat on the south coast of Ireland. They came ashore in collapsible boats but were soon detected and arrested before they could 'stretch their legs'.

These incidents make clear the reason why Germany would not have successfully outflanked Britain by occupying Ireland. For instance, it was often speculated during the war that Germany might break out with some elements of her High Seas Fleet and attack the weaker and slower British ships patrolling the southwest coast of Ireland. The issue came up for consideration again during World War II, and in both instances the strategy proved to be inoperable for similar reasons. The fact remained - it suited Germany's purposes considerably more, to support a rebellion from within Ireland than actually having to invade and occupy it. The latter would have meant establishing and securing a supply line from Germany via a protected navigable route, probably to the north. A southern route was ruled out, as there was not sufficient prospect of occupying strategic amounts of French territory, in order to establish a naval base from which such a force could be launched and protected. And as long as the sea link across the Irish Sea remained under British control, the Ireland buffer would remain England's protection in the west.

The occupation of Irish territory by German forces would have been heavily dependent on the acquiescence of a considerable number of Irish citizens on the western seaboard and elsewhere, to yet another invader. For all these reasons, such a strategy would have failed. Although it may seem that Britain's intelligence-gathering procedures and its forces were rather lax in Ireland, prior to the 1916 Rising, and during Roger Casement's attempt to land German arms, Britain unmistakably ruled above the waves in the waters around Britain and Ireland. However, this margin of dominance had been seriously diminishing, and was regained only just in time after America declared her support for the Allies.

Chapter 3

A WELL KEPT
SECRET

'For the safety of all'

A Well Kept Secret
'for the safety of all'

From the time man set forth on the sea, he has provided 'lights' for his safe return. To warn of shallows and reefs, and for to guide the sailor who travels there, he has erected these in some of the most dangerous places on earth.

Alone on craggy rocks far from shore or on vessels swinging on chains in violent storms, the keepers of the 'lights' performed their duty faithfully.
Occasional signals from passing ships, the solitude shared with fellow keepers, and the sea, were their only companions.

The keepers have all gone now, and the stories of the sea's awesome power, its shipwrecked mariners, and witness of their brothers' destruction during wars, are fading.
The 'lights' are now kept by electronic signals and cannot marvel at the full sail that drives the slender vessel nor the beauty of the ocean.

It would be a mistake to presume that the Admiralty's eyes at sea were confined to her ships only. With the exception of one occasion, on which a light-vessel came under attack from a U-boat, the safety of defenceless light installations (lighthouses or light-vessels) around Britain and Ireland during World War I, would not appear to have been an issue. Consequently, issues concerning their operations have failed to stimulate any notable stud, (where in fact, quite the contrary was instead the case), and the important roll these installations played in the battle against the U-boats, was very much on the mind of the Admiralty.

During his exploits in the Irish Sea, Commander Hashagen had some interesting encounters with light installations. He described one of these in the memory of his patrol in December 1917, when *U-62* approached the *Caernarvon* light-vessel.

'Cautiously we creep up to the Lightship, aft in the cabin a light is burning. No doubt they are sitting there, the old sea dogs over their grog and cards, or perhaps they are entering in their logbook all the calls for help they are receiving on their wireless aerial that day . . . Neither do we trouble these Lightship folk; sea marks, so to speak, are neutral. They show the way to friend and foe.'

An interesting aspect of Commander Hashagen's remarks was his reference to the lightship having had a wireless facility. The use of such an asset will be seen as having played a crucial part in the defeat the U-boats. The conclusion might also be drawn from his words that the lightships were considered by both sides to be 'neutral', and were allowed to remain so. Their function, understood to have been to warn of 'danger' (the interpretation of this word becomes an interesting point of argument), and to show the way to mariners abroad on the sea. When manned, they could also report on vessels and mariners in distress. Without this understanding, lighthouses or

lightships would not have had any special exemption from attack during World War I, or any naval war for that matter, and the fact remains that with only one exception, there were no attacks against light installations. This was a result of the mutual benefit derived from having a light and a navigation mark in places of danger. (According to *British Vessels lost at Sea 1914-18* there was only one other light-veesel sunk during the war. This was the *Corton* lightship off Lowestoft, when she was struck by a mine on 21 June 1916. Five lightkeepers were killed.)

The importance of these 'lights' or 'marks' was recognised by mariners from both sides of the conflict. In the case of German submariners, this is evident from the numerous references made by them on their charts, some copies of which are included in the illustrations. These clearly show the track of their journeys to and from these strategic waypoints, and the manner in which they used them for taking bearings. This was especially important whenever they were laying mines.

Most of us understand that the blackouts during World War II were to deprive enemy aircraft of the ability to identify or orientate themselves with their intended targets. Although there were no enemy aircraft over the Irish Channel during World War I (two German airships were reported over Rosslare in County Wexford during 1918 by a US naval intelligence officer stationed there.), there were many enemy submarines operating in it, against which you might expect similar precautions to have been taken. Especially when it became known that the German submarines were constantly lying in wait outside of brightly lit harbours.

As far as it went, and seemingly in contravention of the spirit of the 'lights order', which was introduced by Admiral Bayly after the Kynoch's incident, city lights do not seem to have been a problem, and they burned away merrily. (It may have been 'ungentlemanly' like or even worse but the Admiralty were known at times to have moved buoys and replaced lightships with misplaced look-a- likes during the war.)
After Commander Hashagen failed to navigate through the English Channel, apparently as a result of being unable to identify any navigation lights, he abandoned his efforts there, and reached the Alley by circumnavigating Britain, north about, by way of the Fair Isle Channel. Having safely reached the Irish Sea, he recorded the following observation in his log on 12 December 1917:

'Steered for *Kish Light Vessel*. Position six miles east of *Kish L.V.* at entrance to Dublin Bay. All navigation buoys alight, Dublin City lit up. Plenty of traffic from Kish across to St, George's Channel.'

He also noted additional illuminations at 4 AM on the following night at Holyhead:

'Surfaced, steered for Holyhead. After two days of observations in the Irish Sea, there is plenty of scope for attack and I have taken the opportunity. The guard is slack and the opportunities very good, because many ships sail with full lights and no zigzag.'
So it can be easily seen that the lights shone – and played an important part in helping

U-boat gunners were well capable of bombarding shore targets on occasions.
The damage to Scarborough lighthouse and Whitby coastguard station shown in the photographs,
was caused by German raiders on December 16th, 1914.

U-boats to orientate themselves and select targets. The two Waterford steamers *Formby* and *Conninbeg* and all of the eighty-three who sailed in them paid the price for the navigational aid provided by the same lights, when they lit the way for Commander Hashagen in the Irish Sea. His escapades in the Alley played an important part in the subsequent formulation of the Admiralstaab's report, which included the recommendation that 'the Irish Sea was an ideal place for attack'.

We might safely assume then, that the Allies required the lights in order that their huge fleet of surface vessels could travel in safety, and that the German submariners desisted from attacking them for much the same reason. However, this was not entirely the case.

During World War II, the instructions to lightkeepers in Northern Ireland were clear. Amongst them were. 'To reduce the strength of the light, and report to the Admiralty the movements of enemy ships and aircraft'. Additional keepers were employed to supplement the existing staff for this purpose. In southern Ireland, the instructions were also clear but quite the reverse. That was, the lights were to appear as normal, and reporting the movement of enemy vessels was prohibited. Despite this, a number of incidences occurred at lighthouses in southern Ireland, where the movements of some enemy vessels were reported on 'humane' grounds. It remains unclear what other instructions were given to the 'Commisioners of Irish lights' by the Admiralty's representative in Dublin Port, in order to facilitate Irish vessels leaving or joining convoys, and to what extent the staff from the Marine Defence occupied some lighthouses for this purpose during World War II.

Until recent researches, it has also remained unclear what instructions were given to lighthouse staff during World War I, although U-boat commanders had suspected that their movements and engagements were been reported to some degree by lighthouse staff. The British ability to contravene what we might believe to be a mutual understanding, was clearly alluded to by Commander Hashagen, when he commented on the wireless facility aboard the *Caernarvon LV*. But was it? Receiving details and reporting a vessel in distress, even if this was a result of being attacked by a U-boat maybe all he referred to. I would presume that those who manned the light-vessels took the risk willingly, but it might be interesting to discover how reporting the sinking of an 'innocent' light-vessel might have appeared in the press.

There is only one example to go by, this occurred when the light-vessel *South Arklow* was sunk by a U-boat on 28 March 1917. Contrary to what one might expect to be an ideal opportunity for propaganda, seemingly the only reference made to it, appeared in the following stark notice posted three days after the event, at the Custom House in Dublin:

'The *South Arklow Light Vessel* has disappeared.'

Censorship was strict and the public was not made aware of things they did not need to know about. Notwithstanding, the above statement is of such unenlightening brevity

that it almost suggests some kind of alien abduction. Time and further research has cleared up some of the mystery surrounding this attack but the following chronicle of events is by no means complete.

Submariners from a U-boat boarded the *South Arklow LV* (It was the custom to name Irish lightvessels after sea birds, the South Arklow light-vessel was name *Guillemot*.) and placed bombs below her decks. The Master of the light-vessel, James Rossiter and his crew were allowed to launch their small lifeboat, and shoved off in the direction of Wexford. Probably due to their extremely stout construction, the bombs apparently failed to sink the lightship, and it was reported that she was finally despatched by gunfire from the U-boat. Some reports state the commander of the U-boat saw the crew of the light-vessel off, with instructions as to where and what time they could catch the train to Wexford or, as in another report, the train to Rosslare. It was also reported that the commander was recognised by one of the lightkeepers, who supposedly had previously seen him at work in Wexford!

The attack on the light-vessel was apparently carried out in reprisal for signals it had made to passing ships, alerting them to the U-boat's position. What means the lightkeepers used to make these signals to the ships is not clear yet, but in sight of the *South Arklow Lightship* on 28 March 1917, a dreadful toll of ships were sunk by an 'Ace of the Alley', *UC-65*. (This submarine sank twenty-five vessels in the Alley between February and May 1917)

This episode began with the sinking of the Greek steamer *SS Delgali* (724 tons), followed by the *SS Ardglass* (778 tons), after it was captured first. Their crews were allowed to disembark in the same manner as the light-vessel, and despatched in a lifeboat. Bombs were then placed in the hold of the steamers, sending them to the bottom. Also on the 28th, *UC-65* sunk the *SS Wychwood* (1985 tons) with a torpedo fired without warning, and resulted in the loss of three of her crew. The toll was mounting at an alarming rate, when once more, on the same day, the Wexford sailing vessel *Harvest Home* (103 tons) was captured and sunk by gunfire after the crew had left the ship. It was reported that this last vessel was the one that the light-vessel had tried to warn. Presumably some of the light-vessel's staff were local men, and recognised the sailing vessel as one of their own.

Two additional vessels were sunk by *UC-65* off Arklow in similar circumstances on the same day, before she crossed the channel and sank the steamer *Snowdon Range* (4662 tons) off Bardsey Island. In this particular frenzy of attacks in the Alley, *UC-65* was responsible for sinking at least thirteen vessels, and possibly more.

Commander Otto Steinbrinck returned to the Alley in *UC-65* during May 1917 and sunk at least another five vessels. This particular U-boat's reign of terror finally came to an end five months later, during one of those rare occasions for submarines, when she was torpedoed off Dartmouth by the British submarine *C-15*. Once a notorious killer, she herself rests with her victims on the bottom of the sea and has become a target for curious divers who report that she has become badly broken up.

It will be observed from the brief notice about the missing Arklow light-vessel, reproduced above, and in keeping with Admiralty policy, the statement is meant to give nothing away to either the public or the enemy. Simply stating, there was no lightship in *South Arklow*'s position after the 28th. The issue in question is not whether 'light' installations had radio, telegraph or semaphore facilities, but to what use these facilities were put during the war.

Reporting vessels in distress is what manned light installations had always done, but informing ships or naval stations of U-boat movements was quite a different matter, and this is where the interpretation of the word 'danger' comes into contention. Reporting a vessel in distress clearly fitted this accepted definition, when the *South Rock* light-vessel reported the loss of the *ABS Stephen Furness* off county Down, and referred to in the following entries from the message log at Kingstown:

'14.12.1917 Tara W.S.S. reports A.T. (Armed trawler.) *Dragon* reports steamer torpedoed sunk 13th in 54.24 N, 5. 11W no further details.

Probably as a result of a reply containing a question of clarification, the following entry was made later the same day:

'My 799 [message above] source of origin report was *South Rock Lightship*.'

It is clear that trawlers, armed or otherwise, carried on two-way communications with light installations during World War I, and relayed the movements and actions of merchant and naval vessels. But how, and by whom, were these messages then relayed to British naval intelligence?

By the end of the war, there was in fact a whole network of lookout and radio directional finding stations situated in most of the strategic outposts of Ireland. And it is reasonable to suppose that the Admiralty acted in much the same fashion in all of Ireland during World War I as it did in Northern Ireland during World War II. These installations, and the coastguard premises which were commonly nearby, were in extreme locations, such as those at Malin Head, Saint John's Point, Elly Bay, Fastnet and Tuskar, and there were important radio stations at Clifden, County Galway (said to have closed mid-1918) and Bray Head on Valentia Island.

The radio stations on the Atlantic seaboard which survived were used again during World War II by the Irish government, and helped to complete a ring of radio direction- finding stations around the Atlantic Basin. Their task once again, was to keep track of the U-boats. (It is reported that the Irish government knowingly or otherwise, supports a segment of a similar type of 'detection ring' on its western shores to this day.) These stations were also supplemented with the erection of eighty-three (this figure varies according to the source) additional 'lookouts'. From these high places, submarines or naval actions could be spotted or heard, and the information relayed by telegraph or telephone to Admiralty intelligence-gatherers.

Even though there was relatively little known about the telegraphic communication with these remote and strategically located lighthouses during World War I, their

existence was not a new concept. Conceived and begun during the 1860s, these valuable connections were introduced to some lighthouses in order to relay intelligence about weather and vessels in danger. A Royal Commission in 1894 recommended improvements to, and the provision of, additional electrical connections to lighthouses, and these were accomplished to varying degrees of satisfaction until the outbreak of World War I.

The telegraph cable to the Fastnet Rock lighthouse from Brow Head is relatively well known, and is understood to have been one of the earliest installed by Lloyds. The same cable was also recorded as being from Crookhaven, and was used for sending messages to the lighthouse, which could then signal routes and port destinations to transatlantic ships rendezvousing at the Fastnet. The facility was later improved upon and was reported to have been used for relaying U-boat movements to 'the Coastguard Station at Brow Head' during World War I.

Less well known were the cables to lighthouses such as Tory Island off County Donegal, and from a facility, which may originally have been put in place by the Admiralty, at a house on Greenore Point, County Wexford, to Tuskar Rock. The latter is also reported to have been the same cable which was later installed by the 'Yanks' from a sonar submarine detection station in the cliff-top house, called 'Four Winds', also at Greenore. The Yanks, in the form of the US navy, came to Rosslare in early 1918 and set up a considerable air base at Ferrybank, from where they operated large seaplanes for submarine hunting. (Aerial photographs of this and another base at Anglesey in Wales appear in the illustrations.)

'Four Winds' was built prior to the war by the Goulding family, of Great Southern and Western Railways fame; their son, Sir Basil Goulding of Goulding's Fertilisers, married the much-admired Lady Valerie Goulding, who is well remembered for her work with the Central Remedial Clinic. The house was requisitioned by the Admiralty during World War I and was returned to its owners after the war, and has remained intact and seasonally occupied by members of the clergy ever since. It is perched on the very edge of a high cliff, at the southeastern tip of Ireland. Local people still remember that the house was also known as 'White Caps', because of the headgear worn by the naval officers who were billeted there. The US naval personnel stationed at Ferrybank were also known as 'White Caps'.

The house has little to distinguish it to the eye from its landward approaches, but facing the sea, the front of the house is striking, and its rare design may reflect the interest in architecture and the arts which flourishes in the family to the present day. It was this house, with its unobstructed views of the seas around the southeast coast of Ireland, which was said to have had the 'sonar cable' installed from it to the Tuskar Rock lighthouse. But according to local man John Hagan, the cable was not run directly from the house but from a small stone hut about fifty yards to the south of the house on the cliff's edge. The small building was known locally as the 'telegraph hut', and its remains could be seen on the cliff's edge until recent years. He also recalled recovering bits of the actual cable from the seabed while fishing and was the cable

understood to have been the 'submarine detection cable'.

Certainly there were 'listening cables' installed at various points around the British Isles, which underwent continual improvement by the Americans for the duration of the war. These may have been the forerunners of the loop of copper cable, which when laid on the seabed, could detect the magnetic interference caused in it by a submarine passing nearby. Although some sources state that this device was not perfected until much later, Robert Kemp in *U-boats Destroyed* alludes to such a device in his description of the loss of *UB-109* at Folkstone on 29 August 1918. Stating, that the 'shore hydrophones' detected the motors and the 'galvanometer indicated' the presence of the U-boat, after which it was sunk up by detonating the nearby mines.

Attempts to listen to the U-boats in this way might have represented early attempts at developing A.S.D.I.C. The more familiar version of which was installed in the fast submarine hunters, and only reached some preliminary degree of effectiveness during the closing stages of World War I.

If this or a similar device was used at the Tuskar, a second listening station might have been required in order to obtain a cross-transit fix. Otherwise, only a single direction, with diminished accuracy in direction and distance to the target submarine, might have been possible. Such a possibility is suggested in the following report received from 'Stockton' and logged at Kingstown Naval Base on 13 October 1917:

'From Carnsore Point X Station to *Lady Blanche* (Yacht). S/M heard on hydrophone, 4 (understood to be miles) South 2.50 PM.'

A later report from Carnsore Point to Kingstown clarified the matter:

'5.20 PM S/M bearing S.S.E. 12 miles, on surface, proceeding slow speed in westerly direction, Guns forward-aft.'

(It is unclear whether 'Stockton' was a listening station situated in the town of that name on the northeast coast of England or the American destroyer based at Queenstown.)

It would appear that in this case, the detection of a U-boat by hydrophone was accomplished at the radio installation at Carnsore Point and then relayed to the armed yacht. Equally, it may have been performed at 'Four Winds' and relayed to the Carnsore station. Given the wording, there is the unlikely possibility that this intelligence might have been radioed to the Carnsore station from another vessel, and then relayed to the *Lady Blanche*. If these 'listening' cables were of any real assistance, why install just one to the Tuskar? Maybe there was more than one cable there? The answer may lie in the suitability of local geography and the customary passage taken by the U-boats.

The theory advanced for the existence of a cable at 'Four Winds', was to enable it to detect submarines passing between the Rock and the shore. Even today, this area is

considered to be extremely treacherous for even the most experienced sailors. And if submarines were to have used this route, the marine conditions in the area provide a compelling reason why the journey might always have been completed on the surface. (Sketches by Commander Lohs, indicate that the light from the Tuskar was obscured from a vessel for a short distance while passing through this channel, as it is today. The Tuskar's light in a reciprocal position on the seaward side is also obscured today, but this was not indicated on Commander Lhos's charts in 1917.)

The cable from 'Four Winds' may very well have been the 'listening cable', which some local people believe it to have been, but it may also have been confused with another.

A more practical use for such a cable would have been, for lightkeepers to use it for transmitting the observed or detected movements of U-boats to a base on shore. This information could then have been passed by telephone or telegraph to the Admiralty station at Rosslare Harbour, and on to Britain. The Eircom maps, included in the illustrations, indicate the trunk and telegraph routes, which were in existence prior to World War I, and clearly show a physical telegraph or telephonic link to the Tuskar.

Quite a different method was sometimes used by lightkeepers on Rockabill Island lighthouse, five miles east of Skerries, County Dublin. Using semaphore, 'displaying the international recognised code KFD' with flags, they warned passing ships of danger from lurking boats.

K = You should stop your vessel instantly.
F = I am disabled. Communicate with me.
D = Keep clear of me – I am manoeuvring with difficulty.

The intended warning seems clear enough, but one wonders how effectively a vessel some distance away, rushing from an attack by a U-boat, or in heavy weather, might receive or give instructions with flags. One might also wonder how well staff on Rockabill could have interpreted flag-signals transmitted to them in similar circumstances.

The Rockabill was another outpost that had witnessed many attacks against steamers during the U-boat war in the Alley. An incident relating to the torpedoing of the Greek steamer *SS Salamania* during March 1918 highlights yet another possible, albeit unclear, 'telegraph' or 'light' connection between the Rockabill and the shore. Details recorded in the Irish Lights magazine *Beam,* in 1974 describe how the steamer was sunk and the subsequent journey by her crew in one of the lifeboats to the Rockabill lighthouse, where they were taken in care by the lightkeepers. In order to inform the authorities of the urgent situation, the lightkeepers fired a number of distress signals as: 'The use of Morse had been temporarily suspended there just about that time.'

The reference to the use of Morse at the Rockabill during World War I is difficult to substantiate if it had been electrical, as there is no record of a cable laid to the lighthouse or the installation of radio in it during the war. The signal may alternatively

have been transmitted by the use of a Morse lamp. If such apparatus was used, it is still difficult to understand how consistent or successful this might have been, over a distance of five miles from the coast in bad weather. It could, however, have been detected more easily from, say, Lambay Island. Halving the distance between the shore and Rockabill, Lambay Island is probably the highest place along the coast between Dublin and Louth. Post Office Engineering records show that Lambay Island had no telegraph cable recorded in 1899 but did have one in 1906. And from at least 1906, Lambay Island had a telegraph or telephone connection from the mainland, probably to the main 'castle' house, or to the coastguard station on the island, for an indeterminable length of time. A telephone service had already been established for a number of years to the coastguard station at the nearby harbour of Rush.

The use of telegraph or signalling cables to lighthouses would have been an extremely valuable asset to the Admiralty, silently overcoming the problem of using wireless, whose aerial and transmissions could be detected by the listening U-boats. If successful, the deception would have lulled U-boat commanders into a false sense of security, giving valuable time to track and hunt submarines, without them being aware that their position had been detected and relayed to the nearest naval base. Such a strategy, if kept secret, would have provided invaluable and secure intelligence to the Allies. This proved to be exactly the position.

Records of the cable to the Tuskar indicate that service may have continued to it in this manner until 1949. What undersea cables to other offshore 'light' installations were out of order from the 1930s is unclear, but by the late 1940s, most seem to have become inoperable. Exactly what services the cable to the Fastnet supplied, and to whom, after 1912, are also generally unclear, but again, Post & Telegraph engineering records clearly show that this connection was maintained during World War I. These records also refer to one, and possibly two, telephone connections to the Tuskar lighthouse. In addition, there are some records of cables to lightships, which were constantly breaking down, and may not have existed during the war.

U-boat logs would seem to confirm what the reader might already suspect. German submarine commanders used the 'lights' for exactly the purpose for which they were intended, and for the most part they seem to have remained out of sight of those operating them. The 1906 maps reproduced from Eircom's archives clearly show that there was a considerable amount of 'electrical connections' to coastguard and lookout stations at the time.

All of the foregoing in relation to light installations, and the part they played in the Admiralty's network of intelligence-gathering, was assembled without the factual information that was subsequently gathered and outlined below.

The following extracts from secret correspondence between the Commissioners for Irish Lights and the Admiralty only came to light as a result of the generous co-operation of the commissioners.

The correspondence confirms most of what has already been suggested, and reveals:

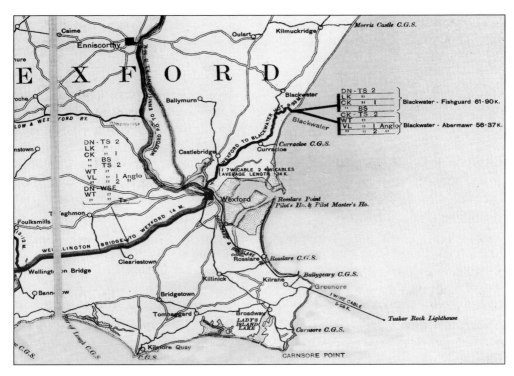

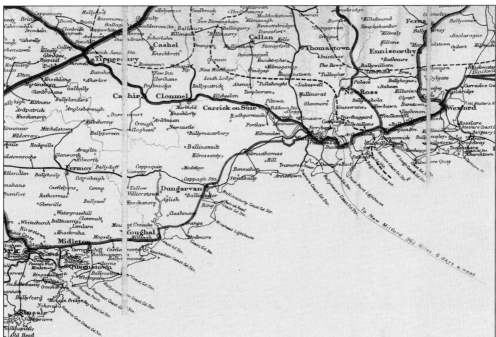

Maps of the telephone trunk routes in 1906.
These show the telephone and telegraph trunk routes and links to lighthouses and coastguard stations.
(Courtesy of Eircom archives.)

In April of 1913, if war was 'imminent' no lights should be moved 'without the previous consent of the Admiralty', and it was 'intended, during war, to extinguish certain lights at various defended ports . . . if these ports were in danger of attack.'

On 22 February 1915 a full list of the lighthouses 'connected with the telegraph system of the country' was furnished to Captain E. G. Barton R.N.R. of HM Coastguard at Kingstown (see list included in the illustrations).

On 28 December 1915 the Admiralty instructed the Commissioners of Irish Lights that 'it had been decided to utilise the Tuskar Lighthouse for communicating orders to the Auxiliary Patrol Vessels under the command of the Vice-Admiral in Charge, HM Naval Base, Milford Haven.'

Further confidential Commissioners of Irish Lights instructional correspondence, dated 18 April 1917, reveals [three weeks after the *Arklow LV* incident] that 'except in the case of certain lighthouses to which instructions have already been issued', recognisable signalling such as 'making visual signals, sound, or wireless indicating the proximity of enemy submarines or other hostile vessels' was prohibited. [Wireless is indicated as being present in some light facilities, which was sometimes recognisable by its aerial.]

The last sentence from this section of the correspondence, confirms the value to the Admiralty of lighthouses that had a telegraph link (a connection by cable) to the shore:

'Any station connected to the shore by cable may, however, send intelligence message by cable.'

The final item contained in the correspondence to the Admiralty, dated 19 October 1917, alludes to the dangers of signalling from 'light' installations:

'(5) In view of the loss of the *South Arklow Lightship* by enemy action on the 28th of March last, and your letter M.039 of the 10th April last, in connection therewith, and further, having regard to recent submarine activity in this vicinity, I am to point out that the use of visual signals to HM Vessels by the Naval Signalmen on the Tuskar may conceivably endanger this lighthouse, whether the signals refer directly to enemy submarine or not.'

The Office of the Commissioners also have in their possession a copy of a memorandum clearly intended for ships but which they believe to have been distributed to lighthouse keepers by the Admiralty during WW1.
It reads in part:

'Memorandum for the attention of Masters and Skipppers of British merchantmen and fishing vessels and the British members of their crew

COMMISSIONERS OF IRISH LIGHTS.

Stations electrically connected with the telegraph service.

EAST COAST.	St. John's Point, Co. Down.
"	Drogheda.
"	Howth Baily.
"	Tuskar.
"	Hook Tower.
SOUTH COAST.	Mine Head.
"	Old Head, Kinsale.
"	Galley Head.
"	Fastnet Rock.
WEST COAST.	Loophead.
"	Kilcredaun.
"	Aran Island, South (Inisheer)
"	St. John's Point (Co.Donegal)
NORTH COAST.	Aranmore.
"	Tory Island.
"	Fanad.
"	Inishtrahul.
"	Inishowen Head.
"	Rathlin Island.

A list of 'Light Stations' in Ireland which were connected by telegraph to the mainland in 1917.
(Courtesy Commissioners of Irish Lights.)

.... It is of the highest importance that sighting of submarines should be reported without delay... substantial reward will be paid to any vessel...... a submarine is never to be reported "en clair"'.

Wireless, semaphore and flash lamps were continually referred to, but just which light installations used which methods is difficult to tell. It might seem obvious, however, that each or all of these methods were in operation by the Admiralty. The correspondence between the Admiralty and the secretary for the Commissioners for Irish Lights on 19 October 1917, would also seem to indicate that little had changed since the sinking of the light-vessel *South Arklow,* and that the Commissioners may have been unaware of the unapproved practices which were being continued by naval personnel installed at the Tuskar. The secretary seemed concerned that as far back as April - 'signals were constantly made to HM Drifters and Mine Sweepers from the Rock by means of flags, semaphore and flashlamp by the Naval Signalman at present stationed there.' This in itself only confirms what has been discovered but would also seem to indicate that naval intelligence concerning U-boats was being acquired at the lighthouse by some means and then relayed to patrols, as the signals referred to were being 'made to' the naval vessels.

It can be said that the radio -direction- finding station at Carnsore Point, together with the 'sonar listening' device at nearby 'Four Winds' and the wireless station at Rosslare, had an ability to eavesdrop over an unobstructed 250 degree arc that stretched from the Irish Sea to the Southwestern Approaches. These stations were conveniently located adjacent to major telephone, shipping and railway connections, which made them very accessible to all the major towns and cities of Ireland and England. The importance of relaying U-boat intelligence to and through these outposts is obvious. Together they formed one of the most important U-boat location and observation areas in the British Isles during World War I.

It was either good fortune or, more likely, a well-kept secret which prevented these stations from being shelled by the U-boats, as was the case when Marconi's 'special wireless station' on St Kilda was bombarded by *U-90* in May–June 1918.

Once again, but on a larger scale, a system of observation stations was established during World War II. Under an Irish government, a considerable undertaking was accomplished by the Office of Public Works when it established an additional network of 'watch houses', 'lookout houses' or, to use their official title, 'lookout posts' (LOPs) around the coast of Ireland. These complimented those already in existence since World War I, and the Martello towers still standing since the threat of a French invasion during the Napoleonic era. A 'coastal watch' service was born or maybe reborn.

The service covered the entire coastline of Ireland, and was established by the construction of numerous small concrete 'houses', which were all connected to the existing telephone network.

The house 'Four Winds' at Greenore, county Wexford. This house was owned by the Goulding family (G.S.N.W.R.) and requisitioned by the Admiralty during WW1. It is is said that a submarine 'listening' or detection cable(s) were in existence between here and the Tuskar Rock lighthouse. A number of 'hydrophone' or listening' stations were situated around the British Isles.

(These posts were actually inspected at times by British attaches.) The posts were in turn connected to a network of regional Command Headquarters, and by radio and telephone links to the Air Marine Defence Headquarters in Dublin.

As Ireland has often been criticised for being unhelpful in the battle against Nazi Germany, one might be surprised to learn what exactly became of the intelligence that was gathered under this regime. What did the Irish army intend to accomplish by their diligent observations of the weather, air traffic, and all the records of shipping movements that were collected by this elaborate system of lookouts? How was such an early-warning system going to alter the inevitable outcome of a German invasion of Ireland, by having just a few hours' notice of the impending event? Or was there an even earlier system of advance warning provided by the secret installation of British radar on the Irish coast? The answer is simple: the information was of more benefit to the British and the Allies than it was to the Irish. For that reason, as the late Commandant Young of the Military Archives at Cathal Brugha Barracks explained to me, the following is roughly what took place.

Information gathered at the 'watch houses' was relayed by telephone to a Regional Command Centre such as those at Castlebar or Limerick. Despite the fact that there were telephone trunk circuits to Dublin from these centres, this information was then relayed by radio to Dublin *en clair*. This was a clear entitlement due to a neutral under the Geneva Convention, after an incursion into or over its territory. It so happens that Britain had supplied the Irish army with the said radio equipment, and British intelligence was able to receive all of these transmissions from a receiver in Northern Ireland.

As this may have been the modus operandi in Ireland during World War II, one wonders what the capabilities of the contentious high-powered radio facilities at the German Legation in Dublin were. Its transmissions were regularly intercepted and decoded by the British, but German operators must also have overheard the same Irish transmissions that the British operators had eavesdropped on. So probably not surprisingly, the Allies persuaded the Irish authorities to shut down this and another secretly operated radio in County Meath, prior to the invasion of Normandy.
The interceptions by the British, although known about, were never actively inhibited, and the implications of these operations for Ireland's neutrality have already been alluded to.

In the case of similarly beneficial operations during World War I, there is every reason to suppose that the 'special relationship' between Marconi, Lloyds and British Naval Intelligence extended to the Commissioners of Irish Lights. In addition to these relationships, in Ireland for some years prior to World War I, the Royal Engineers were controversially substituted into positions within the then National Telephone Company 'for training purposes'. Their numbers grew, and from 1909 until the outbreak of the war, the Royal Engineers remained in control of the Southern Ireland Post Office Engineering Branch, until the outbreak of hostilities gave them an opportunity to put their training into practice.

Considerable grounds now exist, and even proof that during World War I, either the staff of the 'lights' or specially installed Royal Navy personnel, in one way or another, collected and relayed intelligence on U-boat movements, and helped warn or inform the authorities and shipping. Did these activities then contravene what Commander Taussig, of the destroyer *USS Wadsworth,* based at Queenstown during 1917, thought was an agreement in relation to the neutrality of the lightships, when he recorded the following observation in his diary on the U-boats' adherence to such an 'agreement':

'They still carry out the agreement which makes lightships immune from attack, but I am sure this is because the submarines use the lightships for their own navigational purposes, and locating them.'

Exactly what 'agreement' is not clear, and even Commander Taussig's remarks might appear to conflict with the operational parameters of his own lighthouse service back home. The 'lights' in America were also considered to be extremely important installations, and this was reflected in the American Naval Appropriations Bill of August 1916. This bill gave executive power to President Wilson to transfer the operation of the Lighthouse Service from civil control to the Department of the Navy, and was put into effect when America joined the war.

A senior member of the staff from the Commissioners of Irish Lights recently, and convincingly, argued that in respect of the lights, no agreement of 'neutrality' (that he was aware of) existed in the British Isles, either then or later. Furthermore, he stated that lighthkeepers at remote installations, would not only have passed on information about U-boat movements but would have considered it their duty to do so. Not only to their employers but also because they were a nation at war with an enemy who was patrolling its warships and sinking ships in their seas.
(Interestingly, this gentleman later agreed that many of the rules and instructions that were given to lightkeepers during both wars were ignored!)

This is of course where the word 'danger', in respect of the lightkeeping service, continues to be the subject of various interpretations. If this was indeed the case, I wonder whether they were prepared for the very dangerous position in which they might easily have found themselves.

The story came late but any doubts as to the role of lightkeeper's in respect of U-boats during WW1, would seem to have been finally put to rest by ex lightkeeper, Jim Blaney, writing in the Irish Lights in-house magazine, Beam, issue 28 of 2004. In it, he gives the full story of the happenings concerning the South Rock lightship and a German submarine on 16 March 1915:

'On 16 March 1915 the Master of the South Rock lightship, J.J. Duff, observed a German submarine bearing east about a half mile outside of the ship at 12.55 pm. There was a torpedo boat about eight miles north of the ship at the time. He spoke to the ship at 1.05 pm and gave them the bearing and distance of the submarine. The torpedo boat Paragon went after it and fired one shot at 1.20 pm. The Paragon spoke to the lightship again at 4.20 pm and said he had got the submarine. The Master

reported to the Irish Lights Office and asked the authorities to claim for his crew the substantial money reward offered by the Admiralty. Not hearing anything to his advantage for several months he wrote directly to the Admiralty which sent £100, of which £50 was for the Master and the remainder to be divided among the crew in shares proportionate to their wages. No information about this payment was allowed to be published by Master or crew.'

As stated, the master got £50, and each of the remaining 9 crew got roughly a fiver each. In view of the fact there is no record of a U-boat been lost in the 'Irish Channel' until September 1917, the payment would seem to have been a little premature. But if one considers the bad feelings that might have been provoked and spread amongst these strategically positioned lightkeepers as a result of a refusal, especially in the light of a reported 'kill' by the RN patrol vessel, Admiralty silence on the issue and its belated award was probably the more prudent action.

Jim's story would seem to dispel any lingering doubt about radio communications by lightkeepers with RN vessels and their warnings of U-boats in the area. Why, as Jim goes on to tell, 'Lightship crews were dismayed to learn the fate of the South Arklow Light-vessel Guillemot, which was bombed on 28 march 1917. The Master, James Rossiter had signalled to shipping that a U-boat was in the area.....' then seems a bit surprising, considering.

It is clear that the operations at lighthouses around Britain and Ireland came under the control of the Admiralty in one way or another during World War I, and that they were extinguished for operational reasons from time to time, and also used for intelligence-gathering. The reader will have to make up his or her own mind, whether or not the commissioners' duty, to provide for 'the provision and maintenance of lighthouses and other aids to marine navigation, to assist the safe and expeditious passage of all classes of mariners in general navigation' was faithfully carried out, and whether the lightkeepers' motto, 'In salutem omnium' (For the safety of all) was maintained during World War I.

On the other hand, was this noble duty, so elegantly expressed in the following sentiment by the Commissioner of Irish Lights, John Gore-Grimes, in 1993, temporarily shelved for the 'greater good':

'The Lights do not belong to us; they belong to the seafarers who earn their living on the deep. Our duty is to serve; to be as faithful as the sunrise and to provide that shaft of light which reassures mariners that they are not alone.'

The importance of the strategic location of Irish lighthouses around its remote coast on the northwestern outpost of Europe, was expressed in another way by Lord Fermoy when he advised that:

'To protect Irish Harbours, gunboats should be stationed at certain points along the coast, and that these locations to have telegraphic communications. All light houses

should be connected up so that, suspicious-looking ships of war being sighted, an instantaneous alarm could be given.'

Lord Fermoy uttered these sentiments when he became chairman of the London & South of Ireland Telegraph Co. in 1861, after only one year of successful trading. It only leaves one to marvel at the knack some people have for anticipating future events.

Listed below are those who died when HM drifters *Guide ME II* and *Deliverer* were sunk in Dublin Bay.

Deliverer
Anderson, Samuel. Deck Hand. R.N.R. 9, Sterlochy St., Findochty, Banffshire, Scotland.
Campbell, Alexander. Engineman R.N.R. Banffshire.
Flett, George. Deck Hand R.N.R. 32 Main St., Findochty, Banffshire.
Grimes, Michael. Seaman. R.N.R.
Jones, Richard. Deck hand. R.N.R. 2 Water St., Hirael, Bangor.
Legg, John. Engineman. R.N.R. Finlochty, Banffshire.
Maher, Henry. Trimmer. R.N.R. 16 Wellington St., Kingstown.
Noble, Andrew. Second Hand. R.N.R. Fraserborough.
Sutherland, William. Skipper. R.N.R.
Thain, Alexander. Deck Hand. R.N.R. 25 Main St., Findochty, Banfshire.

Guide Me II
Archbold, John. Deck Hand. R.N.R. Craster, Lesbury, Northumberland.

View of German Submarine U-100

Chapter 4

FOR KING
OR COUNTRY?

For King or Country?

Some commentators continue to claim that post World War I, Irish governments and even the Irish people as a whole developed a convenient lapse of memory in respect of the Irish men who fought alongside British ones in 'defence of the realm'. The insinuation contains a criticism that was often double-edged. One, that they betrayed their fellow Irishmen who had rebelled against British rule in order to free Ireland, and alternatively, successive Irish government's willingness to allow these men and this part of Irish history to quietly disappear. It is a cruel and pointless criticism.
We count ourselves lucky not to have been faced with such a dilemma as theirs. We have never seen our parents battered and broke by discrimination and despair (in this respect, it may be argued this remained the case for Catholics and Nationalists in Northern Ireland until the end of the 20th century.); or our children or siblings face hunger every day. We have not earned the luxury or achieved the wisdom to criticise our forefathers for a decision made at a moment in their time we know little of.

Irishmen and women enlist and fight in the British army to this day, and in the Irish army, they 'keep peace' with so many other nationalities around the world. If nothing else, our forefathers have earned us the right to presume that the men it is claimed we have been unable to remember, made their decisions and died for the most honourable motives. It is now a time to remember, commemorate and even to celebrate.

Despite constant cries in the press proclaiming the existence of German plots with Sinn Féin activists, some of which were perfectly true, did the majority of Irish people actually prefer the Crown to 'the Hun'? Essentially, many may have thought that only a bad choice could be made. If an Irishman considered it his duty to fight the 'Monstrous Hun', he enlisted, and suffered the wrath of criticism by nationalists for having supported the Crown. If he tried to avoid this unpleasantness by refusing to enlist, he was criticised by the Home Rulers, Redmondites and the recruitment media for being cowardly. Irish women did not escape tongue-lashings either, and were often similarly accused of being disloyal and cowardly.

The irony of the Irishman's conflict of conscience extended right into the trenches. Sometimes jeered at by German soldiers, their placards announced that while British soldiers were shooting Irish freedom fighters at home, their fellow Irishmen were aiding the British by shooting Germans. W. B. Yeats encapsulated the kernel of the dilemma in the following lines of his poem 'An Irish Airman':

Those that I fight I do not hate
Those that I guard I do not love.

Remarkable observations on similar conundrums were alluded to in an obscure booklet entitled *The Germans in Cork*. This was published by the Talbot Press, Dublin,

in 1917, and although not credited, it is known to have been written by Lady Mary Carbery, when she resided in Cork. The publication is quite humorous, not only due to its quirky derogatory comments about the Irish people, but also by being so obviously propagandist. Its content alludes to a situation in which Germany had won the war and occupied Ireland in 1918. Not being able to trust traitors, the Sinn Féiners, who had aided and welcomed the invasion with open arms, were deported to Germany and Russia for re-education by the new conquerors. Her work mainly comprises of a number of fictitious letters written by the new 'German Governor of Cork, Baron von Kartoffel', and addressed principally to the 'folks back home'. She also referred to a very unusual subject when she prophetically suggested that the new German rulers might exterminate the inmates of Ireland's asylums, the aged and uncooperative, by 'gassing'. And only leaves one to wonder just who had the morbid idea first? One cannot also help wondering, what the outcome might have been for the citizens of Ireland if Germany had successfully occupied her?

Aside from the potential for recruits, Ireland's part in the war was to have been simple. Along with important military facilities, she provided deep water and well-protected bases at Queenstown and Lough Swilly, from where Britain could guard the approaches to her shores and those of northern Europe. Ireland also provided essential quantities of livestock and agricultural foodstuffs, and to a lesser extent, heavy industrial exports, such as engineered iron or steel and munitions. These were exported almost entirely through the ports on the east coast, and from Waterford and Cork.

Conscription was not introduced into Ireland, but the threat of it, and the many unkind references to Ireland's 'special position', received persistent airing in British and American newspapers. Nevertheless, over 200,000 Irishmen enlisted, and many marched quite willingly to war against a foreign dictator in far-off lands. With the exception of these brave fellows, and those who worked long hours, albeit for good money, in the war-related industries at home, it was hoped that role played by Irish people during the war might not be so troublesome, and even passive.

The general public did not seem to have had any ideological dispute with this position, or were not widely reported to have formed a disagreeable opinion of Germany's aggression in Europe. This was noted by some of the US naval commanders who came to Queenstown in 1917. Commander Taussig of the *USS. Wadsworth* formed the following opinion as early as 6 May:

'I have learned since that the Irish people have generally held aloof from any participation in the war and do not consider themselves a party to it.'

Commander Taussig may have confused being 'aloof' from the war with a people's willingness to defend their long-held aspirations of freeing their country from British occupation. He may also not have known about the large numbers of Irish volunteers who had already died in British uniforms on foreign battlefields. Irish blood ran just as red as British or German.

For Ireland to provide young men for the battlefields of Europe, and for the Allies to continue to enjoy full access to Ireland's food and strategic geography without too much obstruction, was possibly all that was required of her. That was, until the dangers of collusion between the German High Command and Irish nationalists became apparent. By then the situation demanded urgent re-consideration. It was not good enough for Irishmen to take no interest in the fact that a German dictator was overrunning Europe and might ultimately threaten the Emerald Isle itself. Worse still, to collude with him was 'a stab in the back' against Britain.

By the time British pleadings in America had borne fruit, the 'Irish question' presented a somewhat different proposition. Until then, Ireland had been Britain's 'backyard', and the British believed that no one else understood the problems of the Irish. Despite some American intellectuals who despised the influence that the Irish and German Americans wielded in the US, when America finally did align, President Wilson regarded Britain's role in Irish affairs as being of special importance. Relayed in correspondence to his president, Ambassador Page in London recalled how he had addressed Mr Balfour on the subject:

'Then it's the effect of the very fact that the Irish question is not settled. You've had that problem at your very door for 300 years.'

The subject prompted a further message, relayed this time to Ambassador Page by President Wilson, with instructions to impress on the British Prime Minister the importance he felt that solving the 'Irish Question' might have on the overall situation:

'If the American people were once convinced that there was a likelihood that the "Irish question" would soon be settled, great enthusiasm and satisfaction would result, and it would also strengthen the co-operation which we are about to organise between the United States and Great Britain. Say this in unofficial terms to Mr Lloyd George, but impress upon him its very great significance.

If the British Government should act successfully on this matter, our American citizens of Irish descent, and to a great extent the German sympathisers who have made common cause with the Irish, would join hands in the great common cause.'

Was this an opportunity that Home Rulers and the nationalist movement were fully aware of? Did traditional animosity for the English, and the rush by some Irishmen to embrace Germany, spoil the chance of a better deal than the one achieved later? It might appear that the future of Europe and Irish freedom hung in the balance during 1917-18.

Alternatively, it is almost certain, that an early victory by Britain in the war would have meant a more prolonged occupation of Ireland under Home Rule or similar.
The nationalists condemned Redmond and his followers for their support of the British, and they seized the opportunity to foster revolution in her time of weakness.

The threat of conscription in Ireland was an issue which inflamed the feelings of many of its citizens. Sinn Féin, and many other nationalists, were totally opposed to its introduction and are said to have been responsible for this anto-Redmond poster. It portrays Redmond's call to arms as a betrayal, and amounting to certain death. (Courtesy of Kilmainham Jail Museum)

Their action was seen as being not only anti-British but also pro-German.

Was there no other way the British aristocracy might have been separated from their view that independence for Ireland 'was a geographical and economical absurdity'? Or was the deal that Ireland finally achieved part of the British price paid to President Wilson and America for siding with the Allies? Although Wilson was not easily persuaded to give way to any kind of minority interests, this might seem to have been the case, as there was sentiment uppermost in the minds of some prominent Irish-Americans for abandoning neutrality at the time.

Some prominent figures, both in Britain's armed services and politics, resented Americans and the benefits they had been reaping from the war. The British could not abide any criticism of their handling of the 'Irish question' by a people they felt were only 'opportunists'.

After the summary execution of the rebels who had led the Easter Rising of 1916, and the declaration by the German ambassador in Washington, Count von Bernstorff, that 'the Irish have come over into our camp like one man', a new emphasis was focused on England's dilemma in Ireland. It then became imperative, as it did again when this unfinished war erupted once more in 1939, that America, Ireland and Britain, in whatever form, should be in full control of the 'Gateway to the Atlantic'.

Considered by some to be an intrinsic part of the endgame was the question of who should be seen to deliver the new freedoms to Ireland – or, more to the point for some, who should not. Pressure to address the 'Irish question' had obviously been applied by America, and as part of a slightly longer article originating in New York, the *Daily Mail* made the following report, headed, 'Ireland the Obstacle', on 5 April:

'There is only one obstacle left to the undiluted outpouring of American sentiment in favour of the Allies. That obstacle is Ireland. No act of the British Government could possibly have such an intensive and immediate effect on American opinion as the settlement of the Irish question. Never in all Anglo-American history would that settlement be so fruitful as now.'

The conscription issue was an extremely thorny one for Britain but she was more than equal to its delicate politics. Irish citizens were threatened with being forced to fight for Britain against Germany. The French agreed with this, or any, plan that might provide enough servicemen to save them and rid Germans from their soil. The 'American problem', as the French saw it, was that insufficient numbers of US servicemen were reaching France speedily enough, and that the bulk of these were perceived as then being dispatched to 'quiet places'. The Americans remained cautious.

Lloyd George understood that it would never be possible to threaten the Irish in this way, and probably thought Lord French's idea, of bombing nationalists into service, was ridiculous.

LANDING OF ARMS

£500 REWARD

The above reward will be paid by His Majesty's Government to any person, or persons, who may give such information as to the landing, or intended landing, of any considerable quantities of arms, as may lead to the capture thereof.

Information should be given to the Commanding Officer of the nearest Military Unit.

This offer does not apply to any officer or man of His Majesty's Navy or Army.

F. SHAW, Lieut.-General,
Commanding-in-Chief, Ireland.

GENERAL HEADQUARTERS,
   IRELAND.

PARKGATE, DUBLIN,
   3rd July, 1918.

(2287).Wt.2778- 45.226 2 2/400 A,T,&Co.,Ltd.

It appears from this reward poster that the landing of arms was of continuing concern for the authorities well after the '*Aud*' shipment.

This would create the very opportunity Germany had hoped for: the creation of another front into which Britain would be forced to pour more of her dwindling resources.

The whole notion of such a scheme, was more accurately described by Sir Henry Duke, the Irish Secretary, when he said: 'We might as well recruit Germans'.

Once America had entered the war, it was clear that Britain would never have to capitulate, but would France? Still bruised and nervous after the widespread mutinies in her army during 1917, would Allied troops arrive in sufficient numbers in order to save her? And might Irish volunteers, cautious about not being seen to support Britain by enlisting, instead, rush directly to the rescue of an age-old anti-British ally? This was the question put to Britain by French politicians; the result was the 'Hay Plan'.

The title was derived from Captain Stuart Hay, who, under Lord Northcliffe, was responsible for delivering the plan. The Plan was the subject of a brilliant article by Jerome Aan de Wiel, published in the *Irish Sword,* 1999 (86).

On the other hand, a rush by Irishmen into the ranks of the French might have been misplaced in any event, if the opinions of the writer R. C. Escouflaire were in any way representative of the thinking within the French administration at the time. In his book, *L'Irlande Enemie?,* he contended that:

'Ireland, in order to justify her rebellion and treason, makes out that she is oppressed. Nowadays (the article was written in August 1918 and published in New York in 1920), the oppression of Ireland by England is a myth, and a very feeble one at that. Macaulay said: "The Irish, on the other hand, were distinguished by qualities which tend to make men interesting rather than prosperous. They were an ardent and impetuous race, easily moved to tears or to laughter, to fury or to love. Alone among the nations of Northern Europe they had the susceptibility, the vivacity, the natural turn for acting, and rhetoric, which are indigenous on the shores of the Mediterranean Sea."'

Escouflaire continued in his preface to criticise the comparison made between the struggle and death of Irish rebel leaders with those of the 'Manchester Martyrs' and the 'heroes of Poland and Serbia and Belgium'. He saw this view as an 'insult to those noble little countries'.

The Hay Plan was conceived in secrecy between French and British politicians, and the Irish Catholic hierarchy. (If this idea was to have resembled conscription, acquiescence by the Catholic hierarchy might seem to conflict with a view supposedly held by the general body of the Catholic clergy at the time, which was reported as having been anti-conscription.) It was hoped to encourage thousands of Irish volunteers to 'join the French army, initially as labourers in specialised battalions'. Its success might suggest resolutions to a number of difficult questions at the time, but after a number of secret meetings, which resulted in poor old Captain Hay being declared unfit for duty, the plan was dropped for one reason or another, and only the threat of conscription remained.

Curiously, it was at this time that a local government circular was sent to workhouses throughout Ireland offering 'three month contract labour' for clerks, railway engineers and labourers in France. Many, if not all of the workhouses at this time had come under the control of the military, and several were used to intern German nationals.

A considerable amount of propaganda was made of the treacherous collaboration between Sinn Féin and Germany during World War I. The colour of this accusation was allowed to run through a similar one directed at all nationalists, and even of the general population. I suspect, however, that the possibility of a widespread flirtation by the Irish psyche with the German High Command was more sensibly reflected by the following contemporary remark on the subject:

'The Irish were pro-German in World War I in the same way as Americans were pro-Japanese.'

When the US finally entered the war, two years after the *Lusitania* incident, she almost at once made an impact on its course. Other than the small but tangible flotilla of destroyers that were sent to Queenstown in May (the USN presence in Irish waters was regularly increased over the course of the war), one of the earliest and most significant developments effected by the new thinking was the introduction of improved mines. Thousands were laid, and they quickly had the effect of restricting and destroying U-boats. From the gigantic undertaking of a barrage of mines that was laid between Scotland and Norway, to lesser ones in the Straits of Dover and off Heligoland. The almost immediate introduction of Convoy and Patrol Lane systems were equally significant, and these measures too, were also said to have begun the defeat of the U-boats. (It is worth noting that even though the convoy system was inaugurated early during WW2 this did not prevent devastating attacks by U-boats against merchant ships and their escorts in the Atlantic. The matter became so serious during 1941 that Irish vessels refused to travel in British convoys for fear of being sunk.)

With the aid of additional American vessels, it became possible to protect the convoys of men and material that passed through the Western Approaches to Britain from the USA. These measures and the effectiveness of tight screens of escorting destroyers, soon forced the U-boat commanders to rethink their strategy, and they did.

They turned with increasing urgency to the entrances of the South Irish Sea (George's Channel), the North Channel and the Irish Sea. Their new strategy was to patrol and lie in wait in strategic geographical areas, such as northwest Anglesey, and off the Point of Galloway, where vessels bound for or coming from Liverpool, or making for the Clyde, made a notable change in course. These and other strategic areas of the Alley also dominated the major cross-channel routes to Liverpool and Holyhead. The individual ships were picked off in these areas as they made their channel crossings or after they were separated or dispersed from a convoy and heading for their individual destinations.

Attacks on solitary ships increased dramatically in the Alley during the last days of 1917, and achieved even greater frequency between February and April 1918. The

number of vessels lost in the Alley during the latter half of 1917 actually increased by more than a third, which reflected the large increase in the number of identified (identified for the purpose of this book.) U-boats that were sinking ships, from eleven in the first half to twenty three. The number of identified U-boats sinking ships in the Alley during the last quarter of 1917 was 17, and this rose to 25 during the first quarter of 1918.

The decimation of ships and seafarers, which had begun to decline in the Alley after May 1918, only abated following the sinking of the mail steamer *Leinster* with the loss of more than 500 (estimated to have been as high as 527) lives on 10 October 1918. The ferocity of the attacks during this period was only surpassed during the height of the U-boat campaign in the Western Approaches during the first quarter of 1917. Gains that had been made by Germany earlier in the war were almost completely eroded within twelve months of the US siding with the Allies, and heralded Germany's defeat.

The Irishman's dilemma was not just confined to those who where undecided about who they must fight for or against. Amid all of this, the thriving one-way commerce between Ireland and England continued. The population had to work, eat, heat their homes, and so on. Fleets of small merchant ships plied the waters around Britain and Ireland, transporting these everyday commodities. There were numerous small steamship companies situated around the British Isles, and were nowhere more prolific than on Ireland's east coast and England's west coast. The reason for this was that between the two, lay the gateways to the Atlantic, which doubled as the conduit for the extensive cross-channel trade with Ireland.

The sailors that were lost when many of these steamers were sunk during the war have not been totally forgotten. This is evidenced by the appearance of some of their names on many fine memorials dotted throughout Britain, and to a much lesser extent, Ireland. But the full extent of the dangers that existed daily from attacks by U-boats, many of which regularly lay in wait outside the entrances to the ports of Dublin, Waterford, Rosslare, Belfast, Bristol, the Mersey, Holyhead, and so on, has never been fully appreciated.

A man had to work, and a ship- owner had to sail his ships. It was of no avail to wait out a suspected U-boat sighting. U-boats quite often only moved on in order to avoid patrols and quite soon afterwards doubled back on their track. And by the end of 1917, when a U-boat's patrol ended and it returned to base, the same patrol area would soon be covered by an incoming submarine. Those ships that were modern might hope to have had some defence against the U-boats with their good turn of speed or by steering a zigzag course, but many, had neither ability, and numerous families suffered because of it. Resolutions passed in the British House of Parliament in 1917, and again in 1919, stated:

'That the thanks of this House be accorded to the officers and men of the Mercantile Marine for the devotion to duty with which they have continued to carry the vital supplies to the Allies through the seas infested with deadly perils.'

There are many fine stories of brave women who served behind the front during WW1.
It is unclear from this poster what 'fun' American women might have been expecting by joining the Navy.

And: 'That the thanks of this House be accorded to the officers and men of the Mercantile Marine for the fine and fearless seamanship by which our people have been preserved from want and cause of disaster.'

Germany's rapid developments in submarine technology had brought her to within a hair's breadth of isolating Britain, and almost forced her to surrender. These advances were not just in minor engineering innovations but in the creation of a whole new concept, a fleet of underwater vessels of varying designs and capabilities, and were being produced in increasing numbers. The scale of the advances represented by these boats can be measured by the fact that the revolutionary qualities incorporated in the basic design of the U-boat during World War I hardly changed until World War II. Alternatively, it is suggested that this only amounted to stagnation in submarine development. This is in part true, and it is also not correct to say that submarine designs were not improved upon at all.

The fact remains, however, that World War I U-boat designs had achieved such rapid and far-reaching advances that further development by the navies who hungrily acquired them during and after the war, was made all the more easy. The German diesel engine was a critical aspect of the U-boat's development, and its technology was eagerly seized upon by many nations after the Armistice. It too remained relatively unchanged for many years after.

Despite many fine accounts of brave engagements by Allied submariners, overall, they played only a minor role in determining the course and outcome of the war. America, for instance, although a manufacturer of submarines, had lagged well behind in the early stages of submarine development, and contributed only twelve in the sphere of European operations. In contrast, Germany had adopted a similar approach to U-boat construction, albeit too late, to that of America's prolific 'Liberty' one with surface vessels, and in 1918 she was turning them out at the rate of three per week. By the end of the war, there were more than two hundred and forty submarines under construction in German yards.

Plagued with difficulties in equipment, Britain's submarines had only limited successes in the Mediterranean, and those at home were often confined to short-duration patrols in anticipation of forays by Germany's surface vessels in the North Sea, or attempts to intercept U-boat patrols. With few German surface vessels to sink, the strategy of British submarines was to block attacks by German ones and to maintain patrols in anticipation of the High Seas Fleet breaking out.

The improved British H-class submarine appeared late in the war, and at least three of them operated with their mother ship, *HMS Vulcan,* out of Kingstown in 1918. These were *H-8, H-11* and *H-12.* With the benefit of intelligence gathered by British agents abroad, and from captured submarines, continuous innovations were being added to British submarine design during the war. This was evidenced in the improved R-class vessels, which were being completed towards the end of the war. These were reported to have been able to achieve a speed of 14 knots while submerged, a speed not surpassed until the close of World War II.

The havoc that the U-boats wrought on shipping cannot be overestimated. Their actions devastated the Allied merchant marine. One has only to study an Admiralty chart of the Western Approaches, the English or George's Channels or the Skerries off northwest Wales and see the scattered shipwreck symbols, indicating the destruction of thousands of vessels and their crews.

Given the relative lack of interest, or at least the dearth of published material by any notable war correspondents, poets or writers, on the U-boat campaign in the Alley, it is not surprising that Irish people seem to be unaware of these operations. Strategically situated as it is, straddling the Atlantic approaches to Britain and northern Europe, Ireland was viewed as being somewhat similarly situated in relation to Britain as Mexico was to America. It was seen as the soft underbelly that had been exploited by Britain's enemies for centuries, the back door through which, with the aid of Sinn Féin, Germany might apply pressure on Britain. The Admiralty anticipated such a strategy, and together with its intelligence service, the Royal Navy would appear to have frustrated several attempts to land spies and munitions in Ireland.

Germany's big successes in the Approaches began to fade after April 1917, and the U-boats soon began to focus their attentions on the Alley. The sheer scale of these attacks, in places like the Irish Sea, are not well remembered, and it is fitting that the details of at least two of them should be retold here. It is hoped these accounts and supporting research concerning two sample Dublin steamers that were torpedoed by U-boats in the Alley in 1917, will help to give some insight into the extent and effect that the U-boat war had on cross-channel traffic and its sailors. And how this aspect of World War I affected the general population, and overshadowed the ongoing battle between Irish nationalism and British occupation.

To this end, these accounts are told in a way that I hope will help demonstrate the ferocity and scale of the attacks that were directed against Irish vessels, and, for that matter, any other vessels that had to ply the Alley. They are events from a period and a place, which sadly remain obscure to this day. The toll of destruction revealed in the following pages, will demonstrate the true debt we owe these sailors, and how any loss of memory that might have existed, is due in great part to censorship during and after the war.

Chapter 5

THE HUNTERS
AND THE HUNTED

The Hunters and the Hunted

They no longer rule the waters:
The genius of the seas
Has invented a new monster,
And they fly from its teeth.

'Lament' by F. S. Flint.

Given today's submarine technology, the strengths and weaknesses of the U-boat during World War I might not be easily recognisable, and in order to help understand their operational difficulties at the time, some of these are at first worth mentioning. The U-boat's disadvantage of being able to remain underwater for a relatively short duration was not exploited by the Allies until a co-ordinated approach to submarine hunting was developed late in the war. Thereafter, the U-boats were increasingly forced to effect attacks from beneath the surface. In contrast to the level of successes that were achieved by them on the surface during the first two years of the war, by the time the war had concluded, the use of torpedoes and mines had almost become the only methods by which U-boats could sink ships. The growing necessity for a U-boat to remain submerged during an attack was further added to by the increased protection achieved after the introduction of the convoy system. The increasing safety from surface -attacks that was later experienced by merchant ships was greatly assisted by the programme adopted of installing improved guns manned by trained gunners.

The growing numbers of fast sub-chasers that were equipped with depth-charges proved to be one of the most effective methods in the battle against the U-boats. Technical improvements made to depth charges and an access to ever-increasing numbers of these made a big impression on U-boat commanders, but again, only during the last year of the war.

Another of the U-boat's weaknesses was its growing inability to engage the improved warships of the Allies on the surface, and were eventually outnumbered and outgunned by them.

It is often wrongly assumed that a World War I U-boat did not have the ability to remain submerged sufficiently long enough to outwit a chaser. The presumption is that U-boats needed to surface frequently to replenish their battery power and refresh their air supply. This was indeed a requirement, but it hampered close quarter operations hardly at all. Some submarines could theoretically remain submerged but stopped for up to six days. This period would decrease dramatically in proportion to the speed of the submarine underwater.

The great strength of the submarine is almost as true today as it was certain then: its ability to disappear. Even if a patrol vessel could get within a short distance of a submarine on the surface without it noticing, and if the U-boat then spotted the

oncoming vessel, it could just submerge and simply disappear. And without tell-tale signs, the approaching patrol vessel would have no idea in which direction the U-boat had taken off, or even if it itself might not come under attack. Apart from operations in very advantageous conditions, submarine detection devices were of little effect until the last months of the war, and are generally believed not to have reached any level of useful refinement until World War II.

Journeys made by U-boats from Germany via Kiel and the Skaggerak around the south-western tip of Norway, and those from the U-boat bases in Flanders through either Dover or the Fair Isle Channel to the Alley, lasted approximately one month. They covered in excess of 5,000 nautical miles, of which only 300 to 400 were performed underwater. So it can easily be seen that the U- boats were on the surface most of the time and were capable of being detected during the most part of their journeys. (Patrols by the UC minelayers from Flanders bases usually only lasted a fortnight.)

The presence of U-boats on the surface presented little threat after a proper convoy protection system was introduced, or while they were excluded to areas where they had nothing to attack. This represented another important strategy in the defeat of the U-boats. It was, in effect, unnecessary to destroy the U-boats in order to defeat them, but if they were confined to target-free waters, they lost the capacity to carry out the job for which they were being designed: to sink ships.

The U-boat war was a race, one in which the new Allied partner needed time to oil the wheels of his war industries, to organise and deploy. It was only after these considerations had been accomplished that the Allies began to taste victory. They very nearly lost this race, and they might have done so if U-boat completions, and crew training in particular, had been advanced by just a few months. Even with additional crews, however, daring and skilled commanders proved impossible to replace in time. This shortfall is highlighted by the fact that there were relatively few U-boat commanders with large numbers of sinkings to their credit, and these people were gradually lost.

From the end of 1917, experienced submariners were repeatedly ordered into the waters around Ireland. A determined effort was made to blockade Britain, but it failed. Many historians reflect on what might have been, if only Germany had possessed as few as a dozen extra U-boat commanders of similar calibre to the most determined few who had created so much destruction.

The change in the U-boats' pattern of attacks during the latter half of 1917 is also described by some naval historians as being the beginning of the defeat of the U-boats, and ultimately of Germany itself. With increasing amounts of supplies and warships arriving from America, and the introduction of a strict convoy-protection scheme, the U-boats were forced to turn to alternative hunting grounds. Where they had previously achieved dramatic and often easy success against soft targets in the open waters to the north and south of Ireland, there was suddenly a lack of them. The bunched convoys were better protected and more difficult to find than individual ships that had been spread out over wide areas of the ocean. These new convoy policies forced corresponding changes in the tactics used by U-boat commanders.

Amongst the areas that suffered most from this change in operational strategy were the channels between Ireland and England. Not only did a sizeable proportion of U-boats move their patrols nearer to the coastline, but there was also a considerable increase in the number of attacks at night, and on the surface. It was bad enough to have your ship explode and suddenly fill with water when you could see where to jump or even help to lower a lifeboat, but to be hurled into the freezing sea amidst flames and explosions during the blackness of the night is unimaginable.

Gross figures produced by Lloyds for losses due to conflict in World War I, clearly show a continuing decline from the all time high figure of 882,227 tons (458 vessels) for the month of April 1917 until the end of the war. The figures from this juncture of the war were at first slow to fall, and from April to June, registered losses were well in excess of 2,100,000 tons (1182 vessels). Figures for 1917 continued to decline overall but showed a sharp trend upwards again from October to December. Although casualties caused by mines amounted to one-tenth of those caused by direct submarine attacks, here too there were sharp increases during November and December.

December's figures were the second highest of the war, and nowhere was this carnage reflected more painfully than in the Alley. Despite this overall downward trend in casualty rates, the numbers of British casualties remained higher during the last months of 1917 than in any month prior to January 1917, when Germany declared another 'unrestricted' U-boat campaign.

Naval casualties also increased alarmingly between October and December. Not least of these, was the significant impact made when the cruiser *HMS Drake* (14,100 tons) was torpedoed and sunk by *U-79* at Rathlin Island on 2 October. This period was a particularly tragic one for the Admiralty, losing the destroyer *HMS Brisk* (780 tons) and the steamer *SS Lugano* (3,810 tons) to the same U-boat on the same day. *U-79* had scattered convoy HH24 but pursued the crippled *Drake* into Rathlin Sound where the fleeing cruiser rammed the steamer *Mendip Range*, which was only temporarily saved by being beached. *U-79* had got amongst twenty to thirty ships that were passing through the Sound and created havoc killing over fifty naval personnel. This U-boat appears to have survived the war.

Compared with the earlier cumulative statistics, there was an overall decrease in these until the cessation of hostilities, but the figures disguise a startling rise in the casualty returns for the Alley between October and December. Furthermore, these continued to escalate for a couple of months thereafter, and remained high until the following April. This resurgence and relocation of U-boat activity can be seen as Germany's desperate and final attempt at isolating Britain. Such a victory had been promised by the German Chief of Staff, Admiral Holtzendorff, by 1 August, 'the beginning of harvesting period'.

The attacks in the Irish Sea were merciless, and turned the Channel into an Alley of maiming and destruction. The U-boats struck terror into the hearts of merchant seamen who were unfairly described as being complacent. They had been accused of having not suffered the full weight of the war, and lucky to be able to sail in waters that some within the Admiralty had described as being a 'quiet lake'.

The policy of protection was completely inadequate, to the point where many felt it to be non-existent at times. This was a situation that many considered relatively unchanged in the Irish Sea since the beginning of the war. (Coastal traffic may have suffered in favour of the increased protection being afforded at this juncture of the war to the growing number of American convoys from the US.) Despite establishing Auxiliary Naval Bases at Larne and Stranraer, Liverpool, Kingstown and Holyhead, and at Rosslare and Milford Haven, from where all manner of vessels and submarine-detection methods were deployed, at times, the Admiralty seemed totally unprepared for the scale of U-boat attacks in these areas. (Kingstown Naval Base was supplemented by an airship base at Malahide Castle. Rosslare was supported by one at Johnstown Castle, and later, by a sizeable American airbase constructed at Ferrybank. Rosslare harbour also supported patrols made by British submarines and was defended by a shore battery comprising of a number of heavy-calibre naval guns.)

As the figure of only two U-boats destroyed in the Alley during 1917 might indicate, detecting and destroying submarines on the doorsteps of some of Britain's most important ports was not a particularly successful pursuit for the Allies that year. The rise in the number of vessels being attacked and sunk in March–April'18 not only reflected another wave of determination by the U-boats, but, because it failed in its objective, also reflected the growing competence and better equipment that was being supplied to the American and British navies. It is also worth noting that there were no submarines lost in this area before America's entry into the war in April 1917, after which many strategies changed on both sides.

The broad operational principle used to combat the submarines in the Alley was an attempt to seal its entrances with special net barrages, and by constant patrolling of the waters between Larne and Stranraer to the north, and between Pembroke and Rosslare in the south. (This southern end, or more correctly the South-western Approaches, was abandoned during World War II in favour of maintaining only the North-western Approaches. Entry by shipping into the Alley during World War II was for the most part, through the North Channel only. The southern end was partly sealed with mines, and by patrolling surface vessels until the last six months of the war.) In the event of submarines successfully evading these defences, and entering the Irish Sea, it was hoped that these might be detected and destroyed by the Irish Sea Hunting Flotilla before they could effect any harm.

This Hunting Flotilla was commanded during 1918 by the most successful Q-ship commander, Gordon Campbell D.S.O., and was composed of vessels from the Auxiliary bases on both sides of the Irish Channel. However, not unlike the rest of the waters around Ireland during the former years of the war, the Royal Navy suffered from a worrying decline in the number of suitable ships for submarine hunting, until the situation was alleviated by the arrival of US naval vessels. The Flotilla was supplemented, with little effect, by British H-class submarines in 1918.

There was one notable success by Allied submarines in Irish waters, when a British E-class vessel sank *U-81,* 180 miles off the Fastnet, on 1 May 1917. There were fourteen British submarines of various classes stationed for a time at Queenstown. It was said that, in order to prevent mistaken identification, these submarines had to operate under the unfortunate restriction of being patrolled only one at a time, and only in areas where Allied vessels had been instructed to keep clear. One of these, *E-54* (this submarine can be seen with other classes of World War I British submarines in the illustrations) was on patrol when *U-81* torpedoed the *SS San Urbano* (6458 tons). Before the steamer sank, *E-54* arrived, and under cover of the sinking vessel fired two torpedoes at *U-81,* sinking her. Seven of the U-boat crew were gallantly rescued by Lieutenant Commander H. T. Raikes and the crew of the British submarine.

Groups of patrol vessels from these auxiliary bases were allocated different patrol areas, and those that the U-boats were known to favour were given particular attention. Channels at the entrance to the Clyde and between the Mull of Galloway and the Isle of Man, areas southeast and southwest of the Isle of Man, from Rockabill to the Arklow Banks, and the approaches from the Skerries to Liverpool Bay, were all high on the list. The approaches to the Bristol Channel, especially off the north coast of Cornwall, were a particular favourite with U-boat commanders.

The U-boats and their hunters employed numerous tactics, and one can see from U-boats' patrol charts that, without an adequate numbers of fast patrol vessels, it must have been almost impossible to track an unseen and undetectable enemy. Exploding mines might be heard off Belfast while at the same time the culprit could be torpedoing vessels off Lambay Island. A pattern of attacks might cease with the departure of a U-boat from Dublin Bay, only so that the ships fleeing out of the reopened harbour might then be caught by an incoming U-boat. Such elusive manoeuvrings are well recorded in Commander Hashagen's log of his patrol in *U-62* during December 1917.

On the day prior to sinking the Waterford steamers *Formby* and *Conninbeg,* which resulted in the loss of all their passengers and crews, he coolly dispatched the small cross-channel steamer *SS Hare* (one of James Larkin's 'food boats') – coolly that is, until the small dying steamer made a last-ditch attempt to bring the submarine down with it.

The practice of attacking on the surface during the night had become popular with the U-boats by that time, and Commander Hashagen describes in his memoirs the action that took place during the night and morning of 14 and 15 December:

'A very big, deep-laden ship was our objective, making, it appeared, for Liverpool. But she was screened by two destroyers, and it seemed hardly possible to get at her. In the pitch darkness we had already got too close to one of them, and were only just been able to avoid her. Evidently some of the oily smells from our diesel exhausts had reached her nostrils; at all events, both destroyers were greatly excited. So were we, for that matter, since the situation was difficult and dangerous. Would it not be better, and above all safer, to dive and deny ourselves the big steamer, though with heavy hearts.

Then suddenly a bright light, away astern and to starboard. My hand flew by instinct to the alarm gong, but hesitated a moment. What was that? Then through the night flashed the abrupt Morse signal: "Keep a sharp lookout. German submarine ahead." One destroyer is warning the other, over our heads! A ray of the enemy's searchlight hovers uncertainly on out bridge. My men laugh. "They'll never see us." And my hand frees itself, trembling, from the alarm gong push. Now to hold out a few seconds longer – tense, nerve-racking seconds. Wraithlike, the slim outline of the second destroyer passes by and fades into the darkness. Behind it, a greater, more gigantic form looms out of the night – the steamship! Now, having broken through the escort, our way is clear.

It was fair game that we offered the destroyer captains. But the Englishmen could not turn it to their advantage. They must pay dearly for their Morse signal. The steamship knew how to defend herself in a manner we could not foresee. Our torpedo took her in the fore hold, and produced a big burst of smoke, mingled with coal dust. Mortally hit, the ship commences to go down on the spot, bow first. We stand by, watching a few hundred yards away. But what is this? The shadow of the vessel suddenly grows larger, grows gigantic. Is she making headway then? Have I misjudged the distance? Will she ram us yet, with her last efforts? But surely she was going down: the thoughts flash through my brain. A hasty order to the engines. The monster advances on us still. At last we gather way.

Like a bull, she makes for us, head down. We hold our breaths. Full speed, emergency full speed. At last, a crashing, bursting, splintering. The stern of the unfortunate vessel rears almost vertical into the night, and we witness the grandiose spectacle of her sinking, with a dull roar, not fifty yards away, into the deep. Ships that pass in the night!'

This is both an exciting and a graphical account, and shows just how difficult a destroyer's job was. As the *Hare* was no 'big steamer', there is some confusion on this occasion as to exactly which vessel was sunk 'six miles east of the Kish', the Norwegian *Nor* or the British *Hare,* after she attempted to ram the submarine before she sank. Commander Hashagen mentions sinking only one vessel on 14 December. A study of the logs from *UB-64* and *UB-65* might throw some further light on these events, as both these submarines were in the Alley on the 12th and 13th.

However, the following report recorded at 14.20 on 14 December in the station log kept at the Kingstown Naval Base, would seem to confirm the ship, date and time – and the difficulty there had been seeing the submarine:

'*Hare* from Manchester. At 2.40 AM.' 'Submarine on surface steering E when first & last seen. 1 torpedo fired which struck amidships. (Starboard side.) Vessel foundered in 3 minutes. Too dark for details of submarine to be noted.5 crew landed Kingstown 14.00. 11 still missing.'

There were some notable successes against the U-boats, but by and large, most U-boat commanders were so confident in their abilities that they continued to enter and leave the Alley by one route or another for the duration of the war, without any apparent risk to themselves. The growing amounts of supplies that were being shipped from America were by then successfully reaching Britain and France, however. This fact again forced the U-boats to alter their attack priorities within these waters.

The U-boats did not remain totally unscathed, and a small but increasing number were lost during the last quarter of 1917, either going to or coming from patrols around Ireland. The number of U-boat patrols increased, and commanders began to take greater risks, resulting in more frequent successes by the Allied patrols. Unfortunately for the U-boat crews, the Allies were growing in strength and efficiency. Although the U-boats' earlier advantages were being eroded, their determination increased, and they took further risks as the spring of 1918 approached. The successes and failures that followed reversed, and the inevitable outcome became more apparent on both sides. Fewer ships were being sunk, and more U-boats were being destroyed.

When World War II erupted, the U-boats returned to visit some of their old hunting grounds around Ireland and England. By then, however, the detection and hunting abilities of the Allies had greatly improved, and had altered the odds considerably. It was one thing during World War I for a submarine to attack a vessel, and then just submerge, or move on without any great risk of being detected, but it was quite another the second time around.

Even though once again the U-boats had it much their own way in the early years of WW 2, the perfection of A.S.D.I.C., and its ability to track a submerged submarine, better destroyers, faster patrol-boats, improved mines, and the extended ability of aeroplanes to hunt and attack with the aid of radar, altered the odds considerably. Against such odds, to enter the confined waters of the Alley the second time around must have been considered almost suicidal, and little attention was given to this area for most of the war. The mine barrage situated across the southern part of the Alley was also instrumental in preventing the U-boats from entering.

Operations with hunting-packs of U-boats in the North Atlantic and in the approaches to the north and west of Ireland achieved considerable success in the early part of World War II, but the U-boats did not patrol into the Alley until the last six months of the war. For one reason or another their sphere of operations did not include these confined waters until much later in the war, and by then their actions there were almost ineffective.

This reluctance by the U-boats to patrol into the Alley during World War II is evidenced by the fact that the number of merchant ships sunk there, amounted to less than the total number sunk during the six months, July to December, in 1917. The comparison highlights the changed fortunes compared to those they had enjoyed during World War I.

Not since January 1940 when *U-33* was depth-charged and sunk in the Clyde, giving

up its valuable Enigma encoding machine to the British, had U-boats sunk ships in the Alley. Almost as if they had reread the tactical manuals from the previous war, the attacks recommenced there, but this time with devastating results. From January 1945 until April, Germany lost ten U-boats and most of their crews, and had precious little to show for it. (See chapter 7 for details.)

Given this dreadful imbalance, Grossadmiral Doenitz must have become demoralised. Although these were critical months, and so many new weapons were being developed by Germany, it remains difficult to understand why so much was being risked by the U-boats in the Alley, so close to the end. Though their submarines had been greatly improved upon by the close of World War II, even so, just what Doenitz had hoped to achieve in this area at such a late stage is hard to understand.

This bold, almost suicidal action in the Alley during the final phase of World War II may have been his last desperate attempt to throw all he could against the British in home waters. Or, as it had almost certainly not escaped his attention, he knew that the Allies were going to accept nothing less than Germany's destruction, the second time around.

His action may also serve to support the opinion that U-boat crews were unique in their bravery, loyalty and bonded-dependency on one another. As an arm of the Fleet, they somehow considered themselves different from its remainder. The fact that the Allies had not 'defeated' them in battle but had only prevented them from sinking ships, was one their commanders found hard to take. In respect of World War I, this boast was tainted by arrogance but might have reflected the difficulties that often exist between politicians and admirals during wartime. In its case, it was the unfulfilled promises that were made in respect of U-boat production levels.

Upon reaching their designated attack areas, the submarines lay in wait for their victims outside major ports, such as Waterford, Dublin and Belfast, or off the Isle of Man and the Skerries, for traffic to and from Holyhead and Liverpool. The journeys that were undertaken by the U-boats were long and perilous, and indicate that there were urgent and rich pickings to be had in the Alley during the latter half of the war. Apart from large convoys coming and going to the major ports of western England, a huge number of relatively minor vessels were carrying large amounts of supplies from Ireland to England. German U-boat commanders had instructions to interrupt these supplies of food, munitions and recruits.

U-boat pack attacks.

The Allies drew a sharp intake of breadth when U-boat attacks subsided in the Alley during the latter half of January 1918. The respite from the ferocious attacks that had begun during the previous November didn't come a moment too soon. It had become obvious from the number and type of these attacks, that an increased number of U-boat commanders were beginning to concentrate on the larger troop-carrying ships, and had become more daring and even reckless. Among them was Commander Lohs in *UC-75,* who sank ships in the Irish Sea for the last time in March. Although the ferocity of these attacks continued until May, the number of sinkings had begun to fall, heralding the defeat of their last major offensive.

The Allies strategy of using liners like the *Leviathan*, was said to have been timely and instrumental in Germany's defeat. This particular ship and her maiden voyage as a troop carrier in the war, was also in part designed to demonstrate America's 'total' commitment to the war, and to some degree, it was a gamble by some senior Royal Navy and US admirals.

The huge ship was packed with American servicemen, and had sailed unmolested up the Irish Sea on the 23 December 1917. Heavily escorted by six US destroyers from Queenstown, under the command of Lieutenant Commander S. W. Bryant, the *AMC Leviathan* was transporting over 9,000 American servicemen and women, and a cargo of 16-inch naval guns for France, on its first transatlantic voyage to Liverpool.

German shipbuilders had proudly launched the ship in 1913 as the passenger liner *Vaterland*, and at 54,282 tons she remained the largest ship afloat in the world until 1931. Unfortunately for Germany, she was interned at New York after her maiden voyage. Its crew sabotaged her machinery shortly before the American government seized her, when it declared war. She was entered into the American Navy in April 1917, as the *Leviathan*. This was not quite what Germany had originally intended for the huge liner, as she went on to play a crucial role transporting thousands of American troops to and from the battlefields of Europe.

On one of these notable voyages, the giant liner's passengers were overcome by a particularly fatal attack of flu. During September–October 1918, the disease rampaged through decks that were thronged with thousands of young servicemen. Shipboard attacks of flu were common during 1918, and on this occasion, nearly 100 seamen died, and a further 2,000 were incapacitated by the disease.

An unforgettable drama began to unfold in the Alley during the Christmas period of 1917, after this huge liner failed to rendezvous with its designated US naval escort of destroyers off the south coast of Ireland. The destroyers, said to have had the 'admiral in company', left Queenstown on the 18th but failed to locate their valuable charge at the first two designated rendezvous positions. The failure to make initial contact was said to have resulted from confused information on both sides of the Atlantic, combined with a failure to adjust shipboard-time aboard the *Leviathan* during the crossing. The poor quality of coal, which reduced her speed, was also, for good measure, added as a reason.

The escorts nevertheless continued their search in the strong north-northeast gales that had persisted with such ferocity during this period. The storm is well documented as having caused widespread and extensive damage both on land and at sea, from the 16th until several days after the destroyers had located the large transport ship off Tuskar Rock on the 22nd. (The Admiral did not join the destroyer escort until after the failure to rendezvous with the *Leviathan* at the first two positions. It was then that he set out from Queenstown in the light cruiser *HMS Active*.)

Tempers aboard the battered destroyers had frayed but these were probably calmed by the subsiding weather, and relief at the sight of the big liner approaching the third rendezvous position. With double watches posted, and all of *Leviathan*'s newly fitted six-inch guns fully manned, the US navy escorts proceeded through the danger zone and nervously northwards along the 50-fathom line into the Irish Sea.

On the 20th, an interesting radio message was sent by *U-94*, which had been operating in the general area of the *Leviathan*'s last rendezvous position. Robert M. Grant, in his book *U-boat Intelligence 1914–1918,* wrote that *U-94* had 'obtained secret orders giving the route to be followed by steamers bound for America.' The information was passed by German command to *U-43,* which was supposedly going to be the nearest submarine in the area but failed to make any contact with a target.

The message is interesting from the point of view of the relayed intelligence that had supposedly been retrieved from the *SS Bristol City* (2511 tons) after she was torpedoed by *U-94* four days earlier. It appears uncertain, however, just how this steamer was sunk, as there were no survivors. If, as stated, she was a war loss, the ship was most likely lost after being struck by a torpedo. This might then suggest that unless some of the crew had survived for a time, it also unlikely that any secret information was subsequently retrieved from the ship. Alternatively, she might have been sunk after the crew of *U-94* had placed bombs in the ship's hold. In either event, one would not expect secret instructions to have been left on board. The net result amounted to two U-boats, both of which were in the general area of the approaching *Leviathan,* being unfortunate or otherwise unable to intercept this important convoy. Good luck will be seen to have played an inordinate part in the safe passage of this particular vessel.

The giant vessel was escorted by no fewer than six destroyers, an airship, and at least one British submarine, on its journey through the Alley. In addition, she was shadowed by several vessels of the Irish Sea Hunting Flotilla, which had already been on special alert. The journey up the Alley proved to be an extremely irritating one for Commander Bryant, who accused Captain Oman of the *Leviathan* of not slowing down for his screen of destroyers, which could not match the liner's speed. It can only be surmised that Captain Oman had his own ideas about what might become of a ship that size, if it compromised its most valuable protection of speed.

Because of her unusually deep draft, on the 23rd, the liner and her escorts anchored in Liverpool Bay in order to wait for the exceptionally high tide, which was required in order for her to make her way across the Liverpool Bar. The following recollection by

Commander Bryant, from E.K. Chatterton's *Danger Zone,* contains a note of sarcasm in his description of the period during which the liner and destroyers were so vulnerable: 'So we all anchored and formed a beautiful target for all the submarines out of Germany.'

The pilot boat *Alfred H. Read* was dispatched from the Mersey, and circled the huge ship until she entered the river at 6 AM on Christmas Eve.

Admiral Bayly seemed almost certain that German intelligence would learn of this particular convoy, when he stated that 'the enemy would make every effort to lie in wait and torpedo her'. Chatterton also recounts that the great liner's risky passage was successfully accomplished, despite 'the gales, submarines and mines'. Curiously, however, he reduced the actual danger that the liner was in from U-boats in the Irish Sea and Liverpool Bay at the time, by incorrectly recording some of the important events that related to this incident. He stated:

'Less than a month before – November 28 – the Mersey Bar examination ship had been less fortunate. She hit a German mine, and with her was lost no fewer than twenty-eight pilots.'

This was incorrect. The steam cutter, the *Alfred H. Read* (probably named after the manager-owner of the British & Irish Steam Packet Co., A. H. Read), was actually lost at the mouth of the Mersey on 28 December, and not a month earlier. It was more accurately reported that this vessel, also known as Pilot Boat No.1, was lost when it struck a mine at the mouth of the Mersey, and that there were forty-one aboard, only two of whom survived. Nineteen pilots were lost; the remaining twenty who died were mixed service personnel and radio operators. The breakdown of the fatalities and survivors is recorded at the end of this chapter.

Vagueness, possibly caused by the lapse of time, may also be the reason for another inconsistency in some records of this event. It is stated in *The World's Greatest Ship* Vol. 1, by F. Braynard, that the *Alfred H. Read* was lost by a mine on the night of the 24th. This date is incorrect but the confusion is interesting.

Whether he knew it or not, Commander Bryant and his flotilla of escorts had been amongst German submarines, and narrowly avoided mines they planted in the Queen's Channel at the entrance to the Mersey on the 26th. The log of *UC-75* clearly shows that Commander Lohs had set out from Brugge through Zeebrugge on December 19th. He had followed in the path of the *Leviathan* convoy up through the George's Channel on the 25th, where he communicated with *U-105,* who appears to have been making for the Alley at the same time.

Another prowler, *U-105,* had gained distinction only two days earlier by torpedoing but not sinking the first American Q-ship of the war. This was the heavily armed *Santee,* on her first mission out of Queenstown. Captain Hanrahan, who had enthusiastically promoted the idea of an American Q-ship, was in command of her.

Unfortunately, it was not long before he had to make the embarrassing call for a rescue tug to be sent from Queenstown. *U-105* passed into the Alley and sunk the *SS Colemere* (2120 tons) in the George's Channel on the 22nd with the loss of four of her crew.

Yet another U-boat, *UC-77,* was lingering in the danger zone at the entrance to the Alley, and she sank the auxiliary Admiralty oiler, *SS Gisela* (2502 tons), with the loss of two crewmen in the George's Channel, also on the 22nd.

Commander Lohs did not strike at any targets here but continued directly to the Skerries, and arrived there at 09.00 on the 26th. Even though he observed several vessels, of 'ten thousand', and 'twelve thousand tons', in the area of Liverpool Bay, he did not attack them. This was a considerable sacrifice. He remained inactive and unseen until nightfall.

At approximately 22.00, *UC-75* laid nine mines across the entrance to the Mersey. Unfortunately for Lohs, the mines were too late for the *Leviathan,* as the liner, full of American servicemen, had just made the tide and moved over the Bar, and by then was some distance up the Mersey.

What course might events have taken if she had delayed any longer remains an interesting question. Commander Lohs's illustrations clearly shows the positions in which he laid his mines across the Queen's Channel on the 26th, and just how lucky this important convoy was to have escaped catastrophe.

UC-75 promptly set off westward across the Alley and reached the entrance to Belfast Lough on the 27th, where she laid her remaining nine mines, sinking the *SS Chirripo* and killing another twenty-eight sailors. Commander Lohs then returned directly to the mouth of the Mersey on the 28th, presumably to view his handiwork. He made no such reference in his log but he might easily have observed the patrol-boats scurrying here and there in search of victims from the *Alfred H. Read* and for any further unexploded mines.

After the *Leviathan* had disembarked her troops, she entered the Gladstone dry dock on 14 January 1918, where she received her long-overdue careening, and her new paint scheme of dazzle-camouflage. War Risk Insurance qualifications made dazzle camouflage compulsory for American merchant vessels in 1918.

Although there are numerous failed attacks by submarines not included in the table of sinkings in chapter 7, it is nevertheless clear that there was an unusually large number of submarines active in the Alley during December 1917. For such a narrow and critical time-frame of just a few days, the presence of this number of U-boats was out of the ordinary. The record shows that at least two, and possibly four, submarines were in the Alley at the time this convoy sailed through, and to have only just missed the opportunity of attacking the *Leviathan* directly, would seem to be down to bad luck. Luck probably contributed to the convoy's good fortune, but the bad luck of the U-boats, or their lack of opportunity, was probably more a reflection of the ever-increasing availability and ability of the Allied patrol vessels.

The conclusion might easily be drawn, that intelligence of this very secret convoy had reached German ears, and was likely to have led to the despatch of several U-boats to the area in order to intercept her. After all, she represented what was one of the most valuable maritime targets of the war. If this were true, it could have been the first occasion on which a combined and co-ordinated attack was carried out by U-boats. Admiral Doenitz later said that the lessons of World War I were put to good effect when the strategy of 'wolf-pack' attacks was developed, and first introduced during World War II.

Despite his comments, the origins of the U-boat strategy of a 'pack attack' continue to be confusing. Most sources say it was not developed until World War II, but Admiral Scheer clearly pointed to such actions being tried during World War I, when he wrote in November 1917:

'That various measures have been tried, including several boats [U-boats] working together as a group etc.'

It may be that the strategy was attempted during World War I but not perfected until World War II.

Tensions in the 'danger-zones' had been rising well in advance of Christmas Day, when a dramatic increase in the number of U-boat attacks occurred in the Irish Sea. Losses quickly mounted, putting the Admiralty on increased alert. The British Q-ship SS Penshurst was despatched to the Alley to lure the unseen enemy into a trap. During this patrol, a submarine was not lured to the surface, but a torpedo fired from a submerged one, sunk the Penshurst. A 'mystery ship', which had achieved so much success against the U-boats in the past, had run out of luck. Fortunately there appears to have been no fatalities as a result of the action.

U-110 had left Emden on the 20th, and, somewhat unusually, was escorted by three destroyers for six hours on its journey to the Dover Strait. After lying silently submerged for a time on the seabed, she surfaced and passed through the strait during darkness, and proceeded to her designated areas of operations in the Bristol Channel and the Irish Sea. After striking the Penshurst with a torpedo, U-110 then surfaced and exchanged gunfire with the Q-ship, before the gallant decoy was sent to the bottom on Christmas Eve. The position in which she is said to have been sunk, is sometimes given as the Irish Sea, but it was in fact somewhat south of that on the north side of the entrance to the Bristol Channel. U-110 returned to Emden on 16 January.

Attacks by this U-boat did not end there. She returned to the Alley once more in March 1918 but this visit was to be her last. After sinking ships in the Alley, and later off Northern Ireland, U-110's luck finally ran out. During an action on the 9th, an aeroplane is reported to have bombed her and damaged the diving gear. She sunk the steamer Amazon (10,037 tons) with a torpedo off Malin Head on the 15th, after which patrol boats dropped depth charges on the submarine.

Keeping up with the U-boats latest innovations was considered by British Naval Intelligence to be crucial in their battle against them. Several sunken U-boats were salvaged by the Admiralty, and were able to provide important details on the latest design innovations. Some of these were subsequently incorporated into British ones.

A frequent visitor to Irish waters, the newly built *UB-110* is shown here in dry dock. She was sunk by the Royal Navy in an action off the east coast of England 1918, and was raised by the Admiralty soon after. A bounty of £1,000 and salvage rights, were awarded for the capture of a U-boat during WW1.

The bell of the torpedoed U.S. oil tanker, *Santa Maria*, which was recovered from the wreck in excess of 60 metres in 1996. She was sunk by *U-19* off Rathlin Island in February 1918. The divers were Olly McElroy, Norman Woods and Simon Nelson. The man or the left was the very popular diver, Tommy Cecil (R.I.P.) from Rathlin Island.

Following two uncontrolled descents to the bottom, she too finally came to rest on it. There were only six survivors from the U-boat. (Some accounts put this figure at four.)

March also proved to be a fatal month for the infamous *UC-75,* and she too was sunk after being rammed by the aged *HMS Fairy* off the east coast of England. Fourteen of the U-boat's crew survived. The gallant destroyer was not up to the collision, and became *UC-75*'s final victim.

Accounts of *Fairy*'s action with *UC-75* are generally basic, and describe how the U-boat was sunk by either artillery fire or ramming by the *Fairy*. This is not altogether how the German sailors who survived the sinking reported it. Their accounts are on file at the U-boat Archives in Cuxhaven, and clearly differ in some important respects from accounts that commonly appear.

Translation of their reports is as follows:

'Report by – Senior Helmsman, Mt – Matrose sailor, Hermann Stengel.
On May 31, 1918, about 3.00 AM the SM UC-75 sank in the North Sea, approx. 8–10 miles South of Flamborough Head at the English east coast. The boat was overrun by the large steamer *Blaydonian* while launching a night underwater attack on a heavily escorted convoy. Her tower and entry hatch were severely damaged enabling large amounts of water to enter the boat. We consequently were forced to surface, and following this we rammed the destroyer at the foreship. Thereupon he made another attempt to ram us, and this time successfully and subsequently opened artillery fire – missing us. As we could no longer manoeuvre – given our damaged state – the Commander decided not to let the boat get into enemy hands, and to sink the boat by opening the ventilation hatches. All men were on the deck at the time of the sinking. As the enemy ships made no immediate attempt to take any of us on board I assumed that all would die by drowning. We were also shot at with pistols from the deck of a destroyer while swimming in the water.'

(A second report by U-Maschinist, MT – Matrose *sailor*, Hugo Zipfel, is similar, and adds nothing new nor contradicts the reports above or below. For reasons of brevity I have omitted it.)

'Report of the Officer on Watch Duty, LzS Otto Freiherr von Recum:
(similar account to above) The destroyer *D35* – has four funnels and is old – begins to rescue the men. When 6 men are on board and many more are hanging onto the side, the destroyer takes on full steam and is gone. Further eight men – amongst the Commandant, W.O., L.I. – are rescued by two scouts (fishing steamers), but they could have rescued more. The reason for the behaviour of the steamer was his own leakage due to the ramming attempts. Destroyer sank a quarter of an hour later. Crew was evacuated beforehand. We were all brought to Immingham, and from there on the same day to London. Stayed there three weeks. Officers kept in solitary confinement with lack of food. The treatment received by LzS v. Recum was unbelievably bad in

accordance with special reasons, which were not justified. A complaint is on the way. Was transferred together with the Commandant into the Officer's camp in Skripton. [?Skipton] '

It is difficult to come to terms with some of the accusations made in these reports but they nevertheless help one to appreciate, that in order to understand events more fully, it is not sufficient to study accounts by one side only.

It was not unusual to move exceptionally successful U-boat skippers to new designs of boats or new commands. Avoiding the particular attentions of the Royal Navy, Commander Lohs temporarily escaped the fate of his old command by being transferred to *UB-57* in January 1918. Alas, the move did not save him, as he and his new crew were lost in August 1918 after their submarine was suspected to have struck a mine, either in the English Channel or near Zeebrugge.

Returning to December in the Alley, yet another submarine was busy sinking ships there. The handiwork of *U-87* was clearly seen, going down with all of her twenty-one crew just a mile east of the *South Rock LV,* at midday on Christmas Eve. A temporary lightkeeper, John Bailie, saw the 'nose cut clean off the *SS Daybreak* (3238 tons)' before loud boiler explosions and her quick disappearance. Relieved in the area by the incoming *UC-75, U-87* sailed south until it sank the *SS Agberi* off Bardsey Island, Wales, on Christmas Day. It seems that this submarine may also have been aware of some unusual activity taking place south of her previous position in the Alley and had hastened there in anticipation of taking part in an action.

As this area had not presented any particular danger for U-boats in the past, *U-87* might not have expected the calamity that shortly befell her. After positioning herself for an 'attack on a convoy', she was reported to have been spotted on the surface by *HMS Buttercup,* who steamed down on the unsuspecting submarine. With no hesitation, the Flower Class sloop drove straight at the submarine, colliding with it but not sinking it. Before the submarine could submerge, *HMS PC-56* also joined the attack. The smaller patrol vessel shelled the submarine as she slipped below the surface, and then immediately dropped two depth-charges on its track.

A submariner's worst nightmare, the massive explosions from these devices could crush the protective pressure hull of a submarine, killing all inside in an instant. The sea erupted in great plumes, and *U-87* was soon forced back to the surface. The submarine hunter, specially designed for her next action, rammed the U-boat, cutting her in two. Although half of the submarine remained afloat for a short while afterwards, this too eventually sank. There were no survivors from her crew of forty-four.

U-61, U-62, U-100, U-105, U-110, U-87 and *UC-75* had all done considerable damage to shipping in the Alley during December and January, but failed to sink the most important target that would come their way for the duration of their U-boat careers. The *Leviathan* reached Liverpool docks safely and, as reported, 'without incident'. Aboard the great ship it may have appeared that there had been no 'incident', but there were certainly a number of incidents in the Alley during the few days she was in it.

One might ask why troops bound for France were landing in Liverpool, seemingly creating an unacceptable risk for this liner to attract an attack? This particular ship had an enormous potential to influence the war; her sinking, together with any loss of life, would have done nothing to increase the confidence of the US or to improve the bruised morale of the Admiralty in its battle against the U-boats.

The effects that such losses have on the morale of American citizens, has always been a burning consideration for American politicians. In a confidential report produced after the war, the US naval attaché in Paris, Commander W. R. Sayles, made the following remark about some of the earlier American troop convoys, which Admiral Gleaves described as falling 'far short of perfection':

'Now that it is all over, and we have won, and so many big historical events have happened since, we are prone to forget the importance and what was at stake on a successful outcome of this expedition. If even one transport had been sunk, it might have resulted in disaster to the Allied cause.'

The importance Germany might attach to an event like the sinking of the *Leviathan* by a U-boat, can be gauged by the resounding jubilation, which was demonstrated after just such a claim. Her sinking supposedly occurred on 19 July 1918. On that occasion, several submarines, said to have been acting together, sank the *Justicia* (32,120 tons) north of Rathlin Island. The outgoing and heavily escorted *Justicia* was almost empty, and Germany's misplaced optimism in claiming to have sunk, not the *Justicia* but the *Leviathan,* with American troops on board, had to be withdrawn when the facts became known.

The combined U-boat attack on the *Justicia* was an example of tactics that were to become more popular during World War II. The operation consisted of a number, or 'pack', of U-boats, acting together to sink a valuable target. It was reported that between three and six submarines were involved in the attack on the *Justicia*, and during their final assault on the badly damaged ship that was being towed by the *Sonia,* the tug's captain, T. H. Hull, recollected that 'torpedoes seemed to be coming from all directions'. Nearing the end of her tow, the *Justicia* gave a final lurch and sank off Skerryvore. Another German claim that the *Leviathan* had been destroyed, was heard in America for several days after her delayed entry to Liverpool docks in January 1918!

It is also worth noting that *UC-75* returned with her new commander to lay mines in Liverpool Bay on 8 March 1918, when the liner *Mauretania* was expected to leave, and the *Leviathan* was once again expected to enter.

(In another operation indicating the development of pack-attack techniques, *U-46, U-55, U-70, U-94* and *U-103* lay in wait on 12 May 1918 in the southern end of the George's Channel for an inbound US convoy. Taken by surprise, *U-103* was rammed and sunk by the White Star Liner *Olympic*. The US destroyer *Davis* rescued Commander Rucker and thirty-four of his crew.)

The period between the *Vaterland* being seized in New York and her safe arrival in Liverpool docks was one during which there were intense public and political wranglings over the role this vessel should play in the war. Statements varied, from proclaiming her seizure to be dishonourable, to suggesting that she should be used only as a 'prison', 'hospital' or 'guard ship' and so on. And the Admiralty was reluctant to agree to the *Leviathan* entering Liverpool, due to the risk presented by her ungainly size and extreme tidal requirements. A lot of admirals' reputations on both sides of the Atlantic were put on the line, in respect of either agreeing or disagreeing with the views of so-called 'experts', and the proposed use of this valuable liner. Some held the view that her size presented too big a target for the U-boats, and that if struck by a torpedo, she would flood and keel over.

After her first voyage with troops to Cuba, during which the liner achieved her top speed of 22.5 knots, Rear-Admiral Albert Gleaves convinced his superiors to proceed with her proposed role as a transatlantic troop carrier. The urgency of using the *Leviathan* was in her ability to move very large numbers of troops and equipment to Europe speedily. Speed was essential if the U-boats were to be beaten, and America was said to have insufficient tonnage of her own to accomplish the task in time to alter the outcome of the war. The danger was that if, in the face of such high-level opposition to her new role, the ship was to have been sunk by a U-boat and American lives were lost as a result, then further expeditions in similar vessels might have been delayed indefinitely.

It was known that the liner required urgent access to one of the only dry docks in the world capable of taking her. Her long-drawn-out coaling operations and troop embarkation in Hoboken did not go unnoticed either. The combination of the highest tide of the period and lack of moonlight at Liverpool on the 27th was a simple matter of reference. So Admiral Bayly might easily have guessed that Germany would have made her play when and where she did. It was afterwards stated by Admiral Bayly that 'submarines were known to be in the area', but was it known how many?

In a letter to Washington on 26 January 1918, advocating the reprimand of Captain Oman for not slowing down for his destroyer escort in the Alley, Admiral Sims, who had initially been strongly opposed to the use of the *Leviathan* for this journey, stated:

'the *Leviathan* had passed through an area where two submarines were known to be operating.'

Two would have presented no surprise, but was he ever aware that there could have been as many as four, or more? What might have happened if the great liner had slowed down during her journey outside the '50 fathom line' up the George's Channel, and in the Irish Sea?

The expedition was a success but the value of landing her troops directly in France soon became apparent to the ever-practical Americans, and only one additional run was made to Liverpool before such voyages were redirected to Brest. There were a lot of battles fought within and by the Admiralty that Christmas.

It was at this point that America asserted the strategy of establishing a second supply line for the transport of supplies and troops directly to Europe. It was decided that larger and faster transport vessels should carry the majority of American troops. As speed and zigzagging had been identified as the best method for these ships to avoid submarine attacks, the transports travelled at twenty knots and would not slow until they approached the coast of France. This strategy avoided the 'danger zones' in the waters at the approaches to, and inside the Alley, and created a dilemma for the U-boat strategists.

A supply line existed across the Atlantic, providing food and material on the slower vessels, feeding into northern France through Ireland and England. Another was opened up with troops and material directly into western France. Given their insufficient numbers, the U-boats were forced to concentrate on either one or the other. In the main, due to the difficulty of locating the solitary troop transports, their speed, and the absence of a narrow danger zone, they chose to concentrate on the former.

Defeating the U-boats.

I suspect that there isn't a published account of the U-boat war in the Western Approaches during World War I, which doesn't mention Admiral Bayly in any light other than a most favourable one. It is clear that he gained the respect and admiration of the vast majority of British and American officers who served under him at Queenstown. He was a man who saw his duty clearly, and overcame the most difficult obstacles in order to protect shipping and defeat the U-boats in the waters around Ireland. For this he was bestowed with great honour and numerous expressions of the most deeply felt gratitude on both sides of the Atlantic.

It is also true, that during the former period of his command at Queenstown, he had come to believe that he was fighting the U-boats with one hand tied behind his back. Admiral Bayly's efforts were severely curtailed in terms of insufficient naval vessels at his disposal, but he also complained bitterly that he was fighting an unseen enemy, in terms of Sinn Féin spies. These, he believed, abounded in the area around Queenstown, and were relaying reports on Allied naval activities to German intelligence. It is certain that such spies existed, but there were also others aboard ships that sailed into and near Cork harbour.

Admiral Bayly's memoirs of those years were collected and published in *Pull Together* by his niece and lifelong companion, Violet Voycey, in 1939. In it, she outlines some of the breaches in security he suspected were causing the 'leakages' out of Queenstown:

'The Admiralty warned me that there appeared to be much leakage of important information from Queenstown and that I should have difficulty in stopping it. On studying the situation it was clear that leakage of information in a country where there were so many people disaffected towards England was fairly easy, seeing that all the messages from Admiralty House (Admiral Bayly's headquarters in Queenstown) were conveyed in clear language to the ships in harbour by visual signal from a semaphore on Admiralty House grounds.'

Very soon after the admiral's arrival at Queenstown, this lack of security was corrected, but the measures did not put an end to the annoying regularity with which German minelayers were dropping their deadly cargoes outside of the entrance to Queenstown. The U-boats' timely visits were said to have occurred 'on every occasion that a fresh division of US destroyers came over from the USA.' At a certain point during his command at Queenstown, the Admiral harboured the belief that he was almost besieged by Sinn Féin spies.

He also expressed another interesting opinion as to why on occasions, American naval vessels came perilously close to being sunk by U-boats. His suspicions were rooted in the little-known about 'communications war', and our old friend the telegraph cable, which he believed might have contributed to the uncanny timekeeping of the German minelayers, when he declared:

'Whether the leakage was from Queenstown or from the cables sent from the USA to Germany it is impossible to say; probably it was a combination of the two.'

Somehow it seems unlikely, that other than the communications which were allowed for the purpose of peace negotiations, US officials were having any kind of regular communication with Germany after they had declared war on her. On the other hand, did some kind of 'roundabout' remain in operation?

It might appear from some writings on the period, that during Admiral Bayly's command at Queenstown, German minelayers only arrived to plant mines, on foot of intelligence received on anticipated arrival of US vessels. It is safe to assume that there were leaks but it is also true that German minelayers had become persistent visitors not only to the waters off Cork but right along the southern coast of Ireland and into the Irish Sea. Cork, after all, was one of the most important landfalls for transatlantic shipping, and was the British, and later Allied naval station, solely responsible for patrolling the whole of the South-western Approaches.

The minelayers had become particularly annoying stones in the admiral's shoe, and he seized every opportunity to strike a blow against them. He didn't have long to wait after the arrival of the first US destroyers before he had successfully dispatched, by one means or another, three of these UC boats in quick succession, and in close proximity to the south coast of Ireland. These events occurred between August and October 1917. Considering that so many vessels were sunk without warning by these submarines, causing the death of so many sailors and innocent passengers, their commanders might not have expected their hunters to show any mercy.

So it was, when British Intelligence supposedly set the trap for one of the three UC minelayers mentioned here. During its June trip to Ireland, she had come through the Dover Strait and laid mines off the Shannon estuary and Innistearacht on 28 and 29 June. She then torpedoed and sunk the Italian steamer *Phoebus* (3133 tons) and shelled the four-masted Norwegian barque *Asalia* (2348 tons) on the 30th. The *Asalia* had been carrying petroleum from New York for Dublin. She can be seen in the illustrations totally engulfed in flames.

The four-masted Norwegian barque, *Asalea* (2348 tons) engulfed in flames.
She was travelling from New York to Dublin with petroleum when she was attacked
and sunk by *UC-44* off the south-west coast of Ireland on June 30th, 1917.

The photograph was reportedly taken after her black smoke attracted the attention of Admiralty vessels.

This minelayer was later attacked by the Q-ship *Gaelic* off the Fastnet on 2 July. The invader was *UC-44,* and she subsequently suffered damage to her superstructure and the death of one of her crew, after some very accurate gunnery by the Q-ship. *UC-44's* cruise began on 23 June and ended on 8 July, when she returned safely to Heligoland after going north about. It was estimated at the time that she might arrive off Ireland again after a period of two weeks. However, due to extended repairs, *UC-44* did not leave until 31 July.

Details of the loss of minelayer *UC-44* are commonly related in two ways. Firstly, while she was releasing her ninth mine off the entrance to Waterford on 4 August (this number of mines amounted to half her full complement), she somehow fouled or struck one of them, causing it to explode at the stern of the submarine. The damage to it was said to have been considerable, and caused her to sink uncontrollably.

An alternative explanation as to why *UC-44* became disabled is suggested by Patrick Beesly in *Room 40,* and is as follows:

'Hall arranged with Admiral Bayly that the port (Waterford) should be secretly closed to all traffic for a fortnight . . . *UC-44* duly reappeared to lay fresh mines and promptly blew up on one of those previously laid.'

German intelligence was credited at this time with breaking the British code that was being used to relay the completion of mine-clearance operations. However, German success in breaking this code was soon discovered by the Admiralty, and the Germans' newly acquired secret was subsequently used against them to lure *UC-44* onto mines that had been laid by another minelayer earlier. It is said hat the trap was set outside the entrance to Waterford harbour, after it was falsely reported by radio that this area had been cleared of mines. The mines in question were supposedly laid during an earlier visit of another UC boat.

The turnaround time for these submarines was two weeks, and even if the earlier laid mines had been anchored, this length of time might seem too long to expect them to have remained in the same positions. Again, Robert Grant has suggested in *U-Boat Intelligence* that the accident might have occurred as a result of striking a mine from 'one of the fields laid by *UC-42* on June 14–15 off Waterford'. This would suggest that shipping at Waterford might have been suspended or diverted for an even longer and more unlikely period. If this suggestion had been fact, it would have amounted to an extremely ironic incident, when one considers the destruction of *UC-42* herself, two months later, in the entrance to Cork harbour.

As it was, three submarines operated and sank ships in an area off Waterford during the two weeks prior to the arrival of *UC-44*. These were *U-53*, *UC-51* and *UC-75*.

In any event, the exploding *UC-44* was heard at the nearby harbour town of Dunmore, where some local men promptly put to sea, and were soon on the scene. It was reported that two local fishermen with surnames, Power and McGrath (familiar local names to this day), rowed out into the estuary and recovered the only survivor. After being treated kindly by some local people, the only surviving German prisoner was whisked off to the Admiralty's inquisitors in London.

This submariner survived the war, and was interviewed much later by another submariner, his friend Commander Ernst Hashagen of *U-62*. The survivor of *UC-44* was its captain, Lieutenant Commander Kurt Tebben johanns, a gentleman of noble birth from the Schleswig-Holsteiner family. The following extract is from the subsequent interview that was held between British Intelligence and Commander Tebben johanns, and later recorded by Hashagen in his book:

'At the time I had been in command of a minelaying U-boat, *UC-44,* for some months. On 31 July 1917 we embarked from Heligoland complete with eighteen mines and after the usual short practice dives we went to sea on our seventh long cruise. It was through the British Channel again to the south coast of Ireland. Orders to lay mines off Waterford and Queenstown and to wage war on commerce en route and in the Bristol Channel.

Apart from the usual excitement at the Dover–Calais barrage and a nasty shower of depth charges off the Scillys, from destroyers, our westward run was uneventful.'

It was off the Scillies, on 3 August, that *UC-44* communicated with the returning *UC-75,* which had just torpedoed the *Beechpark* (4763). *UC-44* continued on his journey to southern Ireland, and arrived off Waterford on the night of 4 August.

She soon began the preparations for mine-laying described here by her commander, Tebben johanns:

'As several hours must pass before the tide was suitable for mine-laying, the boat was taken to the bottom. Shortly after midnight we surfaced. Clear, starlit sky; moonshine and sea as flat as glass; no wind at all. Under these circumstances I decided that, in order to remain unseen at all costs, I would lay the nine mines intended for the blocking of the bay while running submerged. As the lighthouses were lit, it was possible to fix our position accurately, and the mine-laying commenced shortly after 12.30 AM. During the laying I personally checked the chart-work of the Chief Petty Officer Coxwain in the control-room, and then turned to the tower to take a bearing. I had given the order 'Lay nine mines' and the report 'Ninth mine gone' had just reached me. The words 'Stand by for a bearing' were on my lips, when there was a dreadful detonation. Instantly all lights went out, and a horrid, suffocating smell of sulphur arose. I was flung head-first against the side of the tower, but retained my consciousness and roared to the control room, "Compressed air to all tanks."

The order was repeated, but on its heels I heard a gurgling rush below. Then all was still. No cry, no human sound. Plainly I felt the boat sink deeper, then it hit the bottom hard. I knew that the water here was about 15 fathoms deep. Meanwhile, the senior Petty Officer from the control-room and an engineer-apprentice had joined me in the tower. Our attempts to get in touch with other parts of the boat by voice-pipe or

telephone were fruitless. We now stood, the three of us, pressed close together in the dark conning tower. The water that penetrated washed round our feet. We were very soon convinced that the boat was doomed and that the crew, except for us three, had met their end.

Yes, it was a fearful, hopeless situation for us three but the will to survive was not yet extinguished. Then again it was quite dark around us, so that we could not read in one another's eyes what each one felt. Perhaps that helped us to subdue our dread. I knew our position exactly and that the possibility of swimming to the coast was slight: for though the sea was quiet, the distance was considerable [the wreck of the submarine was said to have been four miles from Dunmore] and the tidal stream strong. Nor was it by any means certain that an attempt to leave the submarine by the conning-tower hatch would be successful, and I had a dreadful horror of death by drowning. A slow relapse into sleep in the tower seemed to me the better end, and I discussed the point quietly and practically with Chief Engine-room Officer Bahnster. He, on the other hand, who had married young and just become a father, urged me for the sake of his wife and child to make the attempt. I could not withstand his plea. We now placed ourselves close behind one another on the iron ladder to the conning-tower hatch. Then I carefully loosened the screws securing it, remembering a conversation about a similar case with the gallant Lieutenant Commander Bratigam of the Submarine Reserve in Kiel – till so much air had escaped that we stood in the water to our waists. The undoubted destruction of the after part of the ship by the explosion, and the consequent inrush of water throughout the boat (the bulkhead doors having been open), until its pressure was now equal to the column of water above the sunken submarine, the hatch was easily opened. It sprang up, the pressure instantly equalising itself. We were thrown out. I sought, by swimming with a downward motion, to guard against a too-rapid rise. In spite of the seemingly endless time before I reached the surface, I felt no lack of air. On the contrary, indeed, the excess pressure in my lungs relieved itself quite automatically, and without conscious effort on my part, through the mouth. (A build-up of a more than adequate supply of air in the lungs, which must be vented, is said to be a common experience by scuba divers practising an 'emergency accent.') Even today, it is astonishing to me. Almost inexplicable, in fact, that it occurred to none of us to remove our heavy suits, and above all our boots, before the attempt.

All at once my head was free, and the compressed and tortured lungs breathed again and unspeakable relief. Now to reach the shore. The brightly burning lighthouse was our mark.'

All three reached the surface and began to swim for the shore but only Captain Tebbenjohanns was saved as described. His escape from the submarine was an exceptionally lucky one. It was also said that, forward of the conning tower, another hatch was later found to be open by Admiralty divers, supposedly indicating that some other members of the crew might also have attempted an escape from that area of the boat. Commander Tebbenjohanns on the other hand, did not indicate that he detected any sign of life in the forward section of the submarine. As the author Robert Kemp has suggested, while *UC-44* was submerged and deploying her mines, it is likely that she struck one of her own mines, rather than one previously laid by another U-boat. The Admiralty was soon on the scene in the form of the well-known diver of the Salvage Section, Commander Davis, who, over a period of two weeks, 'bumped' the wrecked submarine into Dunmore Harbour, with the aid of rising tides and wires slung under the U-boat from barges. It is interesting to note that the Admiralty was equally generous to divers as it was with those who either sighted or sank submarines, and rewarded their successes with a bounty of £100, a considerable sum of money at the time.

Admiral Hall obtained very valuable information from being able to observe the construction of these UC boats first hand, and retrieved valuable documents and apparatus from *UC-44*, such as its code books and radio transmitter. It would appear from the diary of Commander Taussig that Admiral Bayly kept the trap that was set for *UC-44,* and the resulting salvage operations, quite secret. The American destroyer captains first became aware of the unusual operations taking place at Dunmore on 8 August, as Taussig's diary entry reveals:

'We have also been intercepting wireless messages between the C-in-C at Queenstown and some mine-sweepers in regard to a stranded submarine which they are trying to save. We do not know whether it is a British or German one. We hope it is German.'

(It is difficult to know who 'We...' was meant to include, or if Commander Taussig and the American officers shared all of the intelligence available to both allies).

Commander Taussig did not refer to the incident at Dunmore in his diary again, until after his briefing-visit to Admiralty House, on 22 August, when he included the following entry for that day:

'Admiral Bayly showed us the report of the information gained from the Captain of the German mine-laying submarine which was recently sunk off Waterford by one of its own mines. It was very interesting but no information of value was disclosed. They have not succeeded in raising the submarine yet.'

Another lengthy period passed before Commander Taussig makes any mention of work being carried out on the sunken U-boat, when on 26 September, he wrote:

'The *Shaw* (USN destroyer) left for Waterford to take officers who wished to see the German mine-laying submarine which blew up on one of her own mines about a month ago and which is now visible at low tide.'

No further mention of salving *UC-44* is made by Commander Taussig in *The Queenstown Patrol* but Chatterton in *Danger Zone,* and Admiral Bayly himself, in *Pull Together,* gave some of their recollections as to what occurred next with the submarine. Firstly, Chatterton recalls what two of his friends had related to him following their visit to see the grounded *UC-44* at Dunmore:

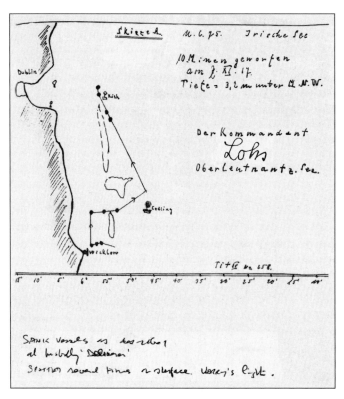

A detailed sketch of mine-laying operations along the coasts of north Wicklow and Dublin by Commander Lohs in *UC-75* during November 1917. Two of these mines are shown having being laid just north of the Kish.

A sketch of mine laying operations along the Arklow and Wexford Coasts by Commander Lohs in *UC-75* during August 1917. The sketch indicates a detailed understanding of the marine hazards so close to this coast and the importance of Arklow harbour and the shipments from Kynochs' munitions factory.

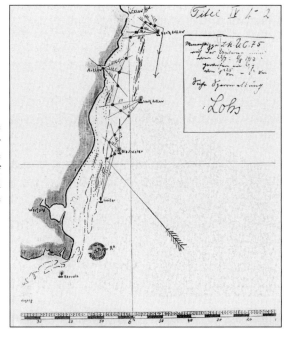

The Commander of *UC-75* Johann Lohs.

'The following month two of my friends drove over to Waterford to have a look at *UC-44*, now hauled up on the beach in Dunmore Cove. There still remained a skull and an offensive odour. It was noticed that besides her mines she carried three torpedoes. All hands apparently slept on spring bunks, and when the explosion took place the watch below must have been killed in their sleep, for in some cases the bodies were still wrapped in their blankets. Part of the submarine had been blown right off, and a torpedo in the stern tube broken in half. Later on she was again taken out to sea, and our depth- charges experimented with, so as to ascertain their effects on the enemy. Some illuminating and very encouraging results were afforded.'

One might immediately wonder why a victim's skull, or the bodies that were observed in blankets, might have been left in the beached submarine. The reference to some of them being 'wrapped in their blankets' is interesting, and might alternatively indicate that they had been entombed in the sunken submarine for some time and suffered from the cold while dying from the lack of air. However, Admiral Bayly informs us as to the fate of the crew and the final resting place of *UC-44* in *Pull Together* when he says:

'so she was towed into the entrance of the river at Waterford and sunk there after the bodies had been taken out of her and buried at sea.'

It was reported that this submarine was later used to test the effects of new depth charges that were been developed by the British navy, and that the wreck was eventually dispersed. It was also reported in the 1930s that the wreck was dispersed once more, and that some of the hull was recovered. It would seem that even in her ultimate destruction, it was intended that *UC-44* should reveal even more about her construction qualities.

One might also wonder, if the bodies had been taken ashore in the submarine, why they were not buried ashore. Expediency, perhaps? Or if this was not the naval tradition then, why were <u>all</u> of the bodies not buried at sea?

Walter Richter, with the German naval rank, 'mascinist', was buried at the Old Graveyard, Duncannon, near Dunmore. His body was re-interred in 1959 at the German Military Cemetery at Glencree, County Wicklow. Neither his tombstone nor German archives reveal whether he was the third man, the 'engineer-apprentice', who had escaped with Commander Tebbenjohanns, but it clearly testified that his death, the recovery of his body or its burial, occurred four days after the loss of *UC-44*. As there is no other record of German naval casualties in this area during the period, it is only reasonable to assume that Walter Richter was one of the crew who had escaped from *UC-44*. The unknown circumstances of this naval rating's death presents some interesting questions.

Commander Tebbenjohanns was later interrogated by naval intelligence, and a summary of his interrogation remains on file in the PRO at Kew. From this report, one might conclude that he seemed to give little away, but it does include some interesting remarks. Firstly, it was reported that a guard-boat rescued him and not the local boat, which Admiral Bayly reported it to have been. Robert Grant in *U-boat Intelligence* said it was a 'row boat' from Dunmore that picked him up. Secondly, Commander Tebbenjohanns only reported having four torpedoes. When asked whether a U-boat could stray into the path of mines laid by a homeward-bound one, Tebbenjohanns is reported to have said he thought this impossible. It was also presumed in the summary of his interrogation that he was able to listen to British naval wireless transmissions and was able to 'read their warnings.' Most revealing was his memory of the submarine's crew, and nearly all of their names. This included a 'machinist' named Richter. A list of the names of the crew that he remembered appears at the end of this chapter and helps to resolve the mystery burial at Duncannon, although not completely.

An interesting, never-reported touch of irony in this episode, occurred after Tebbenjohanns was taken from Dunmore and transported to Queenstown, where he must have stirred more than a passing interest. He was then transported 'first class' by train to Dublin and on to Kingstown, where he and the escorting officer boarded the mail boat, *Leinster,* for Holyhead. During the passage, the escorting British officer was taken to have a drink in the saloon, and on Tebbenjohanns' honour as an officer, his keeper allowed him to walk free about the ship. After being made aware of a U-boat captain walking about the deck of his ship, the commander of the *Leinster,* Captain Birch, was none too happy, and threatened to have both of them confined, if he was not removed below immediately. The submariner was hurriedly confined below, but Captain Birch and many of his passengers were later sent to their graves when another U-boat commander torpedoed his ship.

The second of these minelayers to fall foul of the Queenstown patrols was *UC-42*. She was lost as mysteriously as – and close on the heels of – *UC-44,* in a position not too distant westward. Operations by the Admiralty on both submarines were carried on simultaneously during September–October 1917. She was the sister minelayer referred to earlier, which was reportedly damaged just outside of the entrance to Queenstown Harbour on 10 September, a full two weeks before *UC-44* was beached in Dunmore. Did she observe the salvage operations being carried out on *UC-44* in one of her old stomping grounds just outside Dunmore? If she had, returning with the intelligence would have been a severe blow to the Admiralty, who had hoped to keep the fate of *UC-44* a secret for some time. In any event, the Admiralty had no cause for concern on this score.

The cause for the loss of *UC-42,* is again, quite often very simply recorded. Just as with *UC-44*, it is supposed that she was unfortunate to have struck one of her own mines, which exploded at her stern, causing massive damage, from which she did not survive. The last recorded entry in the U-boat's log was 10 September. But how do we know this, when there were no survivors?

Some histories go on to state that diving operations by the Admiralty on the sunken submarine commenced almost immediately, during which time the divers reported seeing the damage to its stern, and recovered several of its fittings and its log book. As with *UC-44*, divers also reported they had seen the forward hatch open, again, supposedly indicating that an attempt might have been made by some of its crew to escape on the surface or from the wreck. (It is important to note that an underwater escape through these other hatches was never intended nor possible, until water had filled the inside of the submarine and the pressure equalised somehow and allowed the hatch to be opened.) None of the victims' bodies were ever recovered, however. The following account of the loss of this U-boat, by Robert Grant, is similar to others but is at odds with some additional features, which are recorded by Commander Taussig further on:

'As for Queenstown, large quantities of oil were sighted off the *Daunt Light Vessel* on October 31, and two patrols dropped depth charges. Two days later, divers went down and found the wreck of a submarine with the stern blown off. One of them brought up the U-boat's starboard sidelight with the number '42' on it. On the 13th, a diver finally identified the submarine as *UC-42*. She had evidently laid three mines, for her forward chute was empty while the others were full. Her bow lay at a depth of 78 feet, the stern at 92 feet. All the hatches were open, thus showing that her crew had evidently tried to escape. The log indicated that she had perished on September 10.'

(HMTB *Sarba* did report detecting a submarine 5miles SW of the *Daunt Rock Light Ship* on 10 September and was instructed by RN vessel *Brock* to go and destroy a mine 3 miles SE of Old Head Kinsale on 11 September.)

For the moment, there are two points worth mentioning here. Firstly, *UC-42*'s forward mine chute was reportedly empty, and if she had been blown up by her own mine, it was most likely to have been the third one dropped. If *UC-44* had laid its mines in the same way, again, tragedy would seem to have struck at the same moment in both operations, that is, just after releasing one of the adjustable mines from its chute. Sabotage was not suggested for the loss of either of these U-boats, but similar events occurred on at least two other occasions, and German submariners had cried sabotage against their boats and equipment on more than a few occasions.

Secondly, it was reported that the final entry in the log of *UC-42* was made on 'September 10'. This need not be quite the same as saying that the boat and all her twenty-seven crew perished on that date. Lastly, it can almost certainly be presumed that letting go the third mine in the entrance to Queenstown was the beginning of *UC-42*'s mining operations, and that she had already dropped the first two nearby. However, this is at odds with the Admiralty's own intelligence reports, which clearly show entries describing how she laid mines in 'deep water' on the 9th, and off 'Bull' and 'Kinsale' on the 10th.

Nothing untoward might be thought of this incident, except that, once again, some questions arise as a result of entries made in Commander Taussig's diary. These include the following account, which was reported to him on the much later date of 3 November.

The Howth fishing vessel *Geraldine*. Sunk off lambay Island by gunfire from *U-96* in March 1918. Six of her nine crew were killed. The *St Michan* accompanied the Geraldine, and she too was shelled and sunk with no loss of crew.

A series of photographs taken of the salvaged German submarine *UC-42* at Dummore East, Co. Waterford, Ireland.

'Commander Herbert, R.N., and Commander Heaton, R.N., were swapping yarns. The former has had some remarkable experience in submarines – and some miraculous escapes. The latter has lost a hand somewhere. I have not asked him how. He is in charge of the minesweepers. He has just brought up the report about the submarine, which was destroyed off the entrance of Queenstown the day before yesterday. It seems that the small patrol boat *P-55*(HMTB 055) was steaming out when the skipper noticed a small streak of oil which seemed to be coming up. He stopped, put over his hydrophone and heard many peculiar and unusual noises, among which was the sound of hammering on metal. He stood off, ran over the spot and dropped a depth charge of the small type – the only kind he had. The amount of oil coming to the surface increased. He then went for the armed trawler *Sarla* (*Sarba*), which vessel dropped a big depth charge, the explosion of which resulted in large quantities of heavy oil and bubbles coming to the surface. He then stopped, put on his hydrophone and dropped his sounding lead. They could distinctly hear the lead striking something metallic. They then dragged, and the sweep caught on something. Yesterday a diver went down (15 fathoms). He reported a large submarine lying on its side and brought up one of its side lights. It is probable that this submarine had either got into trouble from engine defects, or had run aground and could not rise. They were evidently trying to effect repairs when they were discovered. The submarine service must be both a miserable and terrible existence. It seems to me that sooner or later a captain who takes any risks with them will lose his ship and its crew.'

(The logs of *P-55* and *Sarla* were not available at the PRO.)

Although relations between US and Royal naval personnel at Queenstown are well remembered to have been very good, there are a number of entries in Commander Taussig's diary which suggest that not all British naval intelligence was being passed on to US naval commanders. Commander Taussig, and most likely just as with some of his RN counterparts, was seemingly not aware of all the facts concerning anti-submarine activity at the time. Nor does he seem to have been aware of the events that were recorded by Patrick Beesly in 'Room 40', about what supposedly transpired between Admirals Hall and Bayly soon after the event:

'On 6 November, Bayly reported that the wreck appeared to be buoyant and enquired if he should raise it. He was immediately told by the 1st Sea Lord, to do nothing because the Admiralty had 'all the information we are likely to get and knowledge that we have recovered her might lead to a change of codes, etc. which it is desirable to avoid.' However, only four days later, German call signs were again changed and considerable difficulty was obviously experienced in identifying new ones. On 18 November, Hall enquired from Bayly if the wreck could still be located. He was told in reply that the divers had already visited it but work on raising the boat, which was lying in twenty-five fathoms, had been stopped in accordance with previous orders. Presumably a fresh haul of papers was then retrieved from *UC-42*.'

This last report presents confusion. Were attempts made to raise *UC-42*? In what way was she 'buoyant', after being so badly damaged in the stern by her own mine, all her hatches being found open, and after divers had entered the wreck and retrieved items from inside the control room? Who or what was banging in the wrecked U-boat before the depth charges were dropped? Why had the earlier reported depth of the disabled U-boat increased from 15 to the later 25 fathoms?

Keble Chatterton in *Valiant Sailormen* (1931) stated that diving operations by the Admiralty began on *UC-42* at the beginning of November, and continued for approximately two weeks. The wreck was supposedly lying at 60 degrees to port at a depth of between 78 and 92 feet of water. He also reported that the divers had seen the corpse of a German sailor and described similar damage to the stern section of the U-boat. They removed some munitions, the periscope, and a lamp, and confirmed the number of the submarine from one stamped on the hatch cover aft of the conning tower. Interestingly, the divers also reported seeing two spare torpedoes secured to the deck.

Before any of the UCII class of minelayer were captured, it was generally believed that they carried only three torpedoes in tubes and one disassembled spare inside the boat. This intelligence was later upgraded to a total of six, which included two additional spares that were secured behind the torpedo tubes on the fore deck. Studies made much later venture a total of seven.

It is also interesting to note that the two British officers that had related the details on the fate of *UC-42* to Commander Taussig, were no amateurs when it came to anti-submarine warfare. Commander Herbert (Captain William McBride was his self-christened nickname), already mentioned earlier, had a considerable and varying pedigree of submarine and anti-submarine service behind him, and had not long returned to Queenstown (July) to take up a position on Admiral Bayly's staff.

Having put his Q-ship adventures behind him, he headed up a small flotilla of submarine-hunting vessels, equipped with hydrophones, out of Falmouth, where he and his boat, the *Sea King,* were responsible for the destruction of another minelayer, *UC-66*. This minelayer was considered totally destroyed on 12 June, as a result of dropping depth charges on her off the Lizard. Notwithstanding his accomplishments in this area, he is also remembered for his successes and failures in command of British submarines. These included *A-4, D-5, E-22* and *K-13,* the last from which he had a similar escape to the one experienced by Commander Tebbenjohanns in *UC-44*. However, he is better remembered for his command of Q-ships, and in particular the *SS Baralong*, which was involved in a controversial incident with the mule ship *SS Nicosian,* and its attacker *U-27*. Commander Herbert sank this U-boat on 19 April 1915, in circumstances, which were reported as being brutal, and without showing any mercy.

The regrettable behaviour was reported to have occurred while German crewmen were scrambling for safety in the water, and against others that had attempted to hide in the *Nicosian*.

It was later reported by one of Commander's Herbert's own crew, Corporal Collins, that during the destruction of *U-27* and all of her crew, Herbert ordered his personally picked crew to 'Take no prisoners'. There were none taken. But there were witnesses, and the cruel incident later hit the headlines in America and Germany. It was not the only accusation of cruelty perpetrated against German submariners that was levelled at Commander Herbert, but on the other hand he was an extremely popular commander, and by all accounts a larger-than-life, swashbuckling, devil-may-care man's man. He was an officer seen to be effective, and one who had certain qualities, which were in short supply.

In a clear reference to some of these qualities, after he was appointed to Admiral Bayly's staff, Keble Chatterton said of him in *Danger Zone:*

'If the whole future of this war with Germany was to rest on anti-U-boat contests, here was a type of mind which could render invaluable aid at Queenstown.'

However distasteful the action against the crew of *U-27* might have been, one might not have expected Commander Herbert to have acted any differently, given the following instruction he is reported to have received prior to assuming his new command out of Queenstown:

'Before he sailed from Queenstown in the *Baralong* he had been summoned by one of the senior officers of the Admiralty's Special Service branch, to be told, "This *Lusitania* is shocking. Unofficially, we are telling you . . . take no prisoners from U-boats."'

Commander Godfrey Herbert was awarded the DSO twice, and retired from the navy as a relatively young officer in 1919.

The second British officer, Commander Heaton, was not as notable then but he did command the mine-sweeping flotilla at Queenstown, and received praise from all quarters for his effective and persistent abilities at keeping the approaches clear of mines.

Another very interesting officer, who joined Admiral Bayly's team for a time in anti-submarine work, was Colonel B. F. Trench, of the Royal Marines. Colonel Trench received the nickname of the 'Borkum Spy', after he and fellow officer, Lieutenant Brandon, were arrested for spying on German naval installations. Both were sentenced to four years' imprisonment but were pardoned and released in May 1913, when they returned to the naval intelligence team attached to Room 40 under Admiral Hall.

According to Commander Tebbenjohanns of *UC-44*, it was Colonel Trench, by then the senior Naval Intelligence representative, who interrogated him after he was transported to London. Colonel Trench was known to have been a most successful interrogator, and served again and with similar distinction during World War II.

The last communication between the Admiralty and Queenstown in relation to operations carried out on the sunken *UC-42* appears to have occurred on 18 November. On the following day, the armed trawler *Morococala,* already mentioned earlier, was lost with all hands after striking a mine near the Daunt Rock. The loss received special mention by Admiral Bayly in a memo of special tribute sent to all under his command. Mine clearance at Queenstown was very effective, and there were no other casualties reported from mines or torpedo attacks anywhere near to the entrances of Queenstown, for some weeks either side of this isolated event.

The Royal Naval Hydrographic Office record the approximate position of *UC-42* as 52.41N, and 08.12W in a depth of 20 metres. For many years divers have attempted to locate this war-grave but have failed to find any trace of her in this general area. Commander Taussig recorded on the 19th that he received a radio message on the 18 November, stating that 'Queenstown was closed owing to mines.' The *Morococala* lies on the seabed in the position 51.41.712N, 08.13.433W. Admiralty's records differ from the Hydrographic Office and indicate that the wreck of *UC-42* was located on 31 October off the Daunt Rock, and included the following entry in their 'listening log' in regard to this submarine:

'10 Sept 1917. – Sunk 51.41N 08.14W. (Own mines)'

This position is quite close to *Morococala* but nowhere near the position recorded by the Hydrographic Office. Have divers been looking for this lost wreck all these years in the wrong place?

The mystery surrounding this submarine's final resting place is not helped by the following confusion embedded in Admiralty records. A submarine was detected SW of *Daunt LV* on 9-10 September by *Sarba* and *Stormcock* (*U-57* sank ships and operated in this area between 6-10 October but did not lay mines and returned to base.) Another submarine was detected 2 miles SE of Roches Point on 31 October, which was depth-charged and destroyed. This was confirmed by divers and contained in Admiralty reports on 5 November. However, yet another U-boat was detected SE of the *Daunt LV* and harassed by patrols on the 16 November – action and sweeps against this sub continued until the 19th. Although oil was sighted, a 'kill' was not confirmed on this occasion. This may have been *U-58,* which was depth-charged and destroyed by USN destroyers on the 17 November, a few miles SW of the *Daunt LV.* Alternatively, it may have been *UC-42* revisited on the 18th, as referred to by Admiral Bayly

The foregoing facts, and the heat of battle, would easily give plenty of room for confusion but the confirmation of *UC-42* lying destroyed on the seabed two miles off Roches Point by Admiralty divers would appear to be conclusive, and give today's divers yet another position in which to search. As the log of *UC-42* no longer seems to be available, locating this wreck and clearing up some of the mystery surrounding her loss might still prove difficult. One of the final reports relating to the destruction of *UC-42* by *Sarba* and *MTB 055* is by Commander Seymour, and is dated, both the 9th and 15th November 1917. It is crossed with the word 'Destruction' and explains:

"The evidence of the hydrophone listeners points to the conclusion that the submarine was lying on the bottom damaged & trying to effect repairs or attract attention. The evidence appears to be more reliable than is often the case with hydrophones."

The Queenstown patrols were beginning to have some of it their own way, and the American destroyers also tasted some success against the U-boats on the 17th. Not mentioned in Commander Taussig's diary, but a convoy of merchantmen had left Queenstown on the 17th; amongst its escorts were the US naval destroyers *Fanning* and *Nicholson*. Seven miles south of the Daunt Rock, during an engagement with *U-58,* the US destroyers depth-charged and finally sank this submarine with gunfire. All of the crew from the U-boat crew were rescued.

Given the rapidly increasing number of US naval vessels patrolling the Approaches after May 1917, it is a most curious feature that it was British vessels that were responsible for the vast majority of successful actions against German submarines.

Admiral Bayly's success against the U-boats had become more promising during the latter half of 1917. His final mine-laying victim off the south coast of Ireland occurred on 26 September 1917. And for some unknown reason, this third minelayer, *UC-33,* is still associated by some with an unusual event that occurred at Arklow town, on the east coast of Ireland, just a few days prior to its loss. *UC-33* had attacked a convoy off Tuskar Rock, but due to damaged hydroplanes, she remained on the surface where she was rammed and sunk by the escort vessel, *HMS PC-61.* In the light of further knowledge obtained about U-boat operations in the Alley, the association that this submarine might have had with the events at Arklow which follow, are dispelled, but will not go away.

Merchant steamers and their crews had no choice but to depart safe harbours and face the menace of the lurking U-boats in the Alley. Harbours themselves and their surrounding areas were not always immune from attack either, and were sometimes the targets of gunfire from U-boats. It was not common for a U-boat to bombard a shore target but such events did occur on several occasions around the British Isles. Three weeks prior to the attack on the Guinness steamer *W. M. Barkley,* a devastating explosion rocked the town of Arklow on the east coast of Ireland, killing twenty-seven factory workers. The cause of this explosion was linked to the saga of U-boat attacks in the Alley, and according to Arklow's folklore, confirmation of this link, supposedly lies at the bottom of the George's Channel, near the Arklow Bank.

A massive explosion occurred at Kynoch's huge munitions-facility on Arklow's north shore, in the early hours of 21 September 1917, and rocked the town and its surroundings for up to twelve miles. The explosion damaged nearby houses and destroyed several buildings in the plant. Press reporting on the inquest of the victims, which was held soon after, was restricted, and returned the verdict on the cause of death; 'cause unknown'. However, many believed, and passed on, the story of a submarine shelling the factory on the night in question.

Although rare enough, shore targets were of some interest to the U-boats, even if such attacks were not widely reported in the British Isles. In this case, a great deal of interest focused on the claims by some witnesses that they had seen a flash of light out to sea, followed by a 'whoosh' noise prior to the explosion at Kynoch's. Attention was also drawn to mysterious 'lights' that were reported to have shone from an automobile on the road above Kynoch's, immediately prior to the explosion.

Kynoch's and Arklow were no strangers to alleged attempts of sabotage, nor to German submariners, who paid particular attention to laying mines across its approaches. In order to demonstrate this, I have included in the illustrations, a copy of sketches made by Commander Lohs from two of his mine-laying missions to Ireland in *UC-75,* once during August, and another in November 1917. Particular attention should be paid in the diagrams, to the way in which he used the lightships to navigate the deployment of his mines, and of his apparently intimate knowledge of the treacherous sandbanks off Arklow and Wicklow. His method of laying the mines across the route entrances to the north and south of the Arklow Bank, effectively created a very dangerous situation for vessels approaching or leaving Arklow harbour, until they were cleared. (Gun cotton and chemicals for the manufacture of the munitions were being imported into Arklow during World War I.)

Kynoch's had their own fleet of ships, and because of shallow tidal restrictions, both harbours, at Arklow and Wicklow, were used to berth them. It can be seen from the record of Commander Lohs' operations that he also laid mines at the southern end of the India Bank opposite the entrance to Wicklow harbour. (Operations at the Kynoch's plant were taken over by the government in 1916, and it is not known just how much of its production capacity was exported directly from Arklow or how much of it travelled to Dublin by train for onward shipping.)

Despite the U-boats' efforts, there were no Kynoch's vessels sunk in the Alley, until the *Solway Queen* (307 tons) was torpedoed in the Irish Sea off Black Head, Wigtownshire, on 2 April 1918. All eleven of the crew were killed, four of them from Arklow town. After the devastation caused at Kynoch's, there was considerable disquiet when rumours of the plant's closure began to spread. The prospect alarmed the 3,500 workers. Local representatives made urgent representations, and production was maintained for a while longer. The factory never really got back on its feet, and amid accusations of commercial jealousy and commercial assassination by key interests in Britain, the works finally closed during the period 1918–19, at an enormous loss to Arklow town and the country as a whole.

The entire works, stretching from the harbour at Arklow for about a mile along the North Beach, was reputedly sold for £90,000 to one D. Frame, who resided in the town of Bray further up the coast.

The persistent rumours of a sunken German submarine off Arklow, has stubbornly remained a tantalising element in the circumstances surrounding the mystery explosion at Kynoch's. In trying to tease out this mystery, it has been difficult to determine which came first, the wreck of a coaster named the *Anna Toop* or the story of a sunken U-boat on the Arklow Bank. Many local people still believe the latter.

In any event, the story of the 'Arklow submarine' was elevated from being a figment of someone's imagination, when the Cardiff coaster *Anna Toop* ran onto the Arklow Bank on 21 January 1958. Not until after the captain had notified the ship's owners in England, was the alarm raised in Arklow, and the lifeboat requested to attempt a rescue. A nurse-stewardess and the ten crewmen were subsequently rescued by the lifeboat in bad weather, and lodged at Hoynes Hotel in the town. Efforts to tow the vessel to Arklow the next day failed, when the *Toop* suddenly sank after taking on too much water through buckled plates in the bottom of her hull.

The loss of the *Toop* may not have come as too much of a surprise for some, as the results of her last survey led to the insertion of the following remark in the Lloyd's Register for that year: 'Class expunged and with reported defects.'

During subsequent salvage operations on the *Toop*'s cargo, or as reported by some, to have been an inspection by an insurance investigator, it is said that a diver reported seeing the wreck of a World War I submarine nearby. The 'Kynoch incident' and the story of the 'Arklow submarine' were at this point inextricably joined.

Insofar as 'submarine stories' go, there seems to be no reason why the circumstances of this particular one should not hold some grains of truth. On the negative side, even though there have been reported sightings of a sunken submarine on this bank by divers on two occasions, the presence of such a wreck in the area has never been charted or substantiated. Furthermore, there does not appear to be any record of a U-boat missing in this area at any time during World War I – or World War II for that matter. In addition, there are no references in the Kingstown (Dun Laoghaire) or Queenstown (Cobh) station-reports from World War I which might indicate any contact with or knowledge of a U-boat in the area at the time of the Kynoch's explosion.

The nearest loss on the nearest date occurred when *UC-33* was sunk on 26 September 1917 by *PC-61*. The only survivor from the U-boat was her commander, Oberleutnant A. Arnold, who had been in the conning tower at the moment she went down. After an underwater explosion, three more bodies came to the surface and the submarine was believed wrecked. Interestingly, *HMS PC-61* was commanded by Frank Worsley, with a fellow-officer and old shipmate, Joseph Stenhouse, who were both Antartic explorers. For his action in helping to sink *UC-33,* Stenhouse added the D.S.O. to a long list of decorations.

It is extremely unlikely that if this submarine had bombed Kynoch's factory, and had been rammed afterwards, losing several of her crew through the engagement with R.N. vessels, she would later have limped back up the George's Channel, only to sink on a sand bank off Arklow. She is in any event recorded as lying at the bottom of the sea in the position given.

The story of the 'Arklow submarine' became even more popular when the diver who had worked on the *Anna Toop,* was allegedly able to determine that the submarine dated from World War I. If by any chance the submarine does exist, and it dates from World War I, there would seem to be very few possibilities.

The first and most unlikely suggestion might be a very secret and undocumented mission. The others lie with the sailing times of four submarines. Firstly, *U-45* sailed on 5 September, and was torpedoed by a British submarine west of the Shetlands on 12 September. As there were two survivors from *U-45*, other than deliberate false reporting, this U-boat is ruled out. The second, *UB-32,* which sailed on 10 September, was reported to have been bombed by an aircraft in the West Channel on 22 September. There were no survivors from this U-boat, and nothing more can be said about the incident, except that the crew of the aeroplane stated that, as a result of dropping their bombs, they believed they had sunk a German submarine. Thirdly, *UC-21*, which sailed on 13 September for her familiar hunting-ground off the west coast of France, was never heard from again. Although the date on which this submarine set out comfortably fits in with the date of the explosion at Kynoch's, she had not previously operated in these waters, and so her complicity and subsequent loss on the Arklow Bank is doubtful.

Lastly, a suggestion that a British submarine might have purposely shelled the factory for some political or propaganda reasons seems quite preposterous. The supposition that propaganda advantages might have been gained by smearing Sinn Féin or the German Navy with responsibility for the closure of the factory is far outweighed by the fallout that might have followed the exposure of such a plot, and there was no serious support for the idea.

In an attempt to shed some light on this persistent and mysterious rumour of a German submarine lying wrecked on the Arklow Bank, a small group of interested divers and myself mounted a number of searches in the area during the summers of 2001-2003. We first concentrated on an area where we believed the wreck of the *Anna Toop* lay. The idea was that, if we located it, we would then continue to search in the immediate area of the wreck, hoping to encounter what the original salvage diver is reported to have seen 'nearby'. The *Anna Toop* and another wreck in the area named *Cameo* were easily found. The *Anna Toop* remains in a remarkable state of preservation for a vessel wrecked almost a half-a-century ago but neither wreck resembled a submarine.

Before we made any further searches, I interviewed some old and accommodating fishermen from Arklow, who were very familiar with the submarine story. Other than stating they had always 'known' of it, or 'heard' of it, they were unable to say how they had come to know of it or how they knew the submarine to be on the Bank. Faced with the question 'How do you know that the snag is a submarine?' the reply was quite simple: 'We know where all the other wrecks are.' Questioning also revealed that the story of the 'Arklow submarine' was in place well before the wrecking of the *Anna Toop*.

The other diver who had reported seeing the wreck of a German submarine off Arklow was subsequently located. He turned out to be a well-known sport-diver and restaurateur from Kilkee, Manuel Di Lucia. He clearly stated that he had been put on the wreck of a submarine off Arklow by a local trawler-man in 1973, and was partially able to describe the event and the wreck he believed to be a submarine. Further questioning and additional searches revealed only more mystery.

Whether or not the Commander of Naval Forces in Ireland, Admiral Bayly, based at Queenstown, gleaned any particular lessons from his enquiries into the Kynoch incident, not long afterwards he was responsible for the introduction of a ban on fishing 'within five miles of Arklow'. He was also responsible for the introduction of a 'light restrictions' order for the coast of Ireland, which came into effect on 10 February 1918. This was enforceable under the Defence of the Realm Act (DORA). The new order forbade the shining of any light within five miles of the coastline that could be seen at sea. Item number two of this order would seem to address the curious observations mentioned earlier, in respect of the lights that shone from a mysterious automobile. It prohibited:

'The use in motor or other vehicles, including trains and omnibuses, of powerful lights,that is, lights visible at a distance exceeding two miles.'

Penalties for contravening this order were, as usual, severe.

The possibility of a submarine shelling the munitions plant at Arklow during World War I has been repeatedly discounted but often for no good reason. After all, it wouldn't be the first time a U-boat turned up in a place where it shouldn't have been! Although there was no other report of a U-boat shelling a shore target in Ireland during World War I, such incidences had occurred in Britain. This compelling extract from the testimony of the principal witness, Private Richard Craig, from his recollections of the events on the night in question, was collected from the marvellous local publication *The Kynoch Era in Arklow,* and is hard to ignore:

'He stated that at a quarter to four his attention was attracted to a very bright light which he took to be a ship in distress at sea, having fired a rocket. Four seconds afterwards a loud explosion occurred.'

The soldier clearly associated the sea, and some activity out on it, with the resulting explosion at Kynoch's.

Admiral Bayly and others were clearly taken with the notion that Irishmen were responsible for communicating naval intelligence to German submarine commanders in some form or other. The Admiral is also credited with issuing an earlier order following the Easter Rising in 1916, by Dr De Courcy Ireland in *The Sea and the Easter Rising 1916.*

This order supposedly read 'that any small boat seen between sunset and sunrise within two miles of the Irish coast is to be sunk without warning.'

Indications of a significant new strategy being adopted by the U-boats in the Alley and its approaches began to manifest itself between December 1917 and March 1918. After the dreadful toll of merchant vessels towards the end of December, larger vessels began to be targeted.

The White Star liner *Justicia* (32,324 tons), in service of the Shipping Controller was first but lucky to escape when a torpedo missed her in the Irish Channel on 23 January. Four days later, the Cunard liner, *Andania* (13,405 tons), returning to America with general cargo and passengers were not so lucky, when she was torpedoed and sunk off Rathlin Island by *U-46*. Fortunately there were only 7 killed. On 4 February another Cunarder was torpedoed and eight were lost. This time the culprit was *UB67* operating off Innishtrahul when she attacked the *Aurania* (13,936 tons). The liner was eventually taken in a tow that reached the Isle of Mull but is where she finally sank. The next victim was the *Tuscania* (14,348 tons) returning from New York with troops and cargo. Forty-four were killed when she was torpedoed by *UB-77* on 5 February entering the North Channel.

When not acting as merchant cruisers protecting convoys, these large liners almost always travelled alone, as they could elude the U-boats with their high speed, and many were heavily armed. When they reached the 'danger zones' they sometimes slowed while rendezvousing with their screen of destroyers which would afford protection from the lurking U-boats.

In the case of the *Tuscania*, she was in convoy with eight other medium-sized steamers, a cruiser and several destroyers. This strong escort did not deter the relentless pursuit of Commander Meyer in *UB-77,* who is reported to have tracked the ship for four hours. However, as a result of being harassed several times by the screen of destroyers, he failed to launch another torpedo at the already sinking vessel.

Several lesser vessels, though of significant size, were also torpedoed in the Irish Channel about this time but were saved by beaching and repairs.

Although nearly always empty, almost equal protection was given to these liners when they were outward bound through the 'danger zones' to America. They were, however, often carrying large amounts of gold, which Britain was settling her debts with in America. This was the case with the White Star liner *Laurentic* (14,892 tons) when she was sunk on 25 January 1917 by a mine laid by *U-80*. The liner's valuable cargo of gold was later salvaged by the Admiralty from the wreck, which lies in the entrance to Lough Swilly. Although many of the cargoes in these vessels were salvaged by the famous salvage company, Risdon Beazley, subsequent improvements made in the diving industry have made it possible for modern-day treasure hunters to pursue the more lucrative cargoes from World War I that lie in the deeper waters around Ireland.

On the first of March there was a significant running battle between the armed merchant cruiser (AMC) *Calgarian* and *U-19*. After several torpedoes were fired at the *Calgarian,* she finally sank off Rathlin Island.

The Royal Mail Steam Packet Company's ship, *Amazon* (10,037 tons), was lost off Malin Head on 15 March when she was torpedoed by *U-110*. The *Amazon's* distress calls alerted patrols, and two destroyers subsequently depth-charged and sunk the submarine. Four of the U-boat's crew were saved and thirty nine others were killed. There were no reported casualties from the *Amazon*. The huge liner *Celtic* (20,904 tons) only barely survived sinking on 31 March by a successful tow to the Isle of Man, after she was torpedoed in the Irish Sea.

The upsurge in the number of U-boat attacks in the Alley during the early months of 1918 showed a new determination by U-boat commanders to tackle the well-escorted and valuable merchant cruisers in an attempt to stem the flow of ships and supplies to Britain. The persistence shown in the case of the attack against the *Tuscania,* was again evident and similar to the one carried out by *U-19* against the *Calgarian*, after she had escorted a convoy of ten vessels from Halifax.

At the outbreak of the war the Admiralty had found itself in urgent need of suitable vessels with which to service the increased demand for materials, troops, food and to provide protection for convoys from America and elsewhere. It was fortunate that this was also at a time when there was a significant number of privately owned merchant vessels being completed in British yards, and many of these were commandeered into service for the Royal Navy.

Such was the case with the completion of two large liners for the Glasgow based Allan Line in 1914. (The Allan Line was taken over by Canadian Pacific in 1917.) Grossing 18,485 tons the *Alsatian* was commandeered into the 10th Cruiser Squadron where she headed up blockading duties in the North Atlantic. She survived the war and was broken up in 1934. Not so her sister ship the *Calgarian* (17,521 tons), which was fitted out with eight six inch guns, transforming her into armed merchant-cruiser in order to provide protection for convoys crossing the Atlantic. She ended her days in the deep waters off Rathlin Island in Northern Ireland, on 1 March 1918, after completing her final transatlantic escort of a number of merchantmen from Halifax.

Times were said to have been hard for families that year, when Peter Kearns from Wolfe Tone Avenue, Kingstown (Dun Laoghaire), had no sooner reached his sixteenth birthday in March 1915, before he took himself off down to the harbour and enlisted in the R.N.R. After a couple of months training, Peter was posted to Larne in Northern Ireland and later found himself serving aboard the admiralty trawler *Thomas Collard*. Peter's war with submarines and mines, and the trawler's valuable sideline of catching and selling fish to locals in Larne, would come to a sudden and violent end, when the little ship bravely tried to save the stricken liner *Calgarian* off Rathlin.

Commander Speiss in *U-19* (this submarine was commanded earlier by Captain R. Weisbach, when she landed Roger Casement and two accomplices on the coast of Kerry in April 1916) had been picking off large valuable targets in the Alley from late February. On the 26 February she torpedoed and sank the heavily laden American tanker *Santa Maria* (5318 tons) (photograph of divers and recovered bell from this vessel included in the illustrations), and the *Tiberia* (4880 tons) in the North Channel. Luckily there were no casualties from either. His next victim would not be so fortunate.

Eleven days earlier ten merchantmen were packed with war materials at Halifax and dispatched with sailing instructions for Liverpool, under escort of the *AMC Calgarian,* herself carrying a cargo of munitions and over 600 Newfoundland, and Royal Naval Reservists, merchant sailors and crew. The convoy, under command of Captain Robert Newton RN (retired) reached a point sixty miles west of Rathlin on 1 March without event.

The convoy was joined off Rathlin by five destroyers, two of which set out with the *Calgarian* at a top speed of nineteen knots, zig zagging a course for Liverpool. The remainder of the convoy followed at a slower speed, escorted by the remaining destroyers.

The *Calgarian* and her two destroyer escort reached a position about six miles north of Rathlin Island at 1640 hours, and in 'broad daylight on an exceptionally fine day' (a fact which did not sit well with the vessel's owners, Canadian Pacific), Commander Speiss spotted the large liner and made to intercept her. Perfectly positioned, he fired at least one torpedo that struck the liner amidships. The explosion blew a hole beneath the waterline in the forward stokehold on the port side, killing a number of the ship's crew. The explosion fractured some of the steam pipes, disabling the ship's steering mechanism and reduced the pressure in the boilers. A number of other destroyers and eleven patrol vessels rushed to the scene and immediately began an attempt to take the vessel in tow.

A smoke screen was put up around the stricken liner as attempts were made to get the tow going, at the same time that pressure was being restored to the boilers. However, despite the presence of a plethora of patrol vessels and a convoy of thirty vessels and escorts passing outwards a little further south, at a greatly improved speed after hearing the news, *U-19* continued to pursue the liner and her escorts, and struck once again an hour later.

By this time the trawlers *Thomas Collard* and *Lord Lister* had been ordered alongside the liner in order to assist a destroyer with the tow. (It might be pointed out that the trawlers, although positioned on either side of the *Calgarian* in order to assist in the tow, would have been vulnerable in the event of a further attack by the submarine, and that their crews would have well aware of this). *Lord Lister's* position became confused, and suddenly found herself damaged and alongside the *Thomas Collard*.

Just then Speiss raised his periscope, aimed, and let go with at least another two torpedoes (it was later testified by crew members that there were three explosions heard at this point). These passed under one of the destroyers and the *Thomas Collard*, and struck the liner amidships on the port side once more. The explosions sealed the fate of the liner and she began to sink. The force of the explosion however, had erupted under the *Collard* and tossed her into the air, and she ended up a ship's length away. The fatal nature of the damage to the trawler became evident almost at once as water began to pour through the buckled plates and into her engine room. *U-19's* periscope had been seen and the destroyer *Anchusa* dropped two depth charges and pot shots were fired by one of the other patrol vessels.

Dwarfed by the towering liner, the *Collard*, although now in a sinking condition, got in under the *Calgarian* again, and continued to rescue crew and passengers from the sinking liner, as well as towing the *Lord Lister* out of danger. Eleven of the crew of thirteen from the *Thomas Collard* were injured, including Peter Kearns, who had been released from beneath strewn debris on the deck of the trawler by one of the *Calgarian's* passengers. The *Collard* by then was sinking fast, and all aboard had to be rescued by the trawler *Corrie Roy*. (A picture of the injured crew recuperating at Larne, courtesy of Peter Kearns's grandson, Peter McGee, is included in the illustrations.)

The *Collard* and the *Calgarian* both disapeared into 76 fathoms off Rathlin Island at 1800 hours. Carried with them were 49 servicemen. Amongst the casualties were Thomas Kennedy of Hillaby Street, county Cork, John Keane, Ballytruckle, Waterford, Patrick O'Dwyer, Corbally, Tramore, Waterford, P. Byrne, Lockbuckland in county Down, and James Kelly of Quinn Place, Belfast.

There are a number of important points in relation to this incident worth mentioning. Firstly, the *Calgarian* was a merchant liner heavily-armed and carrying a cargo of munitions. To some, the circumstances of her sinking would appear similar to the *Lusitania* incident, even though the deck mounting plates that had been fitted in her case, had not yet been mounted with guns. The action by Commander Speiss in *U-19* and other capable U-boat commanders showed just how vulnerable some valuable targets were to attack, even when screened by a number of patrol vessels. By 10 March it was known by British naval intelligence that *U-19* had returned to base, and had claimed credit for sinking the *Calgarian*. The smoke screen put up around the stricken vessel was totally ineffective and was said to have even assisted the U-boat during its attack. The U-boat's main defence of becoming invisible and undetectable below the water, being so evidently effective. Determined although the efforts of these submarine commanders were, it had become equally evident that there were too few of them.

Lastly, small vessels and the bravery shown by their crews time and time again during WWI, has not been well remembered. The merit of the majority of *Thomas Collard's* crew was not recognised in any particular way, despite the following mention by the Admiralty:

'2. We exonerate Skipper William Buchan, and the crew from all blame, and we further consider that the '*Thomas Collard*' was handled with considerable ability, that Mr. Buchan showed most conspicuous gallantry under very trying circumstances, in that there were 7 explosions close to him, and that he did not lose his presence of mind although badly hurt, but took his ship alongside '*Calgarian*' twice to take her in tow and take off the crew, and also towed the '*Lord Lister*' clear. His action in remembering his depth-charges is commendable, (ensuring that these were set, so that when the vessel sank, they would explode).

3. We also find that the discipline and zeal on board '*Thomas Collard*' was admirable, and particularly commend Engineman T. Lyons, in that blown on deck by the force of the explosion in the first instance, he went below on regaining consciousness and continued to work his engines until up to his neck in water.'

There were four submarines lost in the Alley and its northern approaches during this period. However, *UB67*, *UB77*, *U80* and *U19* all appeared to have survived the war. These attacks and the number of vessels sunk, signified a determined effort by the U-boats to prevent the large ships transporting soldiers from America to Europe.

Both sides knew that moving large volumes of troops quickly onto the battlefields might seriously influence the outcome of the final land battles that were about to commence in France. German attacks on the troop-carriers only partly succeeded, as by then, so many American troops were being landed from the large, fast liners that were travelling directly to France.

Although they were said to be an unseen enemy, it has been shown that U-boats spent the vast majority of their time on the surface. There has, however, been very little account or folklore of the conflict handed down by sailors or fishermen from towns around Ireland. There were numerous sightings and encounters by Irish sailors, fishermen and boats with German submarines, but no memory of them remains. This is difficult to explain, but it might appear that these omissions result from the subsequent political situation in Ireland, a time during which involvement by a family member in the Royal Navy or British Army would not have been proclaimed too loudly. Or it may simply be that these memories were forgotten when they were overshadowed by the more horrific events of World War II, or perhaps both.

The U-boat was truly a new and lethal weapon, and at first it was one that the Allies found difficult to combat. The evidence of the extensive carnage caused by it in the Irish Sea during World War I is plain to see. Every sea captain and yachtsman that has sailed in these waters has seen the evidence. They have scribbled on it, plotted their voyages on it and left their mug stains on it. More often, it is confined to the damp lockers of small boats. It is the mariner's road map, an Admiralty chart of the sea. The speckling of shipwreck symbols (+++) on charts covering the Bristol Channel to Wexford, Anglesey to Dublin and in the area of the North Channel and Isle of Man, bears testimony to the legacy of shipwrecks from this period.

Prior to World War I there was almost no visible record on admiralty charts to indicate sunken ships in these places, i.e. out in open water. And as there were no naval battles, and relatively few casualties, in the Irish Channel during World War II, the vast majority of shipwreck symbols indicated in the open water on the contemporary chart in the illustrations, represent World War I casualties. (Only one fifth of the number of ships sunk in the Alley during World War I, were lost during World War II, and these were mainly caused from attacks by minelaying aircraft, many of which were in, or close to, Liverpool port.) The devastation is obvious, and it is a fact that has received no special mention hitherto.

British citizens have had no difficulty remembering and honouring their dead heroes, from the battles fought on land and at sea during World War I. This is plain to see on the thousands of monuments that have been erected in prominent places all over Great Britain and Northern Ireland. With the exception of recent celebrations commemorating Ireland's casualties on the battlefields of Europe, there is, in contrast, very little Irish maritime history from this period recorded.

The charting of these tiny 'shipwreck' symbols on the sea charts includes numerous sunken Irish ships, and represents many brave Irish seafarers that went down with them. This fact remains shrouded by a veil of mystery and ignorance. It is a veil I venture to suggest that might have fallen over this period during Ireland's liberation.

The names below are the crew of *UC-44* (this submarine had a complement of twenty-nine), as remembered by Commander Tebbenjohanns during his questioning by British Naval Intelligence. All but its commander were lost when an explosion wrecked their submarine off Dunmore East on the night of 4 August 1917:

Bendler, *Reserve sub Lieut.*
Seifarth, *Engineer with W.O. rank.*
Schleuter, *Navigating W.O.*
Pabsch, *1st Class P.O. Boatswain's mate.*
Heur, *2nd Class P.O. Boatswain's mate.*
Fahnster, *Engine Room P.O. 1st Class.*
Lehmann, *ditto.*
Bienart, *ditto.*
Klein, *Engine Room P.O. 2nd Class.*
Muller, *ditto.*
Schmitz, *ditto.*
Rosner, *ditto.*
Clause, *(Engine Room probationer).*
Richter, *ditto.*
Dusing, *Leading Seaman.*
Burger, *ditto.*
Bartz, *Able Seaman.*
Idseliks, *ditto.*
Zielosko, *ditto.*
Schickendann, *Leading Stoker.*
Kerster, *Stoker.*
Fehrer, *Stoker.*
Kramer, *Telegraphist.*

Chapter 6

LAST ORDERS

**The loss of the Guinness ship
W.M. Barkley**

Last Orders

The loss of the Guinness ship W. M. Barkley

Sail and timber had remained synonymous with maritime trade from the time it had begun. Within the space of half-a-century, both were almost totally replaced by engines and steel. During the course of World War I, the submarine, which had earlier been considered by many to be a useless curiosity, would threaten all of the developments made by naval shipbuilders during the previous half-century. The romance of the sea was soon replaced by the fear of the threat emerging from below it.

We understand that it is a very rare occasion when the single action of a lone sailor or soldier alters the course of a war. During World War I some did, and others came close. Admiral Hall altered the course and determined the outcome of World War I with his decision to reveal the Zimmermann Telegram at the time and in the way that he did. It has also been said that when Commander Schwieger in *U-20* sank the *Lusitania* in 1915, his action led to the defining moment that ended America's indecisiveness, persuading her to join the war. The latter event certainly had far-reaching ramifications but it did not persuade America to declare war on Germany. Although not applicable in the sense intended, the occasion is nevertheless recalled by many as one in which Commander Schwieger altered the course of the war with a torpedo. (Commander Schwieger was lost with his submarine *U-88* and 42 of her crew, after striking a mine in the North Sea on 5 September 1917.)

So, too, did Commander Lohs in *UC-75* only barely avoid a similar place in history while patrolling the same area off the Cork coast almost two years to the day after the *Lusitania* incident. Lohs had an uncanny knack of being in the right place at the right time, and once again on Christmas Day 1917, he only barely missed striking what would have been a decisive blow for Germany.

Shortly after assuming command of the minelayer *UC-75* on 4 April 1917 at Brunsbuttel, Commander Lohs proceeded to Hamburg for arming at the Blohm & Voss works. After returning to Brunsbuttel, he sailed on the 26 April for the south coast of Ireland. There were some engagements off the south coast of England, but he resumed his journey to Ireland and took up station off Cork on 3 May. Whether or not Lohs was aware of the impending arrival of some very important vessels, and the impact that these were going to have on the course of the war, is unclear. But with the exception of the Armistice, the occasion probably became the most significant of World War I. During the very early hours of the 3rd, Commander Lohs laid his full complement of eighteen mines in a staggered pattern across the approaches to Cork harbour. After the unusual tactic of deploying all his mines in a single area, Lohs guided his submarine to a position fifteen miles southwest of the Fastnet. Later that morning he placed bombs in a number of local fishing vessels and recorded the sinkings in his log as: *S850, S271 (Sir Edward), S333, S237 (Clan Dore), S1101, S92 (Hibernia)* and *C154*.

Drawn from a variety of sources, it is reckoned that these were the *North Star, Carberry King, Sir Edward Birbeck, Hibernia, Eleanor, Lucky Lass* and *Fastnet*. The French sailing vessel *Marie* (118 tons) was also sunk in this area on the 4th, when bombs were placed in her hold by the crew of *UC-75*.

It would appear from events which followed, that Commander Lohs might have shown his hand a little too early by sinking the fishing vessels exactly when he did. It seems unlikely, but his action might lead one to believe that he was unaware of the historic event that was already unfolding westward. His action might alternatively be interpreted as intended to be a lure, designed to draw out patrols from Queenstown, and into the path of his web of mines, or even to divert the course of the incoming vessels. It was in any event a mistake. Had he not forewarned the Admiralty of his presence and alerted their suspicions, the first American destroyers to go to war against Germany, were already in sight of land, might otherwise have received a welcome they had not expected.

April 1917 was the month during which the destruction of Allied shipping tonnage by the U-boats reached its zenith, and America declared war against Germany on the 6th. In order to expedite the relief that Admiral Bayly was in urgent need of, no time was lost dispatching a vanguard of six destroyers from the Navy Yard at Boston to Queenstown on the 24th, under the command of Lieutenant Commander Taussig. After its ten-day crossing, the flotilla of American destroyers was greeted by the sound of exploding mines or fishing boats during its approach to Cork harbour. Having safely berthed within the confines of the harbour on the 4th, Commander Taussig gazed at the entrance to Cork harbour from the safety of Admiralty House, and recorded in his diary the following details of his ship's narrow escape:

'We had come up through the channel there, and only the previous night the German submarines had planted ten mines [actually eighteen] only six feet from the surface. This was the first time that mines had been found so near to the surface, although hundreds of them have been swept up by the minesweepers, which are continually at it day and night. The sweepers picked up these mines before we arrived so we were probably saved from an accident at the very beginning. There is no doubt but that the Germans knew we were coming to Queenstown and the approximate time of our arrival in spite of the great show of secrecy made by the Navy Department'.

Unaware of the culprit's identity, Admiral Bayly later recollected the narrow escape of the incoming American destroyers in his memoirs of 1939:

'The night before the arrival of the six destroyers from the USA. Admiral Sims and his staff came down to Queenstown to stay at Admiralty House. During dinner the party were startled by a series of explosions, and recognised the seriousness of the situation when it was explained to them that the noise was caused by the mine sweepers blowing up mines that had been laid to catch the US destroyers on arrival'.

Lord Decies, Chief Censor for Ireland 1916-1919.

Author, E.K. Chatterton, was stationed at Queenstown at the time, and he too recorded the event similarly, in his work *Danger Zone*. His recollections were:

'We had, at the time when the *New York* passed, been busy sinking mines within half a dozen miles of where *Lusitania* foundered. It was beastly weather, and the mines were not easy to see as they bobbed and rose, but we managed to finish the lot, and presently the time came to enter Queenstown, where we were due for refit and leave.'

Chatterton later went ashore and dined with the admiral and his fellow officers, where they were informed of the impending arrival of the American destroyers the next day. Despite Admiral Bayly's apparent disdain for publicity, the occasion was one of jubilant celebration, from which the maximum propaganda was to be extracted. Film crews, reporters, and a large number of high-ranking officers from both navies were to be present for the first public display of America's commitment to the Allied cause. On the morning of 4 May, the motor launches set out with all the high-ranking brass aboard to welcome the destroyers. Chatterton, who was aboard one of them, remembered the occasion on which Commander Lohs so narrowly missed sinking some of the destroyers. If successful, it could have meant a number of these high-ranking personnel scrambling for their lives in the sea. And as the motor launches could not prove to be any match for a surfaced U-boat, men like Admiral's Sims's secretary, Commander Babcock, the American Vice-Consul, Mr Sherman, and an Englishman whose head the Germans supposedly had a high price on, Captain Evans, might have been killed or captured.

Having put the Royal Navy pilots aboard the American destroyers, Chatterton recalls what happened next:

'We had barely signalled her to stop, got alongside, and put Captain Evans on board, than a few cables to the southward up went a couple of violent explosions; for the Commander-in-Chief had suspected the enemy might have cognisance of his arrival. A submarine had actually plastered the approaches with mines only a few hours before, but now the trawlers had discovered the "eggs" and were sweeping them up'.

Not knowing which U-boat had laid the 'eggs', Chatterton wondered what might have been the result if things had been just a little different, or in my opinion, if Commander Lohs had delayed a while longer before striking at the fishing vessels. His chapter on the matter concluded:

'I have since wondered if that submarine did hang about to report the definite arrival of America's first warships, and to note whether the mines had their intended effect. It has also been a subject for thought that had this minelayer torpedoed *M.L.181* and taken prisoners the two officers sent by Admiral Sims, together with "Evans of the Broke", this submarine might have won half a dozen Iron Crosses on her return home.'

Chatterton was not to know, but *UC-75* had returned to the area without further incident on the 4th, before finally setting out on his return course for Germany.

The mopping-up of the German mines had not been as thorough as was thought. Commander Lohs did not record the event in his log, but the subsequent loss of the British steamer *Lodes* (396 tons), when she struck a mine between Cork and Ballycotton on the 5th, killing seven of her crew, was probably another victim of *UC-75*'s handiwork. Following close on but not suspected to have been the result of minelaying by *UC-75*, Admiral Bayly also lost one of his pluckiest auxiliary patrol vessels, the *MFV Ina Williams* (337 tons). She too struck a mine off Berehaven on the 30th. (Fleet memo dealing with this incident is mentioned earlier.)

Commander Lohs's return journey was not uneventful: he sank several more vessels with his torpedoes in the English Channel, including the sloop *HMS Lavender* on the 5th. (This loss is recorded in the U-boat archives at Cuxhaven as having occurred off Mine Head, County Waterford, and accounts of the incident differ significantly from Allied ones.) The loss of this latest sloop brought the toll of this class since March, to a worrying four of the admiral's 'flowers'. Strangely, there was no mention ever made on the sinking of the French sailing vessel or of the seven fishing vessels from Cork and Skibbereen, in the recollections of Taussig, Chatterton or Bayly.

Some 120 miles further to the east, off the coast of Waterford, another event was unfolding that was never reported. The *SS Feltria* (5254 tons) was torpedoed without warning eight miles off Mine Head by another minelayer, *UC-48,* on the 5th. The *Ardmore Journal,* Vol. 5, 1988, recalls that before the ship sank as many as could got away in the small lifeboats. The journal goes on to quote Sir Edgar T. Britain's account of the incident, in which he said:

'The submarine came to the surface and ordered this boat [No.6 boat] alongside of her. Questioning the Chief Officer as to the nature of her cargo, the submarine made off but stopped to pick up Mr Scott, one of the *Feltria*'s engineers, and returned him to the lifeboat. From the U-boat's deck Mr Scott was assisted back into the water, whilst Mr Burt, the *Feltria*'s quartermaster, very gallantly jumped into the sea and helped him to the lifeboat's side, where he was pulled aboard in a very exhausted condition.'

Despite the humanity shown by the U-boat commander in this regard, Mr Scott died later. Forty-four others of the sixty-nine aboard the *Feltria* also died.

So, from the moment that the first American warships were sighted off Ireland, the new German minelayers, and *UC-75* in particular, matched the event, and gave Admiral Bayly considerable cause for concern. During his first operations off Cork in May, Commander Lohs signalled his unrestricted intentions to sink any vessel considered to be making a contribution to an Allied victory. However cowardly these attacks on fishing vessels were considered to be, Johannes Lohs proved himself to be an extremely able and bold commander. And, as we will see later, he also showed some compassion for his victims on occasions.

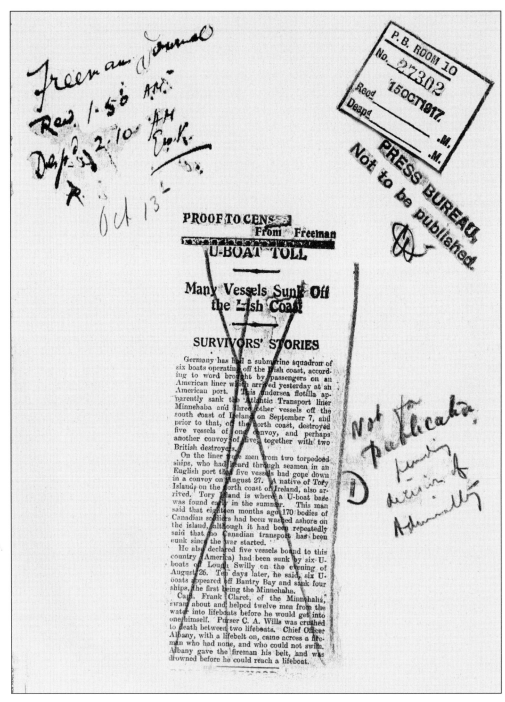

This controversial article by the *Freeman's Journal* was issued with a 'D' notice prohibiting its publication.
The issues were : escalating losses of valuable ships and the very unusual reference to a U-boat base at Tory Island. October 1917.

CONFIDENTIAL. NOT FOR PUBLICATION OR COMMUNICATION.   P.C. 1038.

The Editor,

"Freeman's Journal",

6 & 7 Townsend Street,

DUBLIN.

Reference proof you submitted October 13th, entitled "MANY VESSELS SUNK OFF THE IRISH COAST". I have requested the authorities in London to give me a decision by telegram.

Personally, I do not think this article can be published as it would violate the Defence of the Realm Regulations, but as soon as I get a reply from London I will let you know, but I would suggest you do not publish this article till authority has been received from London.

PRESS CENSOR,

IRELAND.

Press Censor's Office,

85, Grafton Street,

DUBLIN.

13th October, 1917.

A copy of the letter sent by Lord Decies to the editor of the *Freeman's Journal* on October 13th, 1917. In it he gives reasons why he has refused to allow the publication of the article (Previous illustration) on shipping losses and the U-boat base at Tory Island. It also explains the procedure adopted with his superiors in London.

A clear example of how determined this commander was, and how lucky Britain and Ireland were that there were not more men like him, can be seen in the archival statistics on U-boat patrols. Between the date he commenced his first voyage in *UC-75* on 26 March 1917, until he relinquished command on 8 January 1918, Commander Lohs completed nine patrol-voyages. (According to its log, there appears to have been eleven 'outings' by this U-boat. Unusually, for a commander who proved he could lay mines off the Arklow Bank with apparent ease, there are no outings shown for his boat for the whole month of September during the Kynochs incident.) During those ten months, he patrolled in the English Channel, off the south coast of Ireland but mainly within the confines of the Alley, where he wreaked havoc on shipping.

In Irish waters alone, he sank no fewer than twenty-eight vessels. Lohs operated in the Flanders fleet out of Brunsbuttel-Heligoland for his first three cruises. His remaining patrols in *UC-75* included visits to the elaborate U-boat pens at Brugge, and the ports of Hamburg, Emden, Wilmshaven and Heligoland, but his submarine operated predominantly out of Zeebrugge. Other than his patrols to enemy-waters, these other journeys were made to complete repairs to his vessel, the fitting of armaments and mines at the notable armaments manufacturer Blohm & Voss, and shore leave. Leave for the crew seems to have been for periods of between ten and fourteen days.

At first glance you might expect the ship's name, *W. M. Barkley,* to reflect that of its owner. For certain it did, but the owner was not to be found in the Guinness family in whose service she was in at the time of her loss. Guinness had purchased the vessel from the prolific shipping merchants of Belfast, John Kelly Ltd, in 1913, but here again there was no one in the Kelly family named Barkley either. Maintaining the name of the ship while in the Guinness fleet might be explained by the age-old superstition of not changing a ship's name for fear of bad luck. Or, as the much-loved scoundrel, Long John Silver, is said to have put it: 'I never knowed any luck as came of changing of a ship's name.'

So where did the name originate? When the firm of William Barkley & Son, also of Belfast, and an old rival of Kelly's, was absorbed into the new firm of John Kelly Ltd in 1911, the stock and vessels were included in the take-over. These included the *Barkley*, a modest coastal steamer of 569 tons which had been built for J. M. Barkley by the Ailsa Shipbuilding Company at Troon in 1898, hence the ship's name.

Outwardly she had little to distinguish her, except that those who served in her had reported that, because her centre castle was situated over her boilers and engines, she proved to be a little unsuitable for the handling of cargoes of stout. They are also reported to have complained that her sailing qualities were a little 'cranky'. Her hull was constructed of iron but much of her upper accommodation was timber. Although she was said not to have been entirely suited for the trade in which she eventually found herself, her construction was perfectly sound. But alas, it was not sufficient to protect its crew nearly twenty years later.

The decision by Guinness to ship stout to Britain in its own vessels was adopted into the distribution-chain of its products purely as a practical business innovation.

A painting of the Guinness steamer *W.M. Barkley* hanging in the Guinness Hop Store Visitor Centre, Dublin. She was torpedoed and sunk by *UC-75* off the Kish Bank in the Irish Sea on October 12, 1917.

Guinness had been in the business of transporting stout to Britain since the middle of the 18th century, and the decision to purchase its own fleet was rooted in the throes of the worst labour dispute Ireland has ever experienced. Guinness stout was produced in its brewery at James's Gate, Dublin, from where it was transported on its own rail system to its barges that berthed opposite the company's lower yard on the River Liffey – an area known in earlier times as Lord Galway's Walk. From this quayside, the stout was shipped down-river in Guinness steam barges to the waiting cross-channel steamers at the Customs House Quay.

During the trip down-river, the barges had to lower their familiar red smoking funnels under Anna Livia's bridges. These were sometimes lined with excited children, and the story goes that, thinking the barges were going to sea, the children often shouted at the 'bargees': "Bring us back a monkey" or "Bring us back a parrot". As the kids could observe the same barges and their crews returning upriver a short while later, these streetwise urchins are unlikely to have thought anything of the sort, but were just having a noisy joke at the expense of the 'river sailors'.

From the barges, the valuable barrels of 'black stuff' were hoisted onto hired vessels, or onto the quayside. This final transfer had been the only operation not in the direct control of the brewery on the Dublin side of its export-operations.

Labour disputes at the docks, and their potential for crippling its export-operations, was an issue that was forcibly brought to bear on the famous brewing family during the infamous 'lockout' of 1913. In order to try and avoid the prospect of its product being stuck on the quay wall as result of disputes, Guinness had bought the *W. M. Barkley* that year, and began to sail her with a company crew. This amounted to a total control on production and export of Guinness products between Ireland and Britain. The brewery prospered from this arrangement, and its fleet grew until it was finally decommissioned through commercial obsolescence some seventy years later. Although the above-mentioned measures might be considered anti union, it is well known that Guinness has maintained a generous and progressive policy of pay and conditions since its foundation.

The historic labour dispute of 1913 taught Dublin workers a lesson they would not easily forget. Led by James Larkin, they fought for recognition and improved conditions against a consortium of well-heeled but stubborn employers led by the Cork-born tycoon William Martin Murphy. What had begun with strikes progressed into a mass lockout of the employees, and lasted for about six months. During what became the largest and most disastrous labour dispute Ireland has ever seen, many unsavoury issues surfaced. Labour unrest at this time was not confined to Ireland alone and had been brewing in Britain, Europe, South Africa and the USA, where there was rising anger amongst the working classes, borne out of a history of exploitation. This erupted in the workplace and in the streets, and their protests continued with a rising confidence derived from collective agitation. In Europe, there was a growing movement towards international socialism or communism, which had already become words and philosophies feared by employers.

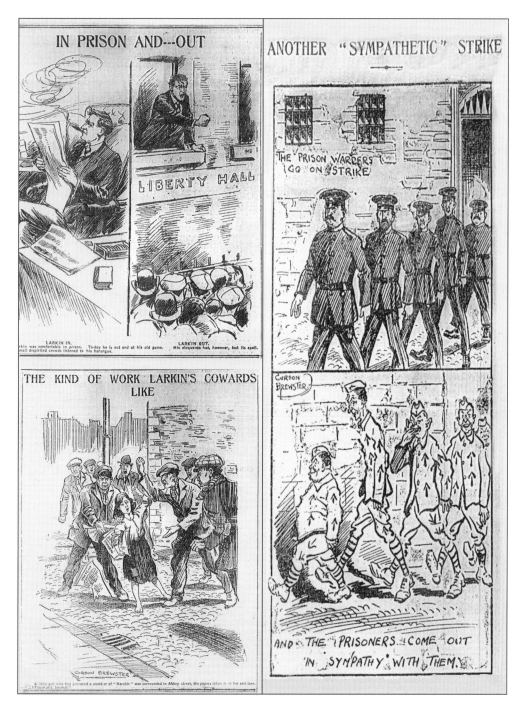

A sample number of anti- James Larkin cartoons from an ongoing series, which appeared in the *Evening Herald* during the labour disputes in Dublin, 1913.

The newspaper was owned by Larkin's arch-rival, William Martin Murphy.

The movement represented an emergence from Victorian values and a flicker of hope for much-needed labour reform and equality, which was temporarily snuffed out when World War I began.

The conditions within Dublin's the inner-city were already deplorable, and degenerated into a legacy of social shame. The overcrowded, unhygienic and unsanitary conditions in large areas of slum buildings led to disgracefully high mortality rates. These were the living conditions that existed amongst those who were excluded from their work in 1913 – a class of downtrodden workers who mistakenly thought they had nothing left to lose.

The growing threat of revolt by the working classes in Britain and Ireland had been flagged by some at least a year earlier. Lady Mary Carbery, who seems to have had a clairvoyant ability of predicting impending doom, remembered the following conversation she had in 1912 with a 'dear friend' of Lloyd George:

'"In Wales" he said, "the nonconformist, the educated workman, felt a terrible anger for the idle rich, and a terrible feeling against the millionaire who motors all over the country, and eats and drinks and enjoys himself, and thinks nothing of the poor."

This wise and gentle lady noted 'that there was much to agree with in what he said.' She also recorded that this 'Welshman' stated that 'Lloyd George and many others anticipated revolution in England, and are straining every nerve to prevent it.'

The strike in Dublin eventually heaped starvation and misery on workers and their families. When the 'food boats' and 'soup kitchens' could no longer cope with increasing starvation amongst the striking families, the unions organised temporary accommodation and patrons in Britain for the starving 'Dublin kiddies'. This led to a regrettable reaction by the Catholic hierarchy, when they claimed that, by sending hungry Irish children to Britain and separating them from their parents, they might suffer all manner of deprivation and immorality. This led to scuffles at railway stations and quaysides, when attempts were made to seize some children from their families. Some of the parents were later held on charges of kidnapping, and those willing to participate in the scheme were shamed, when their names were printed in the papers. This was an issue that can be viewed now as a case of hysterical reaction, as indeed it was, or something more sinister and quite different. Although it seems that the kidnapping charges against parents were dismissed, these events portrayed the labour movement in an unfavourable light, and the plan was discontinued. The incident was regrettable from everyone's point view.

Not unlike many others, the Catholic hierarchy seemed divided on the issue of voluntary enlistment in Ireland, they nevertheless generally appeared to reject conscription. It is, however, notably inconsistent and even ironic that, when so many young men and women left Ireland to work and fight during the war, and once again during World War II, amongst the 'immoral British hoards' in the munitions industries, they received the blessings of the very same people.

When 'scab' labour was hired to do the work of the strikers in 1913, the army and police were ushered in to guard the distribution of coal and other essentials, and to help policemen baton strikers in the streets. Riots followed. Every method, fair and foul, was used to break this strike, which was seen by many as a threat not only to the selfish disposition of the well-off but also to the authority of the Crown.

While children in the city of Dublin starved, princes landed from their yachts at Kingstown, bound for the Dublin Horse Show. Other vessels – not princely yachts, but little steamers of a different kind, known as 'food boats' – were hired by the labour movement. These came with supplies from Britain and sailed up the Liffey to the eagerly waiting families on the quaysides. The handouts provided much-needed nourishment, but it must surely have been a pitiful sight to see so many proud but hungry people pushing and shoving for food parcels on Dublin's quaysides during the winter of 1913.

One of these heroic little steamers was the *SS Hare;* a photograph of her, which appeared in the *Evening Herald,* is included in the illustrations. Sadly, she was later torpedoed in the Irish Sea and sunk with all twelve of her crew. The attack on the *Hare* took place several miles east of the *Kish* light-vessel, when she was torpedoed by *U-62* on 14 December 1917.

By Christmas 1913, small numbers of men reluctantly began to return to work. Despite a unanimous vote by strikers in early January 1914 in support of the strike, some had already given in. By the end of January, James Larkin conceded defeat and the strike ended. For those workers who luckily managed to return to their old jobs, many were compelled to bow to conditions more harsh than those they had endured prior to the strike. They finally surrendered their only remaining possession, pride.

It was a battle won not only with the weapon of starvation but also with the help of another very valuable instrument, available mainly only to the employers, namely the news media and propaganda. The *Independent* and *Evening Herald* newspapers were both controlled by William Murphy, and he used them. Propaganda is a weapon we tend to associate only with governments and war; its power is quite often applied in other ways, however. The *Evening Herald* ran a series of anti-Larkin cartoons, some of which are included in the illustrations. Their consistent and derogatory portrayal of Larkin and his strikers is an interesting testimony to the attitudes of the newspaper and its owners.

Was this turbulent episode in Ireland's labour-history a battle between two giant egos? Or was it a miscalculated adventure into an industrial conflict at a time when workers and employers had not yet achieved the maturity with which to resolve it? Or again, was it just the workers' moment, their time to cast off the yoke of Victorian exploitation, or simply a period of pure desperation?

The employers won that particular battle but they lost the war against the awakening aspirations of workers. The seeds of bitterness were sown, and although they were ultimately deserted on that occasion, the workers discovered the power to be had from the organised withholding of labour.

Bringing food to the starving strikers, Larkin's 'Food Boat', *SS Hare*, is seen in the photograph alongside the quay in Dublin port during 1913. The small steamer was later torpedoed and sunk in the Irish Sea on 14 December 1917 by U-62.

MEMORANDUM.   23rd Oct.1917

The City of Dublin Steam Packet Company's advertised sailings are

From DUBLIN - Tuesday,Thursday and Saturday to Liverpool

do.   Thursday   to Manchester

(Extra Cattle Specials when required)

Subjoined are the sailings of the S/S "Cork","Kerry","Carlow" and

Wicklow during the current month.

Monday	Octr.1st	----------
Tuesday	do 2nd	"Kerry"
Wednesday	do 3rd	----------
Thursday	do 4th	"Cork","Carlow"(special with Government cattl. "Wicklow"(to Manchester)
Friday	do 5th	"Cork"(special)
Saturday	do 6th	"Kerry"
Monday	do 8th	"Carlow"(special)
Tuesday	do 9th	Port of Dublin closed on account of submarine
Wednesday	do 10th	ditto ditto
Thursday	do 11th	ditto ditto
Friday	do 12th	"Cork","Carlow"(special with Government cattl
Saturday	do 13th	Port closed on account of submarines
Monday	do 15th	ditto ditto
Tuesday	do 16th	City of Dublin Co.did not sail waiting for orders from the Government.
Wednesday	do 17th	ditto Ditto
Thursday	do 18th)	ditto ditto
Friday	do 19th)	ditto ditto
Saturday	do 20th)	Company informed that orders were coming from the Government and made special arrangement to sail ships on Sunday.
Sunday	do 21st	Orders received and risk undertaken by the Government: "Carlow" & "Kerry" sailed to Liverpool "Wicklow" to Manchester.
Monday	do 22nd	"Cork"(Special)

The foregoing particulars make it plain that the
congestion and consequent damage to cattle that arose in Dublin
between the 8th and the 16th October was caused entirely by the
Ports of Ireland being closed by order of the Naval authorities,
and that congestion began to be relieved on the 16th when the port
of Dublin was opened.   The City of Dublin Company's steamers
were ready to sail back as soon as the Government took the risk;as
a matter of fact threeboats sailed immediately on the SUNDAY and
another on the MONDAY,neither day being regular sailing days,so
that the Company actually got away the same quantity of cattle as
in ordinary circumstances they would have done on the regular
sailing days.

Following the sinking of the *Barkley* this memo dated October 23, 1917, was sent from the City of Dublin
Steam Packet to the Dublin Port & Docks Board. It outlines the company's shipping schedule for the
period and its interpretation of the events, which grearly angered the company.

Their brush with the ascendancy taught the newly-emerging-labour movement a valuable lesson. Working men and women had defied the aristocracy in a way they had never done before, showing in real terms the potential power of collective action. Although the workers starved, Dublin came to a virtual standstill. Since that lesson, the labour-movement has had many more battles, but its course has been irreversible and continued from strength to strength.

Although unions and workers were to experience general improvements in their pay and conditions partly as a result of the war, a dejected and exhausted Larkin left Ireland for America in 1914, where he continued to further the cause of socialism and workers' rights.

William Martin Murphy died five years later in 1919, while Larkin was incarcerated in Sing-Sing Prison. Larkin returned to Ireland after being deported from the USA in 1923, and continued his sometimes stormy contribution to the strengthening labour movement. Although he went on to form another union, the Workers Union of Ireland, his star never again shone as bright as it had in 1913. And despite winning a seat in the new Irish Parliament, he was unable to take it up after having been declared bankrupt.

The emerging labour-movement failed in 1913, but success later came to it, not least because of the courage and sacrifice that had been shown earlier, and from its growing abilities to organise. Monuments now stand commemorating the great James Larkin, and the pain suffered by his followers has never been forgotten.

Some employers said that William Murphy bullied them into continuing the strike in order to overcome Larkin and subdue the strikers. Others said that Murphy was a fair employer and a generous man, but however true either opinion might have been, this great industrial battle is probably viewed by ordinary Dubliners today, in a similar way as Bill Sweeney did, when he recounted the following incident.

Bill was a young man of sixteen when he followed his father and joined the City of Dublin Steam Packet Company in 1912. He was later promoted to assistant-purser aboard the *RMS Leinster,* and survived its sinking when she was torpedoed outside Dublin on 10 October 1918. He recorded an audio-interview many years later, from which I have extracted this part of his charming story:

I usually traveled on the tram from Bachelors Walk to the Park Gate in the morning time, about twenty to eight. I was on the ships at the time, and I used to go to my Aunt's to collect clean laundry. The tram was always full of men, all going to their work in the Phoenix Park. They were belonging to the Office of Public Works. I used to love going on the tram. Their foreman was a little bowler-hatted chap. There was a little stool in the tram, and when the driver would be changing ends, he would pick up this stool out of the plug-hole and plug it in the far end. It would make an extra seat. But this little foreman, a bowler-hatted gentleman, he used to sit on this. Oh the tram would start, and out would come the Independent, *and he'd read it. The headlines, "Oh hello," he'd say, "30,000 Germans Captured." This was the war news.*

And then the next morning, "Three British Cruisers Sunk." And I can remember the names of those cruisers. The Hogue, *the* Cressy *and the* Aboukir. *And one German sub sank the three of them.*

But anyway, this morning, this fellah opened up the newspaper. About half an inch of black edging all around it and he read out the headlines. "The Death of Mr William Martin Murphy." And he had a look around the tram over his eyeglasses, and says he: "The curse a Jasus on him anyway." Well I thought I'd have to be carried out of the tram, I laughed so much. Such an epitaph.

Partly as a result of the reducing numbers of merchant seamen, and their ability to obtain higher rates of pay in American ports, their wages, and indeed wages in general, increased during the war. Overall, however, there was generally no improvement in the living conditions of most, and in many countries they even worsened. In Ireland, for instance, inner-city conditions for many became intolerable during 1917. Food became scarce and extremely expensive. City folk became weak and starved from the lack of nourishment. Fuel was in very short supply and was prohibitively expensive. Women's groups came to the fore in a campaign for change, which might have pointed to a lack of menfolk. If so, this may have been the result of emigration and war, or it may have stemmed from the fear of reprisals by employers. It may simply have been a reflection of the successes experienced by women's groups in Britain.

The average weekly industrial-wage was said to be four to five times greater in Britain than the twenty-shillings in Ireland. Return passage in steerage on a Tedcastle's steamer to Liverpool was five shillings and sixpence. Many times greater than the same relationship with earnings today, this prevented many aspiring Irish emigrants from reaching British cities for work.

Just as they had done during the strikes of 1913, the people from the inner city again suffered disproportionately during the Great War that begun only six months later. Six months is all the time it took before the same employers were pleading to the nation's manhood to enlist, to do their duty for King and country, and to kill other workers. This was the case even after fifty citizens had been gunned down by rifle volleys from two companies of the King's Own Scottish Borderers at Bachelors Walk on 26 July 1914. This incident began after the landing of arms by Erskine Childers in his yacht *Asgard* at Howth. The violence erupted after the soldiers returned from Malahide, where they had disarmed a number of National Volunteers. Soldiers were said to have felt threatened by a jeering crowd, which was later testified to have been capable of dispersal by a small number of policemen.

An inquest was convened on the deceased Mary Duffy, from No. 26 Lower Liffey Street, Patrick Quin from No.1 Gardiner Place, and James Brennan of No.7 Buckingham Street. The Dublin Corporation, the military, the Irish National Volunteers, and the next of kin were represented at the proceedings. On 3 August, Mr. Hanna KC, representing the Military, expressed a need to complete the evidence of the soldiers from the King's Own Scottish Borderers, as they were expecting to mobilise

the following day. Mr A. M. Sullivan for the Dublin Corporation boomed the stinging reply: 'The next time I hope to hear from the King's Own Scottish Borderers will be from Antwerp.'

World War I was declared the next day, and despite later reports that the officer in charge at Bachelors Walk had been reprimanded, the inevitable outcome of what began as a very public inquest faded in favour of more dramatic newspaper announcements, such as the 'run on gold'.

News of the hostilities in Europe reached Irish newspapers at the same time that news of the departure of thousands of volunteers from the city's quaysides was omitted. Long being the practice, many of Dublin's inner-city dwellers who lived in the area of the docks suddenly found that there was an increasing demand for labour, and for more seamen to man the hundreds of little steamers that were plying in and out of Dublin. The *W. M. Barkley* was one such vessel, and all of her crew were recruited in Dublin after she entered into service for Arthur Guinness in 1913. The little steamer, bought from Kelly's of Belfast, had a chequered but short life thereafter. Guinness's new enterprise was an unqualified success, and three more vessels were purchased from Kelly's between 1914 and 1915, the *Carrowdore, Clareisland* and *Clarecastle*.

Not long after the *Barkley* was put to work carrying stout on the Dublin-to-Liverpool route, war erupted, and the Admiralty requisitioned the ship. The remaining Guinness ships were also requisitioned in 1916, and returned safely to shipping stout in 1919. It had been intended that the *Barkley* would operate around the British Isles, carrying coal and feedstuffs, and the crew were given the option of remaining with the ship. All but one refused to stay with her, and a fresh crew was recruited from Belfast. The exception was Mr Thomas McGlue, who hailed from the town-land of Baldoyle, an area in north Dublin well-known for its sailors who served on cross-channel vessels. Mr McGlue joined the ship at the age of thirty-two in 1914, and remained with the *Barkley* as steward. Unlike the other three vessels, the *Barkley* was found by the Admiralty to be unsuitable, due to its slow speed and high fuel consumption, and she was returned to Guinness in 1917. Some of her original crew returned to the ship, and along with Thomas McGlue, they remained with her until the end.

Nervousness at Dublin Port had been increasing well before the *W. M. Barkley*'s final journey. A growing number of rumours concerning the U-boat attacks taking place just outside the harbour had the port in a heightened state of tension. Along with a small number of other vessels, the little steamer sailed from Dublin on a day when some of the bigger ships remained in port, in fear of the whispered 'invasion by submarines'. The war had raged on land and at sea, and had decided nothing. People had become weary of it. Except on rare and brief sorties, none of the German High Seas Fleet would 'come out'. This tactic completely frustrated many in British Naval operations, including the Admiral of the Fleet, David Beatty. Not the only Admiral 'of old Irish stock' to command foreign navies, he had long hoped for what might be the final engagement. By April 1917, Admiral Beatty was informed that the monthly figure for

lost tonnage had reached in excess of 875,000. The situation was described as desperate. It was simply the case that ships were being lost faster than they were being replaced, whereas U-boat production seemed unstoppable. Amid some personal and political difficulties with the Admiralty and Whitehall, Admiral Beatty wrote to his wife on 3 May, indicating some annoyance and despair:

'I do fight the enemy when I meet him. Ye gods, was there ever such an astoundingly humorous situation? How they must laugh, and in the meantime our magnificent Mercantile Fleet is rapidly being destroyed. And the task is gradually assuming proportions that the Archangel Gabriel couldn't put right under six months. What is to be done ?'

Co-operation between Naval Intelligence, and he admirals and officials at Whitehall had suffered from infighting, and was undergoing a degree of undesirable strain. It is difficult to get an accurate picture as to the extent of the disagreement that permeated to the highest level, and perhaps it is unnecessary here. The situation had become critical at a time when a great deal of co-operation and determination by all was required. Given the urgency of the situation, and whether the Americans brought with them such qualities, they arrived in any event, and the tide was turned, but not before there had been many more harrowing scenes of ships tossing their sterns to the sky on their journey to the seabed.

By 19 June, the situation had become so grave that Admiral Beatty saw the need for a certain amount of risk to be taken. In respect of the pursuit of an 'invisible enemy', he wrote again to his wife:

'I am in the middle of a big operation against enemy submarines, which I pray may be successful. I have denuded myself of all Destroyers, Subs., Patrol-vessels, Sea-Planes, Air-Ships, etc, in the effort, so the Fleet is immobilised for the time being, it's no use pecking at it.'

The frank admission of an 'immobilised Fleet' was remarkable (it is unclear whether or not the Admiral's correspondence was censored at the time), but such a strategy could not have been countenanced without access to good intelligence. Whenever possible, this intelligence was being supplied to the admiral, by his old captain and friend, Admiral Hall. By 22 June, Admiral Beatty took the view that his 'big operation' had 'no luck', and had not got 'more than one sub'. It must have been a nail-biting time and a demoralising failure for Beatty, who had deployed thirty-four valuable destroyers and fifteen submarines during the operation.

Despite America's entry in the war, during a conference on 20 June 1917, the First Sea Lord Admiral Jellicoe frankly admitted that: 'owing to the great shortage of shipping due the German submarines, it would be impossible for Great Britain to continue the war in 1918.' Even so, after the welcome alliance with America, a new optimism

began to spread through civilian and military life in the British Isles. Admiral Jellicoe's gloomy opinions soon became unpopular but he was not deterred from expressing his continued frustration. He further remarked that: 'There is no good discussing plans for next spring. We cannot go on.'

In the meantime the slaughter continued. Although the overall casualty-returns had begun to decrease, attacks and encounters with U-boats in the Alley began to rise. These occurrences showed a marked increase in the third quarter of 1917, and continued to rise steeply until the following May. The level of casualties and encounters with U-boats in the Alley between the all-time-high figure reached in April 1917 and those in April 1918 detailed in chapter 7, clearly demonstrates the sharp rise in these events. The urgency of the situation focused minds and changed attitudes with regard to the new threat posed by the U-boats in these waters.

Although the number of shipping casualties off the coast of Ireland in areas such as the Approaches well exceeded those in the Alley during given periods, the local inhabitants of these coastal areas were largely unaware of them. Some of the most important industrial and shipping centres of Ireland and England straddled both sides of the Alley, and the threat of attacks on the ships and seamen serving out of these ports existed from day to day. The north and south coasts of Ireland did have traffic with other major ports, but in the main, this was less frequent deep-sea traffic and was subject to the protection inherent from sailing in convoy and in a vast expanse of water. In other words, the traffic was more international there by comparison to the closely-knit maritime commerce between both sides of the 'Irish channel'. They also had the advantage of being screened by the Allied warships when they approached the 'danger zones'. The following account, and the one describing the loss of the *SS Adela,* will give the reader some idea of the perils that were faced in the Alley by cross-channel vessels and their crews from 1917 onwards.

It had been a week of gloomy anticipation around Dublin port. Arklow-born, Captain Gregory of the *W. M. Barkley* had travelled to the Guinness shipping office at No.17 North Wall Quay on several occasions, to see if the suspension of sailings had been lifted. The port had been closed from Monday night, and all merchant-shipping traffic was halted. Reasons for the closure were never made public, but it was common knowledge in the port that the number of fatalities from submarine attacks in the Alley was escalating. After Dublin authorities exerted pressure on the controlling office at Liverpool naval base, Captain Gregory was informed on Thursday evening that the port might reopen the following day. The crew was also notified, and the next morning, Friday 12 October, Captain Gregory returned once more to the Guinness office on the North Wall.

Restrictions on sailings had indeed been lifted, and Captain Gregory collected the *Barkley's* papers and her crew, and made ready to sail with a cargo of stout for Liverpool. Two other ships were also cleared and had already sailed. These were the steamers *Cork* and *Carlow*. Four other sailings had also been approved from Liverpool to Dublin, and these too had already begun the crossing.

They were the *Wicklow*, *Kerry*, *Hare* and *Belfast*. Whether or not Captain Gregory, or anyone else for that matter, was aware of it, the port would close again, almost immediately after the Guinness ship had left, for exactly the same reasons as before.

Most of the shipping controllers in the region of the Irish Sea were well-aware of the submarine threat in the channel at the time. The rising tension amongst officers and crews on escort duties was palpable. Since the 8th, Commander Taussig of the American destroyer *Wadsworth* had been out on convoy duty from Queenstown with six other destroyers. Having successfully seen off an outbound convoy on the 10th, the American destroyers rendezvoused with an incoming one, consisting of eleven vessels from Dakar and their large escort cruiser, the *Moldavia*. The convoy was destined for Liverpool, but they too had been warned of the impending dangers on the 11th, as this entry in Commander Taussig's diary shows:

'Received wireless reports that the Irish Sea was closed on account of submarine activities – this was on Thursday. On Saturday received report that Irish Sea was again open.'

The convenient and short-lived reopening of the Alley at that important moment allowed the small steamers to make their unescorted dash across the channel. Although warned of the dangers, Commander Taussig seemed to be unaware of the sudden opening and closing of the channel to traffic, until he was informed of the 'all-clear' on the 13th. During the opening of the channel, and the progress of the incoming convoy, another six British destroyers were sent to accompany the already heavily escorted convoy. The number of escorts at this point being in excess of the number of merchant vessels in the convoy.

Was the opening of the channel at that moment a clever ploy to lure the U-boats in the direction of the scurrying little cross-channel steamers, in order that the more valuable incoming convoy from Dakar might escape attack?

This was also a period of protracted and acrimonious disputes between the City of Dublin Steam Packet Company, the shipping controller and the Admiralty, over sailing instructions and the administration of the War Risk Insurance Scheme. The C.D.S.P.Co. Dublin had disagreed not only with the shipping controller and the Admiralty but also with its arch-rival, the London and North Western Railway Company. It is difficult to determine precisely what was going on between these two companies, other than what has been described in *Death in the Irish Sea*. That is, that the L.N.W.R.Co. was somehow seen as 'patriotically British', and the C.D.S.P.Co., as being 'Irish'. Both companies also seemingly trying to position themselves for a time not too distant, when escalating operating costs would force the rationalisation of the whole shipping industry.

Whether politics, religious bigotry or just overly-active competitive spirits were at the root of it, relations worsened considerably when the managing director of the Irish office of the L.N.W.R.Co., Mr G. Burgess, was appointed as the 'Director of Cross

Channel Transportation for Ireland' in 1915. His counterpart and rival, William Watson of the C.D.S.P.Co., protested vigorously, but to no avail. Both were hard-headed businessmen, with an acumen in maritime commerce that been acquired over a lifetime. They had both witnessed the birth of steam travel and belonged to many prestigious boards connected with harbours and shipping. Mr Burgess was an active member of the prestigious Kildare Street Club, where he must also have come into regular contact with another well-known public figure, Ireland's Chief Censor, Lord Decies.

At this point, Mr Watson might have been forgiven for thinking that his competitors were beginning to 'gang up' on him, following the awarding of the government appointment, 'Controller of Cross Channel Traffic', to another of his competitors, Mr A. H. Read. Read, who was manager and owner of the British and Irish Steam Packet Co. He had no sooner taken up his new position, when he broke with long-standing agreement and practice, and entered his company into direct competition with the C.D.S.P.Co. on the Liverpool route.

The week that the *W. M. Barkley* sailed out of Dublin in October 1917 marked the beginning of a serious deterioration in relations between the two companies. One of the main bones of contention centred on the risk to vessels from attack by submarine, and the way that risk was covered by insurance. The L.N.W.R.'s vessels sailed from Dublin under orders from the government and the Shipping Director, and the British government directly underwrote their risk. Despite pleadings by the C.D.S.P.Co. that its own vessels should be allowed to operate under similar considerations, this was denied, and it fell to the company to provide its own insurance.

Losses which occurred as a direct result of enemy action, and where Admiralty instructions had not been contravened, were ultimately underwritten and reimbursed by the British government under the War Risk Insurance Scheme, albeit only after long delays. This was a serious commercial disadvantage for the C.D.S.P.Co., as it meant that their greatest rival could get cover in any event, while it suffered the disadvantages of having to wait for clearance to sail. Even if clearance was given, but ship-owners suspected that the Channel was too dangerous, they had in conscience to remain berthed and lose out.

The C.D.S.P.Co.'s October schedules were maintained at a heightened state of nervousness but without event until the 8th. On that day, the port of Dublin was closed by the Admiralty 'due to submarines', and except for twenty-four hours on or around the 12th, it remained so until the 16th. The exceptions were the departure of the *W. M. Barkley,* and two 'specials', on the 12th. The C.D.S.P.Co. was to later learn of the loss of the *Agricola, Eskemere* and *Barkley,* on the 12th and 13th, and refused to take any further risk by putting its remaining vessels to sea, even after the port was reopened again by the Admiralty on the 16th.

The Shipping Director, Mr Burgess, who was considered to be exploiting his official office in favour of his own company, ordered the City of Dublin's ships to sail. After officials had refused once more to give orders for the ships to sail, the four steamers

were requisitioned and handed over for management by the L.N.W.R. They later sailed on the 21st under the protection of the government's War Risk Insurance Policy but were subsequently transferred to, and operated by, the British and Irish Steampacket Company.

The C.D.S.P.Co. frequently appeared and felt that it was on the wrong side of the fence, but the company was nevertheless noted for putting the welfare of its workers first. One of the company's 'two 'specials' that had sailed on the 12th with the *W. M. Barkley*, was the *SS Cork*. (The other was probably the *SS Carlow*.) As a result of the continuing threat from U-boat attacks, the company did not sail the *Cork* again until the 22nd. The concern shown by the company for its steamers was commendable, but in the case of the *Cork*, her good fortune lasted an additional three months only, before she was torpedoed on 26 January 1918 in the Irish Sea by *U-103*, during a voyage from Dublin to Liverpool. On that occasion, twelve more crewmen were lost.

The *W. M. Barkley* shoved off at 17.00 hours and steamed down the River Liffey, flanked by Dublin's fading lights. Little did the crew of the *Barkley* know that, as soon as they would lose sight of Dublin's lights, the luck the ship had enjoyed during her escapades in the English Channel would finally run out. Given the particular U-boat commander who had patiently lain in wait at this time, her fate had almost certainly become inevitable. It was her misfortune that this submarine commander, known to be one of the most determined in the Fleet, had taken command of the Flanders minelayer, *UC-75*, from Captain Paech, on 4 April 1917, and he seemed to be thoroughly familiar with the waters between Ireland and England.

It can be deduced from his sketches in the illustrations, that Lohs possessed a daring ability, and was equally capable of operating his vessel in and around the dangerous sandbanks off the east coast of Ireland, as he was in the narrow channels of important harbours in the Alley. His patrol sketches also reveal a full understanding of the 'danger zones' within the Alley. Some of the favourite areas for lurking U-boats in the Alley were off Galloway, the Isle of Man, the northwest coast of Anglesey, Bardsey Island, St David's Head, the Tuskar Rock, Arklow, Rockabill and South Rock. Indeed the navigational importance of the Rockabill was as old as shipping itself, as is evidenced in the following quote from a paper submitted to the Board of Trade by the harbour office at Drogheda in 1857, outlining the need for improvements to be made to the harbour of Skerries.

'That there is no other point on the north-east coast more frequented by ships passing and re-passing from the different ports of the United Kingdom (including Liverpool, the greatest naval port of Great Britain) than the island of Rock-a-Bill, situated about four miles seaward of Skerries'.

U-boat commanders seemed to know only too well that, in order to harass shipping travelling to and from Liverpool, it was not necessary to enter the well-patrolled bay itself. It was only necessary to patrol the sea-lanes stretching between the Skerries and Dublin, and from Belfast to the Mull of Galloway, and to the Isle of Man. These patrol areas not only covered the approaches to and from the north-west coast of England, and from the south, but also the traffic from all the major ports of Ireland.

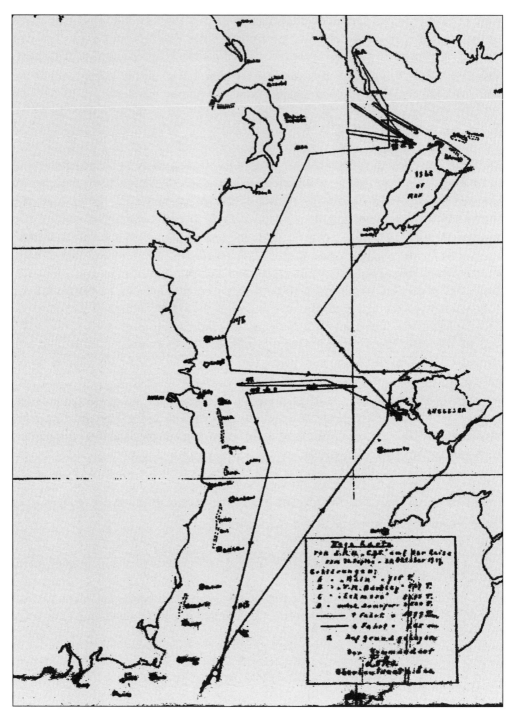

A sketch of the route taken by Commander Lohs in *UC-75* on a patrol in October, 1917, when he sunk several vessels in the 'Alley'. Amongst them was the Guinness ship *W.M. Barkley*.

Note the particular attention given to the positions of all the 'lights'.

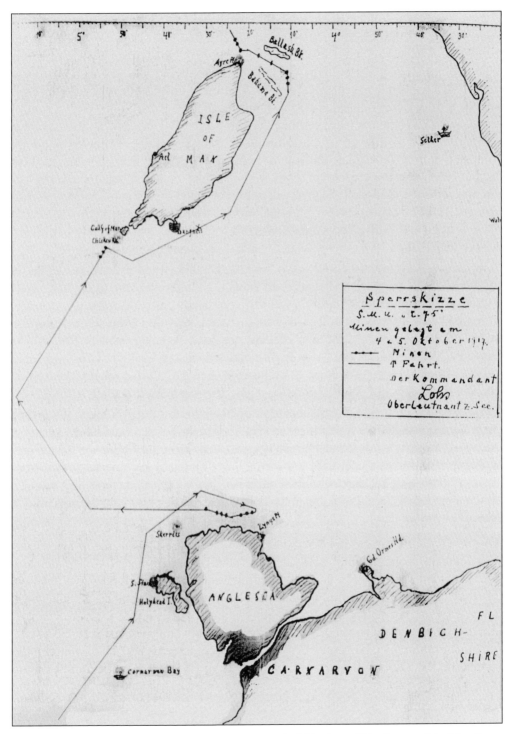

A sketch by Commander Lohs in *UC-75* showing where he laid mines off Anglesey and the Isle of man prior to sinking the *W.M. Barkley*

After Oberleutenant Johannes Lohs took command of *UC-75,* his first three patrols were made with the Flanders Flotilla out of Brunsbuttel. During his following six patrols, he visited Hamburg, Emden, Wilmshaven, Heligoland and the elaborate U-boat pens at Brugge. These latest UC minelayers were 162 feet in length, and were about 500 tons' displacement. Quarters for the crew, numbering between twenty-nine and thirty-two, were cramped into areas immediately fore and aft of the central control room situated beneath the conning tower. The area ahead of the forward accommodation was taken up almost entirely with submarine equipment, and six through-hull mine tubes that were almost vertically positioned from an exposed entry in the upper deck to a deploying exit in the bottom of the submarine. Aft of the conning tower was equally congested, with the twin diesel engines and electric motors, the petty officers' mess, and one torpedo tube fitted in the stern. The craft's surface speed was twelve knots but, submerged, they could equal the rarely-performed maximum speed of seven knots, rated to most other classes on battery power.

A minelayer's primary function was to lay mines, and this was usually carried out at night and across busy channels, or in the mouths of harbours. Due to the dangerous nature of these operations, the UCs suffered very heavy casualties. The practice was to proceed directly from their base to pre-designated areas, and to lay mines under the cover of darkness. This did not exclude attacking valuable targets they might encounter during the voyage. After laying mines their duty was to attack opportune targets with their torpedoes or her 22-pr. forward deck gun. Surface endurance for this class of minelayers at 8 knots was 6,000 miles. This could be extended.

These minelayers carried a complement of eighteen mines, three in each tube. All of these were pre-set before a patrol began. The top six, however, could be readjusted if necessary, but only while the submarine was surfaced. The mines were about three feet in diameter and were sometimes laid with a thirty-minute delay release device. That is, after mines were released with their anchoring device attached, congealed salt or a similar component would dissolve in the release mechanism, allowing the mine to rise later to its pre-set depth.

These UC boats were designed to carry four torpedoes, one stowed and disassembled spare, another preloaded into the inboard stern tube, and the two remaining twenty-inch (19.7 inches.) torpedoes preloaded in the two forward external tubes. However, this complement does not always appear to have been adhered to, and the actual number of torpedoes carried sometimes varied. The two external torpedo tubes were contained in the outer hull, and were not accessible from within the submarine, except for firing adjustments. After laying all of its mines, the submarine had then only four (4-7, varies with source) torpedoes and a deck-gun with which to make any subsequent attacks on shipping. Whether or not all of the mines were laid or all of the torpedoes were fired, UC minelayers could and did surface to fire on ships with their deck-gun. Their cruises lasted for about half the length of time as those of the U- or later UB- class boats, which in the case of the latter two, lasted for approximately one month.

Commander Lohs left Brugge on 29 September 1917 and passed once more through the Allied patrols and minefields at Dover with seemingly repetitive ease. The Tuskar Rock was left to the south on 4 October, and Commander Lohs then steered a direct course for the northwest of Wales. Familiar with the way traffic in the Irish Sea sometimes hugged the shelter of the north Anglesey coast, he passed first to the north of the Skerries. He then altered course eastward for a short period, before returning southward until the north shore of Anglesey was again in sight. Again he altered his course, this time to westward and proceeded close in along the coast, where he laid seven of his deadly mines. The manoeuvre was intended to leave the mines to the stern of the vessel while she completed the operation. Minelaying was almost always carried out at night, and against wind and or tide. Previous miscalculations of these natural forces by some U-boat commanders had resulted in their destruction.

Mine laying completed, *UC-75* continued north and laid the remainder of its eleven mines to the south and north of the Isle of Man. Commander Lohs then patrolled the channel between the Isle of Man and the 'Point of Galloway'. His victim at Galloway was the steamer *Main*, which he sank with gunfire in Luce Bay on the night of the 9th. There are few detailed accounts of attacks on minor vessels, i.e. below or around 500 tons, but Commander Lohs' log does describe this attack in detail, and the unusual quirk of fate, which played a hand in her loss. The unfortunate experience of the small steamer *Main* began when she sought shelter from bad weather in the lee of Galloway, on 9 October 1917. The story continues in this translation of Commander Lohs' log from *UC-75*:

'KTB 09.10.1917. East Tarbert Bay (under Mull of Galloway)
In stationary position a few hundred metres off the coast. Upper-deck torpedoes regulated and reloaded. While working, steamer comes into bay.

11.30pm. Barometer rises.
Torpedoes are loaded. Followed the steamer, which must have anchored in the bay, which does not have a harbour.

09.10. 02.00h am.
Had a look at the steamer, too dark to make out anything, in the course of this we rammed him with our net-saw.

02.45h am.
Opened fire on the steamer, which has a mounted gun aft. During this the sailor Rodat is flung overboard, because of the gun recoil. As he is swimming on the lee side we are able to fish him out at the screw propeller housing, by means of hard-rudder and reversing of the lee screw. The sailor has severe bruising on his thighs and has to be brought below.

After the crew of the steamer had gone into the lifeboats alongside, we sank it with artillery fire, as there was still a strong gust.

English armed steamer – six-pounder gun, the 'Main' 715 T empty en route from Belfast to Liverpool. The steamer had sought shelter near the coast because of heavy seas from aft.

According to the crew of the submarine, the captain and thirteen men had been killed. Eight men and the first mate were in the boat. The steamer never had a chance to fire. It sinks in its anchoring position, 2 miles offshore.

06.15h am. Below Galloway. NW 6. Seastate 6.
On the steamer route a ship is sighted, course 300. Got the gun in position, gave up on it as it was a small steamer, only 100 tons and I am already right up on front of him. Submerged. Stayed at bottom, 28, 42, 45 m. Looked out repeatedly. No traffic, sunshine, steady westerly wind, force 7–8.

07.15h pm. Seastate 6. Wind W6.
Surfaced, went under East Coast of Ireland, as there was too much sea motion for the purpose of firing.

10.10 0300h am.
Attack on steamer. Did not fire as it was only 800 tons. Not able to work with artillery like yesterday as there is too much sea motion.

It's the same type of steamer as the 'Main'. With the engine aft. In the dark one often erroneously takes these to be tanker steamers.'

It can be seen from the entries in Commander Lohs' log, that the *Main* had obviously sought shelter from heavy weather but had unfortunately fallen from the frying pan into the waiting fire of *UC-75*.

The interesting remarks made by Commander Lohs concerning the reloading of the external torpedo tubes would suggest that he was not a man intending to waste any opportunities that might arise during his patrol. They also indicate that he had set out with more than the normal one spare torpedo. Some commanders of minelayers carried an additional two torpedoes, lashed behind the forward external torpedo tubes, in order to achieve the maximum success from their patrols. Reloading the tubes with these spare torpedoes put a submarine in a very exposed position, and at great risk. One might also wonder if he only assumed the *Main* was empty from the level of her load line?

It is also obvious that the sailors in the *Main* had no chance, and were fired on from very close range. The master and all eleven of the *Main's* crew were killed during the attack.

The final remark by Lohs is also interesting, as he describes how some U-boat commanders wrongly identified the silhouettes of vessels, and confused them with tankers. This was the very mistake made by Commander Loe in *U-100,* two months later, off Anglesey, when he sank a very similar steamer, the *Adela*, with equally disastrous consequences for her crew.

UC-75 set off in a westerly direction until it reached northern Ireland, and took shelter in the vicinity of the *South Rock LV*. Lohs made no attack there, and later proceeded south for about fifty miles until he identified the lighthouse on the small island of Rockabill, situated about four miles off Skerries (*harbour town*) on the east coast of Ireland. Not surprisingly but unbeknownst to Lohs, there was a dearth of targets as a result of the port closures, and he continued a little further south until he picked up Lambay Island. There was no delay here either before he promptly altered course eastward back across the Irish Sea towards Wales. When *the* Skerries hove into view once more, he continued with his patrol in this vicinity for a short while. Having had no luck, he then proceeded south, and reached the South Stack off Holyhead in the early hours of the 11th.

His expertise had brought him through supposedly some of the most densely patrolled areas of the British Isles with no apparent difficulty. And from the entries in his log, his patrol would seem to have been almost casual, avoiding Allied patrol vessels with near-impunity. No targets were attacked off the Welsh coast, and Commander Lohs began a patrol of the Irish Sea on the 12th, and remained there until the 13th.

It wasn't long before several vessels appeared on the horizon. These were most likely the steamers that had made a dash for it after the ports had first opened temporarily. However, by the time Commander Lohs was able to position his submarine for an attack, the lucky vessels had passed out of range. The evening of the 12th arrived without any significant event, and Commander Lohs found himself lying in wait off the *Kish* light vessel, seven miles from Dublin.

Not long after the light had begun to fade, several more vessels approached from the direction of Dublin at 6.45 PM. Again, he was unable to position the U-boat for an attack until after another hour had passed. Finally, his patience was rewarded, when he observed through the periscope, another steamer approaching from the direction of the Kish lightship. The little steamer was belching out its black smoke, as it struggled along at about seven knots, on a course which would bring it fatally close to the lurking U-boat.

The attack commenced at about 19.45, when Commander Lohs surfaced about 300 metres from the *Barkley,* and let loose with one of his forward torpedoes. The torpedo erupted from the submarine in a burst of compressed air and sped with its load of high explosives towards the Guinness steamer containing all those barrels of stout.

The log of *UC-75* proved very difficult to interpret, even by proficient linguists, as its style is said to be 'old German'. The task was further complicated by it being available in longhand only, and proving very difficult to read. However, the gist of Lohs' record of events seems to confirm the survivor, Thomas McGlue's, very fine account of the attack on the *Barkley.*

McGlue's account appeared many years later in the Guinness in-house *Harp* magazine, under the title 'Recollections of the *W. M. Barkley*':

'I was in the galley, "baft of the bridge". I was just reaching out to take a kettle off the fire to make a cup of tea for the officers. When we got the poke, the kettle capsized

and shot the boiling water up my arm to the elbow. The galley was filled with steam and I said a few hard words, but apart from that there wasn't much noise – not a murmur, in fact.

The port side of the ship was locked to keep it dark, so I went through the engine room and out on the starboard deck. There was a lifeboat hanging there, hanging by one end to the forward fall. The Barkley was doing her best to go down, but the barrels were fighting their way up through the hatches and that kept us afloat a bit longer – in fact, it's the reason any of us got out of her.

The master gave three blasts on the siren and then I didn't see him any more. I climbed into the boat and a mate gave me a knife to cut the fall and the painter. The boat dropped clear and dipped under a bit and we had to do some fast bailing. The other fellow was all for us getting away while we could, but I said "No there's more than two of us here and they'll want to come along". Then the gunner came up – we had one gun on the after deck but he wasn't at it when we got the poke; as a matter of fact, he was in the galley with me, waiting for some hot water to do his washing with. I don't know where he'd got in between.

The gunwale of the lifeboat had been ripped when we were hit and the gunner gashed his leg on it, getting in. Then another A.B. [Able-bodied seaman] jumped in and that was four of us. We rowed away from the Barkley so as not to get dragged under, and we saw the U-boat lying astern. I thought she was a collier, she was so big. There were seven Germans in the conning tower, all looking down at us through binoculars.

We hailed the captain and asked him to pick us up. He called us alongside and then asked us the name of our boat, the cargo she was carrying, who the owners were, where she was registered, and where she was bound to. He spoke better English than we did. We answered his questions and then asked if we could go. He told us to wait a minute while he went below and checked the name on the register. Then he came up again and said: "I can't find her." He went back three times altogether. Then he came back and said: "All right we've found her and ticked her off." We said can we go, but there were two colliers going into Dublin and he told us to wait until they were to windward and couldn't hear our shouts. Then he pointed out the shore lights and told us to steer for them.'

In certain respects, World War I was no different from previous wars, or from those that came afterwards, and atrocities were committed during it on both sides. In respect of Germany, and with the exception of it being the first to introduce chemical weapons onto the battlefield, the U-boats and their commanders bore the brunt of this type of criticism. To what extent these alleged atrocities were accurate remains obscure, and is tainted by a considerable amount of propaganda of the day. However, on lecture tours across America after the war's end, Admiral Sims stated the following:

'Within the past few months, in speaking to various audiences on the operations of the German submarines, I have stated that their commanders were specially selected and thoroughly trained men, and that most of the accounts of atrocities popularly attributed to them were untrue'.

It has been difficult to understand fully what might have gone through a U-boat commander's mind while he prepared to attack an utterly defenceless steamer like the *W. M. Barkley*. However, Ernst Hashagen, commander of *U-62*, figured prominently in the attacks against shipping in the Alley during December 1917, and he has left us with some insight into this particular moment of fate.

He recorded his wartime experiences in *The Log of a U-boat Commander,* published in 1931, and it includes several accounts of attacks on shipping. It also includes what is believed to be a record of the events aboard *U-62* leading up to the fatal attack on one of the two Waterford steamers in the George's Channel. Both vessels were devastated from the huge explosions that ripped through them, and not a soul survived from either ship.

His words shed some light on the thoughts that might have passed through the minds of U-boat skippers during similar attacks on unsuspecting ships – attacks with high explosives that were propelled at victims at up to 30 knots from beneath the sea and almost certainly spelt death for all aboard:

'Towards midnight, a vessel passes to the westward. We leave our station and creep nearer. She is a large, deep-laden ship, unescorted. It takes hours for us to haul sufficiently ahead to be able to carry out a surface attack.

To get a safe shot, we must know the course and speed of the ship with accuracy. So first we run along for some time about a thousand yards from the ship, and match our speed exactly to hers. It is by now so dark that, with the naked eye, only a vague mass can be made out beside us. Nine knots, we calculate from out own rate of revolutions. It is rather dreadful to be steaming thus alongside one's victim, knowing that she has only ten or perhaps twenty minutes to live, till fiery death leaps from the sea and blows her to pieces. A solemn mood possesses the few upon the bridge. The horror of war silences us. Every one of our orders, every movement, every turn of a wheel is bringing death to our opponent. All is exactly settled in advance. We, too, have become a part of Fate.'

From McGlue's account, and Commander Lohs' log, we know that the attack on the *Barkley* was carried out on the surface about five miles east of the *Kish* light vessel. The practice of attacking by night on the surface had by then become more prevalent, and was in large part due to the fact that at this juncture of the war there were more targets available after dark in the Alley. A feature of underwater attacks at night was that it was almost impossible for a U-boat commander to track a target through a periscope, thus forcing him to surface for a better opportunity. Although the submarine was then exposed, the situation had its advantages.

For one, it was extremely difficult for Allied patrol vessels to spot the small superstructure of a submarine on the surface during darkness. And once having closed on his target, the experienced U-boat commander had a better chance of success with his torpedoes on the surface.

There are some additional observations in McGlue's account that we might draw

attention to. Firstly, there was no abuse of survivors. Secondly, and striking, was Commander Lohs' fluency in English. Surprise was often expressed during these confrontations, in respect of German officers' English-speaking abilities. If in this case we put Lohs' fluency in English, along with his expert knowledge of the Alley, particularly in respect of the treacherous sandbanks off the east coast of Ireland, one might suspect that he or another of his officers could have visited the region during more peaceful times.

It is, as I have said before, difficult to know what one's own ability to remain calm might amount to when faced with the same catastrophic circumstances which merchant sailors endured in the Alley. To his great credit, McGlue seems to have taken the event somewhat in his stride, and his cool-headedness was undoubtedly of great assistance in helping to save the lives of his fellow survivors in the small lifeboat. As he said himself:

'The submarine slipped away and we were left alone, with hogsheads of stout bobbing all around us. The Barkley had broken and gone down very quietly. We tried to row for the *Kish* [*Kish* light vessel] but it might have been America for all the way we made. We got tired and my scalded hand was hurting. We put out the sea anchor and sat there shouting all night.

At last, we saw a black shape coming up. She was the *Donnet Head,* a collier bound for Dublin. We got into Dublin about 5 AM and an official put us in the Custom House at the point of the Wall, where there was a big fire. That was welcome because we were wet through and through and I'd spent the night in my shirtsleeves. But we weren't very pleased to be kept there three hours. Then a man came in and asked "Are you aliens?" Yes, we're aliens from Dublin. He seemed to lose interest then, so we walked out and got back into the lifeboat and rowed it up to Customs House Quay. The Guinness superintendent produced a bottle of brandy and some dry clothes and sent the gunner off to hospital to have his leg seen to. The rest of us went over to the North Star for breakfast. And later, after I'd had my arm dressed – the doctor said the salt water had done it good – the superintendent gave me a drayman's coat to wear and put me in a cab.

I was glad to get back to Baldoyle, because I'd left my wife sick and was afraid she'd hear about the torpedoing before I could get home.'

Somewhat unusually, a report on this attack, preceded by the line, 'As passed by the Censor', promptly appeared in the newspapers the next day. It included a list of the casualties, and a short account given by the surviving R.N.V.R. gunner, Ernest Nye. His account covered the outward journey, the subsequent explosion and sinking, and their rescue by the steamer *Donnet Head.* There was no mention whatever of their encounter with the submarine. The gunner also stated that the ship had been showing no lights, which he might have intended to mean, navigation lights, or else the statement would have contradicted McGlue's story that only the 'port side was locked to keep it dark'.

It is very likely that Thomas McGlue was subsequently offered the opportunity of alternative employment in the Guinness brewery, but his choice was to remain at sea where he served out the remainder of the war. He narrowly escaped further dangers in the war aboard another Guinness steamer, the *Clarecastle*.

Thomas McGlue retired from Guinness in 1947 at the age of 65, but even then, he could not contain his love for the sea. He attempted to re-enlist at a Dublin shipping office, where he was kindly advised that enough was enough, and unlike many of his earlier shipmates, Thomas lived a 'gentleman's life' for many years.

Commander Lohs did not dally in the area to where he had brought maiming and destruction to sailors. He turned eastward for the Welsh coast once more, and the next day intercepted a Liverpool steamer travelling in ballast from Belfast to Barry. He fired one of his two remaining torpedoes and sank the ship, killing twenty of her crew. According to station reports, there were at least four survivors. These were picked up by the SS *South Stack* and brought to Dublin.

The unfortunate vessel was the one-year-old Admiralty-hired collier SS *Eskmere* (2293 tons), which had nothing but empty spaces into which the seawater poured. A huge hole had opened in the side of her aft hold, sending her to the bottom in just a few minutes off a headland with the same name as the rescuing vessel, the South Stack, near Holyhead.

It is interesting to note how reports by survivors from the *Eskmere* described the offending U-boat as being between, 200 and 350 feet long. This is at odds with *UC-75*'s actual length, which was 162 feet. Station reports containing descriptions of *UC-75* by survivors from the *Barkley,* were also at odds with her actual specifications. These anomalies might have occurred as a result of observers being inexperienced.

There was a tendency by some U-boat commanders to overestimate the size or presumed importance of their victims. So, too, were some victims so inclined when reporting on the enormity of their attacker.

In order to help the Admiralty gain as much knowledge as possible about the U-boats, they had given instruction to sailors that, when they found themselves in close proximity to them, to observe as much of the submarine's features as possible. U-boat commanders, on the other hand, were conscious of this, and not unlike the Allied 'mystery vessels', they too employed false guns, erection of sails and so on, in order to confuse their enemy. It is also true to say that some of the early accounts of U-boat attacks have often attributed the wrong U-boat to the event.

It can be noted from the data compiled on attacks and losses in chapter 7, that the UC minelayers were quite frequently in the same patrol areas as the bigger and longer-out and larger U-class vessels. Given the confusion which must have been caused by the continual movement of attacking U-boats in these waters, the effectiveness of the UC-class might easily have been made to look even more destructive than it was. In practical terms, ships could be sinking in the Mull of Galloway and off Belfast after striking mines, at the very same time that others were being sunk off the Skerries or

Dublin by torpedoes fired from the same submarine that had laid the mines. In the case of *UC-75,* during October, *U-96* was also patrolling in the Alley at the time.

UC-75 departed from the Alley on 14 October and passed through the Dover Straits to reach Zeebrugge. During the return leg of his patrol, Commander Lohs was also credited with sinking the *SS Britannia* (765 tons) with his remaining torpedo in the English Channel on the 19th. As was his habit, Commander Lohs turned about in a very short time and began another patrol in the same area between 28 October and 12 November. This cruise was very similar to his previous one, except that during its most northern extremity he entered into the North Channel, and daringly penetrated the Firth of Clyde, where he torpedoed and sunk the French steamer *Longwy* (2315 tons) on the 4th. He also sank the *Marquis* (373 tons) with gunfire off Lambay Island.

He further claimed to have sunk a steamer named the *SS Atlantian* (9339 tons) in the Irish Sea. This last claim proved to be premature however, as the *Atlantian,* although suffering comprehensive damage to her stern, decks, gun and steering, reached port safely. However, the *Atlantian*'s survival was only a temporary reprieve, for this Leyland steamer was attacked once more, and sunk the following June when she was torpedoed by *U-86* west of Donegal. (Mistakes of this nature were not uncommon in U-boat logs, as many of the attacks and sinkings might not be confirmed until well after the war's end.) After the final attack on the *Atlantian,* her chief officer and wireless operator were taken onto the U-boat and became POWs.

In June of 1917, during one of its frequent trips to the Alley, *UC-75* torpedoed and sunk another ship of the same line, the *SS Anglian* (5532 tons), southwest of Bishop's Rock, with only one life lost. The Liverpool-based Leyland line fared particularly badly during the war, in the main due to the prolific number of ships it had in service. These made repeated transatlantic voyages, carrying large volume of animals, grain and general cargoes, and many were sunk by the U-boats.

UC-75 and its persistent commander were frequent visitors to the Alley, and knew its waters well. Despite the fact that the British had begun to construct a new mine barrage across the Dover Strait on 21 November, Commander Lohs would pass through it with customary ease in December, and return to the Alley to sink more ships and seamen. This next voyage might have changed the course of the war if the 'World's Greatest Ship', the *Leviathan,* had not had a very lucky escape.

From the time he took command of *UC-75* until he relinquished it on 8 January 1918, Commander Lohs completed nine cruises. During those ten months around the coasts of Ireland and England he wrought havoc, destroying 78,798 tons of shipping.

Nothing more might ordinarily be said about the loss of the small steamer *W. M. Barkley* and her popular cargo of stout but for Guinness's own records, which contain copies of a number of interesting letters that were sent by shipping companies after the incident. The letters from across the channel mainly consisted of claims for compensation, for the recovery of the company's casks, or simply requests for arrangements to be made for their return.

The Canadian Pacific liner *Calgarian* (17,521 tons), sunk by *U-19* near Rathlin Island, 1 March 1918. The Admiralty trawler *Thomas Collard* was alongside and assisting in the rescue when she was sunk by a subsequent torpedo strike.

The crew of the steam trawler *Thomas Collard* who were injured when she was sunk along with the AMC *Calgarian* by *U-19* off Rathlin Island on 1 March 1918.
Peter Kearns from Kingstown (Dun Laoghaire) is second from the right, front row.
Photograph is courtesy of his grandson Peter McGee

A *UC-75* class mine-laying submarine in dry dock during WW1.
Note the six forward (through hull mine tubes).

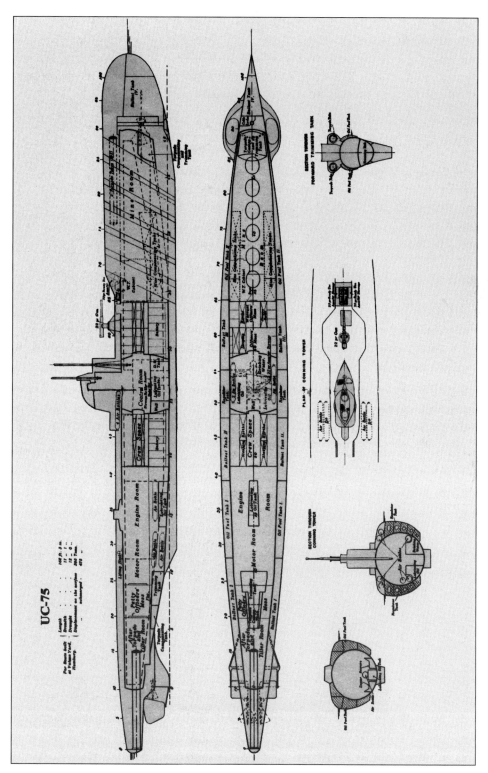

Layout of a *UC-75* class mine laying submarine.

The casks had been recovered by beachcombers or picked up by passing vessels over a wide area of the Irish Sea. It was forty miles from the site of the disaster to the English coast but only ten to the Irish side, where there were no casks reported to have come ashore. This might leave one to wonder just how serious Irish beachcombers took the brewery's old advertising slogan 'My goodness, my Guinness'.

The men who lost their lives when the *W. M. Barkley* sank after being struck by a torpedo fired at it by *UC-75* on 12 August 1917 were:

Gregory, Edward. *(Captain)* No.2 Meadows Lane, Arklow.
Corry, Alexander. *(Ist.Engineer)* No.3 Victoria Villas, Malahide Road, Dublin.
Murphy, Owen Francis. *(2nd.Engineer)* No.105 South Main Street, Wexford.
Kendall, Ernest A. *(A.B.)* No.3 Meany Place, Dalkey.
Murphy, Thomas. *(Fireman)* No.36 Sheriff Street, Dublin.

The remains of the *W. M. Barkley* lie in about fifty-six metres, six miles east of the Kish Bank, off the coast of Dublin. Divers are profoundly curious about shipwrecks, especially those that remain unexplored. Although the wreck of the *Barkley* is reported to be unspectacular, and lies in excess of the recommended depth for normal sport diving, it nevertheless continues to attract a small number of hardy individuals in pursuit of its darkened recesses.

Obviously, the historic association with the most famous brewery in the world might spur those beyond recommended practices in order to obtain mementoes from this particular shipwreck. I hope it will be borne in mind that the loss of this historic little vessel should not become responsible for any additional victims.

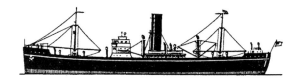

Chapter 7

U-BOATS
AND SHIPPING

Casualty statistics for the Alley and around Ireland

U-boat and shipping
Casualty statistics for the Alley
and around Ireland, 1917-18 and 1939-45.

No matter how often or detailed the casualty statistics are presented, there seems to be no way in which the sheer vulgarity of the slaughter that occurred during World War I can be fully comprehended. Young men from all over the world were pitted against each other in the most horrible conditions, and in ways that had never been experienced in any previous conflict. Sensitive men, poets on both sides, cried out in their writings of the terrible deeds that were being perpetrated against humanity. Siegfried Sassoon was only one of those, and in the following few verses he despairs at the horrible reality faced by those in the field of battle, a reality which was in stark contrast with the one which was presumed by their loved ones at home:

> *You love us when we're heroes, home on leave,*
> *Or wounded in a mentionable place.*
> *You worship decorations you believe*
> *That chivalry redeems the war's disgrace.*
> *You make us shells. You listen with delight,*
> *By tales of dirt and danger fondly thrilled,*
> *You crown our distant ardours while we fight,*
> *And mourn our laurelled memories when we're killed.*
>
> *You can't believe that British troops 'retire'*
> *When hell's last horror breaks them, and they run,*
> *Trampling the terrible corpses – blind with blood.*
> *O German mother dreaming by the fire,*
> *While you are knitting socks to send your son*
> *His face is trodden deeper in the mud.*

Merchant and naval-shipping casualty figures for World War I are usually presented cumulatively, and generally not for any specific geographical sector. In order to determine which U-boats were attacking which ships in any given area, it is necessary, in-so-far as it is possible, to extract and compare all of the available and relative reports from archives and historical publications for the period. This has been an endeavour pursued in order to produce the following tables and graph, which it is hoped will demonstrate the true level of attacks carried out in the Alley during 1917-1918. There may remain however, a significant number of attacks and sinkings by U-boats that were not identified in the course of this research.

The monthly chronicle demonstrates, how sailors and their ships, who had little to protect them from these dangers, were attacked and sunk by and unseen enemy. How they viewed their lot, we may never know.

Although the casualty figures for 1917 show a dip in November's returns, encounters with submarines (with the exception of the following graph, attacks are not included) and the devastation wrought on shipping actually increased in the Alley until the following May. There were many actions and sightings of U-boats in close proximity to the large port cities on both sides of the Alley, and the infamous *U-62* was amongst them.

We also know that *UC-75*, who was a regular visitor to the Irish Sea, had operated off Dublin during October, and returned to Germany without any damage or difficulty. Following a prompt re-supply at Brugge, she entered the Irish Sea again in December to hunt for more ships. This month heralded a depressing resurgence in the cumulative casualty figures, which rose to 408,655 tons.

This level of destruction was never again attained by the U-boats. (Note: Unless stated, the casualty figures quoted have been extracted from 'Lloyd's Shipping Losses World War I').

During the period between the sinking of the *W. M. Barkley* and the valuable British steamer *Apapa* at the end of November, there were seventy-seven fatalities from U-boat attacks in the Alley. This figure might not seem to be excessive, and give the impression that this must have been a relatively quiet period. It nevertheless included the loss of no fewer than seventeen vessels. The protagonists were *UC-77, UC-75, U-96* and *UC-31.*

It is also recorded that the latter half of December 1917 was one of the stormiest periods ever seen in the Irish Sea, and one wonders what the total carnage might have amounted to, were it not for this very unusual bout of bad weather. The conditions recorded were so extreme that they should ordinarily have been considered extremely dangerous for shipping, but in reality the weather may have saved many.

The period between January and April of 1918 produced even greater losses of vessels in the Alley, and was directly related to Germany's 'Spring Offensive' in France. The accompanying graph of losses clearly demonstrates that during the first half of 1917, there were very few actions by U-boat in the Alley. The situation was quite the reverse elsewhere, as April 1917 remains the month during which the highest number of casualties were recorded.

U-BOAT ATTACKS

A graph which shows the sudden and then continual increase in the number of u-boat attacks in the 'Alley' during the period, April 1917 to May 1918. It clearly shows a dramatic rise in these attacks at a time when overall loses were actually declining. These figures indicate a concentration in an area that was considered to contain vital shipping lanes for the Allies, during a critical period of W.W.1. And although U-Boat numbers in the Alley remained relatively high, after April their numbers began to decrease. This was reflected in a diminishing number of attacks, which was also due to diminishing opportunities.

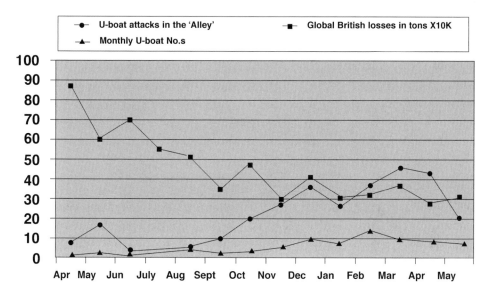

The graph also demonstrates, that immediately after early summer 1917, there was a clear switching of tactics by the U-boats, and this precipitated the beginning of a dramatic rise in the number of U-boat attacks in the channels between Ireland and England. This period of intensified U-boat activity in the Alley climaxed at the end of spring in 1918.

Allied losses had risen sharply in the Alley, at a time when the overall trend was actually downwards. It can be concluded from this that the German High Command obviously recognised, that, in order to achieve victory, it was necessary to increase the number of U-boat attacks in these waters at that time

Losses in the Alley between 1917 and 1918.

Date	Name of vessel	Tons	How	Place	Caused by
14-Apr '17	SS Hermione	4011	Mine	Tuskar, off	UC-33
17-Apr	SV William Shephard	143	Bombs	St. Anne's Head, off	U-boat
17-Apr	SV Dantzie	108	Bombs	St. Anne's Head, off	"
19-Apr	SV Jewel	195	Bombs	Tuskar, off	"
23-Apr	HT Rose II	213	Bombs	Belfast Lough, off	"

There were three failed attacks recorded in April '17.

Date	Name of vessel	Tons	How	Place	Caused by
01-May	SV Ivrig	?	?	Co. Down, off	U-boat
01-May	SS Dora	296	Bombs	Mull of Galloway, off	"
01-May	SS Helen	322	Bombs	Copelands, off	"
02-May	SS St. Mungo	402	Bombs	Co. Down, off	"
02-May	SS Derrymore	485	Bombs	Co. Down, off	"
02-May	SS Taizan Maru	3569	?	Irish Channel	U-boat
02-May	SS Amber	401	Bombs	Co. Down, off	UC-65
02-May	SS Morion	299	Bombs	Co. Down, off	UC-65
02-May	SV Ernest	111	Bombs	Skulmartin LV, off	UC-65
04-May	FV Victorious	39	Bombs	Strumble Head, off	U-65
04-May	FV Strumble (ex. Q-ship)	45	Bombs	Strumble Head, off	U-65
04-May	New Design	66	Bombs	Tuskar, off	U-boat
04-May	Pilar De Laringa	4136	Torpedo	Tuskar, off	UC-65
07-May	*FV Mande	93	Bombs	Bardsey Isl., off	U-boat
30-May	*FV Aloya	?	?	Irish Sea	"
30-May	*FV Queen Bee	?	?	Irish Sea	"

There were 4 failed attacks recorded in May '17.
* Mention of these three vessels appeared in the Irish Censor's files and are not substantiated elsewhere.

Date	Name of vessel	Tons	How	Place	Caused by
10-Jun'	SS Keeper	572	Torpedo	Irish Sea	UC-66
17-Jun	SS Raloo	1012	Torpedo	Tuskar, off	U-61
18-Jun	SS Kangaroo	76	Gunfire	Wexford, South of	U-boat
18-Jun	SS Violet	158	Gunfire	Tuskar, off	U-boat

Up to this date, successful attacks were mainly registered on the surface and against minor vessels.

Date	Name of vessel	Tons	How	Place	Caused by
20-Jul	SS Atlas	2070	?	Tor Head, off	U-boat
24-Jul	SS Mikelis	2430	?	Antrim, off	Submarine
29-Jul	SS St. Marcouf	1117	Torpedo	Irish Channel	UC-75

There are no records of unsuccessful attacks by U-boats in the Alley for this month.

07-Aug'17	*SS Ant Cassar*	3544	Torpedo	George's Channel	*UB-118*
12-Aug	*FV Eleazer*	111	Gunfire	St. Anne's Head, off.	U-boat
23-Aug	*SS Helen*	235	Missing	Kish LV., off	?
25-Aug	*SS Cymrian*	1014	Torpedo	George's Channel	*UC-75*
29-Aug	*SS Lynburn*	587	Mine	Wicklow, off	*UC-75*
07-Sept	*SS Haakoa Seven*	?	Torpedo	Irish Sea, Sth. of	U-boat
15-Sept	*SS Saint Jacques*	2459	Torpedo	Miford Haven, off	*UC-51*
26-Sept	*UC-33* (German)	395	Rammed	Tuskar, off	*PC-61*

There were six failed attacks recorded in September 1917.

There seems to have been a distinct lack of U-boat action – or successes by them, at any rate – during this month. It was also during this month, on the 19th, that the Kynoch's munitions production plant at Arklow was badly damaged by a mysterious explosion.

02-Oct	*HMS Brisk*	780	Torpedo	Rathlin Island, off	*U-79*
02-Oct	*HMS Drake*	14100	Torpedo	Rathlin Isl., off	*U-79*
02-Oct	*SS Lugano*	3810	Mine	Rathlin Isl., off	*U-79*
03-Oct	*SS Hurst*	4718	Torpedo	Skokham Isl., off	*U-96*
04-Oct	*FV Young Clifford*	47	Gunfire	Lundy Isl., off	U-boat
08-Oct	*SS Memphian*	6305	Torpedo	Arklow LV., off	*U-96*
08-Oct	*SS Greldon*	3322	Torpedo	Arklow LV., off	*U-96*
09-Oct	*SS Peshawur*	7634	Torpedo	Co. Down, off	*U-96*
09-Oct	*SS Main*	715	Gunfire	Luce Bay	*UC-75*
09-Oct	*AMC Champagne*	5360	Torpedo	Isle of Man, off	*U-96*
10-Oct	*HT Waltham*	161	Mine	Isle of Man, off	*UC-75*
11-Oct	*AY Kethailes*	611	Collision?	Blackwater LV., off	?
11-Oct	*SS Rhodesia*	4313	Torpedo	Tuskar, off	*U-61*
12-Oct	*SS W.M.Barkley*	569	Torpedo	Kish LV., off	*UC-75*
13-Oct	*SS Eskmere*	2293	Torpedo	Irish Sea	*UC-75*
13-Oct	*SS Dui*	?	Lost	Wexford, off	?
15-Oct	*HD Active*	81	Mine	Milford Haven	U-boat
23-Oct	*HT Earl of Lennox*	22	Mine	North Channel	U-boat

There were three failed attacks recorded in October 1917.

03-Nov	*HD Deliverer*	97	Mine	Dublin Bay	*UC-75*
05-Nov	*SS Longwy*	2315	Torpedo	Irish Channel	*UC-75*
07-Nov	*SS Umgeni*	2662	Sub.?	Irish Channel	?
08-Nov	*SS The Marquis*	373	Gunfire	Rockabill, off	*UC-75*
10-Nov	*SV Lapwing*	95	Lost.	George's Channel	?
12-Nov	*SS Ardglass*	4617	Torpedo	The Maidens, off	*UC-31*

14-Nov '17	SS Unknown	?	Lost	South Rock LV., off	?
18-Nov	SS Gisella	2502	Torpedo	Skokham Isl., off	UC-77
19-Nov	SS Admiral Zede	5980	Torpedo	Milford Haven, off	UC-77
22-Nov	SV Conovium	86	Gunfire	Sth. Arklow LV., off	U-boat
22-Nov	SS Elsena	335	Gunfire	Sth. Arklow LV., off	U-boat
27-Nov	SS Apapa	7832	Torpedo	Anglesey, off	U-96
28-Nov	SS Angenoria	2977	Sub?	The Copelands, off. (Beached?)	?
30-Nov	SS Derbent	3178	Torpedo	Lynas Point., off	U-96
30-Nov	SV Piere	?	Lost	Wexford, off	?

There were twelve failed attacks by U-boats recorded in November 1917.

02-Dec	SS Copeland	1184	Torpedo	Tuskar, off	U-57
07-Dec	SS Earl of Elgin	4448	Torpedo	Carnarvon Bay	UC-75
09-Dec	SV Sea Fisher	297	Lost	George's Channel	?
12-Dec	SS Charleston	1866	Bombs	The Smalls, Wales, off	UB-65
12-Dec	SV Bellville	992	Sub ?	Tuskar, off	?
13-Dec	SS Stephen Furness	1712	Torpedo	Irish Sea	UB-64
14-Dec	SS Hare	774	Torpedo	Kish LV., off	U-62
14-Dec	SS Nor	1418	Torpedo	Irish Channel	UB-65
14-Dec	Eimarjari	?	Sub ?	Wexford, off	?
16-Dec	HMS Arbutus (Q ship)	1290	Torpedo	George's Channel	UB-65
16-Dec	SS Formby	1282	Torpedo	Irish Sea	U-62
17-Dec	SS Conninbeg	1279	Torpedo	Sth. Arklow LV., off	U-62
22-Dec	SS Colemere	2120	Torpedo	The Smalls, Wales, off	U-105
24-Dec	SS Daybreak	3238	Gunfire	South Rock, off	U-87
25-Dec	SS Penshurst (Q ship)	1191	Torpedo	Georges/Bristol Ch.	U-110
25-Dec	SS Agberi	4821	Torpedo	Bardsey Isl., off	U-87
25-Dec	U-87 (German)	850	Rammed	Carnarvon Bay	HMS Buttercup
27-Dec	SS Adela	685	Torpedo	The Skerries, off	U-100
28-Dec	SS Chirripo	4050	Mine	Black Head, off	UC-75
28-Dec	SS Lord Derby	3757	Torpedo	St. Anne's Head, off	U-105
28-Dec	SS Robert Eggleton	2274	Torpedo	Bardsey Isl., off	U-91
28-Dec	PC Alfred H. Read	457	Mine	Liverpool Bar	UC-75

There were twelve failed attacks by U-boats recorded in December 1917.

There were six U-boats operating in the area of the Alley during the last week of December 1917.

The position in which the *SS Penshurst* was sunk is some distance south of the geographical boundary of the Alley. It is included, however, to demonstrate the heightened U-boat and Allied activity there was during this period, and the dangers posed to sailors on Q-ships. Another two Q-ships were sunk by the U-boats in February.

01-Jan'18	*SS Nadejda*	3489	Sub?	Irish Channel	?
01-Jan	*SS Almanack*	1455	Torpedo	Antrim, off	*U-37*
02-Jan *	*Bucuresti*	?	?	Irish Channel	?
02-Jan	*SS Boston City*	2711	Torpedo	Saint George's Channel	*U-91*
03-Jan	*SS Birchwood*	2756	Torpedo	Blackwater LV., off	*U-61*
04-Jan	*SV Otto*	96	Gunfire	St. John's Pt., off	U-boat
05-Jan	*SS Rose Marie*	2220	Torpedo	Nth. Arklow LV., off	*U-61*
06-Jan	*SS Knightsgarth*	2889	Torpedo	Rathlin Isl.	*U-91*
06-Jan	*SS Spenser*	4186	Torpedo	Bardsey Isl., off	*U-61*
06-Jan	*SS Halbardier*	1049	Torpedo	Bardsey Isl., off	*U-61*
07-Jan	*SS Egda*	2527	Torpedo	Tuskar, off	U-boat
26-Jan	*SS Cork*	232	Torpedo	Irish Sea	*U-103*
26-Jan	*U-84* (German)	850	Rammed	Tuskar, off	*P-62*
27-Jan	*SS Andania*	13405	Torpedo	North Channel	*U-103*
29-Jan	*SS Ethelinda*	3257	Torpedo	The Skerries, off	*U-103*
29-Jan	*SS Gelfruin*	3097	Torpedo	Holyhead, off	*UC-31*
30-Jan	*UB-63* (German)	502	D/charged	Irish Sea	*P-68*

There were nine failed attacks recorded in January 1918.

* This report appears in records of the City of Dublin Steam Packet Company. and remains unconfirmed.

04-Feb	*SS Treveal*	4160	Torpedo	The Skerries, off	*U-53*
05-Feb	*SS Tuscania*	14348	Torpedo	North Channel	*UB-77*
05-Feb	*SS Cresswell*	2829	Torpedo	Irish Sea	*U-46*
05-Feb	*SS Mexico City*	5078	Torpedo	Holyhead, off	*U-101*
05-Feb	*SS Alamance*	4955	Torpedo	The Maidens, off	*UB-73*
07-Feb	*SS Ardbeg*	227	Gunfire	Liverpool Bar, off	*UB-73*
07-Feb	*SS Limesfield*	427	Torpedo	Isle of Man, off	*UB-57*
07-Feb	*SS Ben* Rein	212	Gunfire	Liverpool, off	*UB-57*
08-Feb	*SV Erica*	167	Gunfire	Bardsey Isl., off	U-boat
11-Feb	*SS Wesphalia* (Q ship)	1467	Torpedo	Irish Sea	*U-97*
11-Feb	*SS Cullist* (Q ship)	1200	Torpedo	Isle of Man, off	*UC-47*
19-Feb	*SS Wheatflower*	188	Gunfire	Tuskar, off	U-boat
20-Feb	*SS Djerv*	1527	Torpedo	The Skerries, off	*U-86*
20-Feb	*SS Hailebury*	2888	Torpedo	The Maidens, off	*U-91*

Date	Ship	Tonnage	Cause	Location	U-boat
21-Feb'18	*SS Rio Verde*	4025	Torpedo	Mull of Galloway	*U-86*
22-Feb	*SS Ulabrand*	2011	Torpedo	Irish Channel	*UC-75*
23-Feb	*SS British Viscount*	3287	Torpedo	The Skerries, off	*U-91*
24-Feb	*SS Renfrew*	3830	Torpedo	St. Anne's Head, off	*U-91*
25-Feb	*SS Sarpfos*	1458	Torpedo	Irish Channel	*U-105*
26-Feb	*SS Santa Maria*	5318	Torpedo	Irish Channel	*U-19*
26-Feb	*SS Tiberia*	4880	Torpedo	North Channel	*U-19*
26-Feb	*SS Dalewood*	2420	Torpedo	Isle of Man, off	*U-105*
27-Feb	*SS Largo*	1764	Torpedo	Isle of Man, off	*UB-105*

There were thirteen failed attacks recorded in February 1918.
The hospital ship *Glenart Castle* was lost when she was torpedoed by *UC56* on the 26th in the Bristol Channel with loss of 168 lives.

Date	Ship	Tonnage	Cause	Location	U-boat
01-Mar	*HT Thomas Collard*	215	Sub	Rathlin Isl., off	?
01-Mar	*SS Penvearn*	3710	Torpedo	South Stack, off	*U-105*
01-Mar	*AMC Calgarian*	17515	Torpedo	Rathlin Isl., off	*U-19*
02-Mar	*SS Carmelite*	2583	Torpedo	Isle of Man, off	*U-105*
02-Mar	*SS Havna*	1330	Torpedo	Tuskar, off	U-boat
02-Mar	*SS Kenmare*	565	Torpedo	The Skerries, off	*U-104*
02-Mar	*H-5* (British sub)		Collision	Irish Sea	*SS Ruthergien*
02-Mar	*MV Bessy*	60	Gunfire	Isle of Man, off	U-98
03-Mar	*FV Sunrise*	24	Bombs	Isle of Man, off	U-boat
03-Mar	*SS Romeo*	1730	Torpedo	North Channel	*U-102*
07-Mar	*SS Tarbetness*	3018	Torpedo	Carnarvon, off	*U-110*
09-Mar	*SV Nancy Wignal*	98	Torpedo	George's Channel	U-boat
09-Mar	*FV Marguerite*	10	Bombs	Beaumaris, off	*UC-75*
10-Mar	*FV Wave*	47	Bombs	Isle of Man, off	*UC-75*
10-Mar	*FV Sunrise*	24	Bombs	Isle of Man, off	*UC-75*
12-Mar	*SS Arno Mendi*	2827	Mine	The Skerries, off	*UC-75*
14-Mar	*SS Tweed*	1777	Torpedo	Tuskar, off	*UC-75*
15-Mar	*SS Sea Gull*	976	Torpedo	Lynas Point, off	*U-103*
17-Mar	*SS Cressida*	157	Torpedo	The Skerries, off	U-boat
20-Mar	*SS Kassanga*	3015	Torpedo	Sth. Arklow LV., off	*U-103*
20-Mar	*SS Glenford*	494	Gunfire	Rockabill, off	U-boat
22-Mar	*SS Trinidad*	2592	Torpedo	Codling, LV., off	*U-101*
23-Mar	*SS Jane Grey*	124	Gunfire	The Smalls, off	U-boat
24-Mar	*SS Anteros*	4241	Torpedo	Sth. Stack, off	*U-103*
24-Mar	*SS Renfrew*	3830	Torpedo	St. Anne's Head, off	*U-91*
24-Mar	*SV John G. Walther*	258	Explosives	The Smalls, off (derelict)	U-boat
25-Mar	*SS Destro*	859	Torpedo	North Channel	*U-96*
26-Mar	*U-61* (German)	820	D/charged	Irish Sea	*P-51*
28-Mar	*SS Inkosi*	3661	Torpedo	Luce Bay	*U-96*

30-Mar'18	*FV St. Michan*	43	Gunfire	Lambay Isl., off	*U-96*
30-Mar	*FV Geraldine*	23	Gunfire	Lambay Island., off	*U-96*
30-Mar	*SS Salamania*	3112	Torpedo	Irish Sea	U-boat
31-Mar	*SS Conargo*	4312	Torpedo	Isle of Man, off	*U-96*

There were fourteen failed attacks recorded in March 1918.

02-Apr	*SV Solway Queen*	307	Torpedo	Black Head, off	U-boat
05-Apr	*SS Cyrone*	2904	Torpedo	Bardsey Isl., off	*UC-63*
07-Apr	*SS Boscastle*	2346	Torpedo	Strumble Head	*U-111*
11-Apr	*SS Lakemoor*	2045	Torpedo	North Channel	*UB-73*
12-Apr	*SV Wilson*	110	Gunfire	The Smalls, off	*UB-73* in area
14-Apr	*SS Chelford*	2995	Torpedo	Bardsey Isl., off	*UB-73*
16-Apr	*SS Lodaner*	3291	Torpedo	Irish Sea	*UB-73*
16-Apr	*SS Ladoga*	1917	Torpedo	Arklow LV., off	*UB-73*
17-Apr	*UB-82* (German)	502	Gunfire	North Channel	*HD Young Fred*
20-Apr	*SS Florieston*	3366	Torpedo	South Stack, off	*U-91*
20-Apr	*SS Lowther Range*	3926	Torpedo	Irish Sea	*U-91*
21-Apr	*SS Normandiet*	1843	Torpedo	Isle of Man	*U-91*
21-Apr	*SS Landonia*	2504	Torpedo	Strumble Head, off	*U-91*
22-Apr	*SS Fern*	444	Torpedo	Irish Sea	U-boat
26-Apr	*SV Ethel*	100	Gunfire	The Smalls, off	U-boat
27-Apr	*Walpas*	312	Sub ?	Irish Channel	?
27-Apr	*SS Gresham*	3774	Torpedo	Bardsey Isl., off	*U-91*
28-Apr	*SS Oronsa*	8075	Torpedo	Bardsey Isl., off	*U-91*
28-Apr	*SS Damao*	5668	Sub ?	Irish Sea/Bardsey Isl. off	?
29-Apr	*SV Johnny O'Toole*	84	Gunfire	Tuskar, off	*U-105*
39-Apr	*SV Christiana Davis*	86	Gunfire	Tuskar, off	*U-105*
30-Apr	*UB-85* (German)	502	Gunfire	Black Head, off	*HT Correopsis*
30-Apr	*SS Kempock*	255	Gunfire	Co. Down, off	*UB-85*
30-Apr	*SS Kafue*	6044	Torpedo	North Channel	*U-86*

There were nineteen failed attacks recorded in April 1918. *U-19* was reported to have been in the Alley again in April.

Despite heavy losses by the Allies in the Alley during May '18, the numbers continued to decline, showing some resurgence again in September. By then the game was up. Despite sinking many valuable ships, the U-boats were unable to prevent the troop carriers delivering their valuable cargoes. No matter if sinkings had returned to the all time high levels of April 1917, this would not have prevented the defeat of Germany.

U-boat statistics for all Ireland during WW1.

There were 119 different known U-boats that either attacked or sank ships around the coast of Ireland during WW1.

In terms of the total number of all classes of vessels sunk in Irish waters during the whole of the war, the most 'successful' U-boat by far, were *UC-75, U-96, UC-65* and *U-57.* (If various criteria, such as type of vessel sunk, length of operations, etc. were taken into account, it could be argued in terms of tonnage sunk, that *UC-65* was equal to if not more effective than any other submarine that operated around Ireland.) These submarines were also very successful and figured prominently in other areas of operations.

U-boat statistics for the Alley during World War I

Seventy-one different known U-boats sank or attacked ships in the Alley during WW1. These were:

U-19, U-20, U-21, U-22, U-24, U-27, U-28, U-30, U-31, U-36, U-37, U-38, U-44, U-46, U-52, U-53, U-54, U-57, U-60, U-61, U-62, U-65, U-79, U-80, U-82, U-84, U-86, U-87, U-90, U-91, U-94, U-95, U-96, U-97, U-98, U-100, U-101, U-102, U-103, U-104, U-105, U-110, U-111.
UB-38, UB-57, UB-64, UB-65, UB-72, UB-73, UB-77, UB-85, UB-87, UB-92, UB-95, UB-103, UB-105, UB-118, UB-120, UB-123, UB-124, UB-125, UB-126.
UC-31, UC-33, UC-47, UC-48, UC-51, UC-65, UC-66, UC-75, UC-77.

The most 'successful' of these were *UC-75, UC-65, U-96* and *U91.* And again, all of the above submarines were also active in other areas of operations.

After the all time high global casualty figures for April 1917, U-boat tactics altered and focus was relocated on the Alley and its entrances, until the launch of the large scale German offensive in France, twelve months later.

During the first quarter of that twelve months in the Alley, there were 6 U-boats sinking ships and 20 fatal attacks made by unidentified others. For the second quarter, the figures were 8 and 7. The third quarter showed a dramatic rise to 17 and 15. And during the final quarter, January to March 1918, the figures were even more startling at 25 and 15. During same period twelve months earlier, the figures were 7 and 16. Again highlighting the dramatic change in emphasis by these submarines.

The foregoing statistics were compiled from *British Merchant Ships Sunk by U-boats in the 1914-1918 War* and *British Vessels Lost at Sea 1914–1918.* Data was also referenced on details of individual ships, U-boat logs, a list of 'Lloyds War Losses' held at Liverpool Maritime Museum, Shipwreck Index of the British Isles by Bridget & Richard Lane, records at the Public Records Office (PRO), Kew, and from a database of Irish shipwrecks, compiled by Compuwreck.

The results are based on all class of vessels (mainly British but also a significant amount of 'foreign' vessels) that were sunk by U-boats. As these include minor vessels

such as fishing boats, if tonnage sunk or unsuccessful attacks were to be used to measure U-boats' successes, the results might appear differently. They might also appear different, if it had been possible to include all foreign casualties. The statistics that produce these figures also included 366 attacks or sinkings by unidentified U-boats around the coast of Ireland.

U-boats lost in the vicinity of the Alley during World War I.

26/09/1917. *UC-33*. Rammed by *HMS PC-61* off the Tuskar. 27 of her crew were lost and 1 survived.
17/11/1917. *U-58*. Depth-charged by *USS Fanning* off Milford Haven.
2 of her crew were lost and 36 survived.
25/12/1917. *U-87*. Sunk by *PC-56* and *HMS Buttercup* in the Irish Sea.
All 44 crew were lost.
26/01/1918. *U-84*. Rammed by *PC-62* in St George's Channel.
All 40 crew were lost.
Jan/Feb 1918. *UB-63*. Destroyed by *HD's Young Fred, Cormorant* or *USS Allen* in the Irish Sea / North Channel. The incident is unsubstantiated.
33 were lost and there were no survivors.
26/03/1918. *U-61*. Depth-charged by *HMS PC-51* in St George's Channel.
All 36 crew were lost.
17/04/1918. *UB-82*. Depth-charged by drifters *Young Fred* and *Pilot Me* in the North Channel. All 32 crew were lost.
25/04/1918. *U-104*. Depth-charged by *HMS Jessamine* in St George's Channel.
All 42 crew were lost.
30/04/1918. *UB-85*. Sunk by *HD Coreopsis* off Belfast Lough.
All 34 crew were rescued.
25/05/1918. *UB-119*. Missing after patrol in Irish Sea. Sank steamer off Belfast Lough on the 25th. All 34 crew were lost.
??/09/1918. *U-92*. Enroute for patrol in Irish Sea. Registered as missing.
Last transmission was from Fair Isle on the 9th. All of her 42 crew were lost.

U-boats lost in the vicinity of the Alley during World War II.

12/02/1940. *U-33*. Depth-charged off the Firth of Clyde. Scuttled by crew. British divers later recovered Enigma 'rotors' from the wreck. (Alternatively, according to some sources, this valuable piece of equipment was said to have obtained from one of the U-boat's crew.) 25 crew were lost and 17 were rescued.
16/01/1945. *U-482*. Depth-charged in the North Channel. All 48 crew were lost.
26/01/1945. *U-1051*. Depth-charged and rammed by *Aylmerand* in Irish Sea.
All of the submarine's 52 crew were lost.
27/01/1945. *U-1172*. Depth-charged in Irish Sea by *HMS Keats* and *HMS Bligh*.
All 52 crew were lost.

00/03/1945. *U-296*. Cause of disappearance unknown but believed to be in or north of the Irish Sea. All of her 46 crew lost.

00/03/1945. *U-246*. Believed depth-charged in Irish Sea or North Channel. Her 48 crew were lost.

07/03/1945. *U-1302*. Depth-charged in Irish Sea. All 49 crew were lost.

05/04/1945. *U-242*. Lost in Irish Sea. Believed to have struck a mine. All 44 crew were lost.

13/04/1945. *U-1024*. Depth-charged, and later sank in fog later while being towed in the Irish Sea. 37 of her crew were lost and eight were saved.

00/04/1945. *U-1169*. Presumed lost between Tuskar Rock and Pembroke or the English Channel. Position unknown.

(Note: U-boat losses quoted above are derived mainly from *U-boats Destroyed* and *U-boat Intelligence,* both by Robert Grant, and *German Submarine Losses* by David Perkins.)

Chapter 8

A CHRISTMAS TO REMEMBER

The loss of the Tedcastles ship Adela

A Christmas to Remember

The loss of the Tedcastles ship Adela.

'But never again will they have to wrestle with its outbursts
or stand fast against the full force of its strength.
For them the battle is over.
There is no victor, no vanquished, but a deep and lasting respect!
Their mettle has been put to its severest test.
They have seen friend and companion succumb.'

Part of 'A Tribute to the Old Sailors', from *Tales of the Wexford Coast*
by Tom Williams.

Lieutenant Colonel Lord Decies was the Chief Press Censor for Ireland from 1916 until 1919, and by available accounts, he is said to have been quite successful at his job. The period was an extremely turbulent one, with World War I and the separate battle for Ireland's independence both in progress. Lord Decies had a brilliant career in the cavalry, and showed a profound love of horses and equine sports until the day he died. He also figured prominently for many years among the horse racing set at the Curragh in County Kildare. He was a man who loved all kinds of sport, owning his own yacht; this included a keen interest in sailing.

His entire army career was a notable one. Amongst his many decorations, he received the D.S.O. for exceptional service in Somalia in 1903. He was an excellent horseman, and was a member of the distinguished team, which won the first gold medals awarded for polo at the Paris Olympiad in 1920. Later, during his posting in Dublin, he became known for his relish of the verbal banters with fellow members during his stopovers at the Kildare Street Club. This bastion of society's upper crust had a world reputation, and had become a meeting place for a section of the community that had no superiors in rank or privilege. A measure of its members can be imagined from the following description, which was sometimes given to it: 'The headquarters of Unionism and Toryism in Ireland'. A very large portion of its members were officers of senior rank, and it was amongst such company that Lord Decies could reflect on world events, whilst imbibing his privately imported brandy.

Having moved from his previous residence at Mount Merrion to the historic residence of Leixlip Castle, a home which he continued to improve with electricity and heating during the war, his stopovers in Dublin city became all the more frequent. The Castle, although a fine home, was impractical for daily commuting to Dublin, where he carried out the duties of his office. Situated just a few doors from the recruiting offices of the Royal Navy Air Services, at 102 Grafton Street, Lord Decies' offices, at No. 85, were only a short stroll from his club in Kildare Street, Dublin.

Recorded in *Thom's Directory* as, 'Crown Bazaar, Head Office', this was where Lord Decies scrutinised the draft copy of the printed word in Ireland.

The work of censoring the media had previously been under the control of the military, at the headquarters of the Irish Command in Dublin Castle. After objections were made against a military censorship of the Irish press and media, the office and its duties were removed to No.17 Ely Place for a short time in 1916, and from there to Grafton Street in 1917. An apparently civilian-run censorship was thus inaugurated, but under the same Lieutenant Colonel Lord Decies and his chief assistant Captain Shaw. The office of the Irish Press Censor was re-established by the Irish government in Dublin Castle during World War II. The remaining censor's files for 1916–19 are now kept in the National Archives, and contain a paper mountain of patronising explanations and apologies by the newspaper editors and printers of Ireland during World War I.

It is impossible to get an overall image of the man from just his working files, but the claim by some that he was a considerate person is well supported by some of the correspondence contained in them. These record a certain determination to 'look after' his employees, and an apparent genuine concern to do favours for ex-soldiers from the ranks when called on to do so. It was also said of him that his relationship with journalists was unusually friendly for one who held such an office, as both would so often come into conflict. Some members of his family have also wondered why, during the subsequent attacks by nationalists on the stately homes of Ireland, his castle home at Leixslip was never touched. He nevertheless appeared to perform his duties as Chief Censor loyally and without flinching, even when swift and firm action was required.

Although one might expect censorship in Ireland to have been absolute during the period 1914–18, there were some exceptions or oversights by the censor's office. These occurred on occasions when proofs of articles, if they had been properly submitted, would have received a 'D notice', preventing their publication. However, some editors and printers appear to have published some risky articles, either knowingly or otherwise, and when seen later by Lord Decies' office, brought swift reprimand, albeit in some cases the equivalent of 'closing the stable door'.

Although the authorities were perfectly willing to apply extreme sanctions on newspaper and printing works, including imprisonment, most offences and reprimand concluded with a written warning. The 'cat and mouse' activities between some editors and the censor's office contributed to the large volume of apologetic but interesting letters from editors and owners that remain on file today.

The examples given further on, and those shown in the illustrations, give the reader an insight into Lord Decies' tolerance. They also provide an understanding of the propaganda operations that existed during World War I, and demonstrate the difficulty there was obtaining crews for vessels on the cross-channel routes. The increasing scarcity of merchant seamen was a direct result of the growing number of attacks during the heightened U-boat campaign in the Alley at the time.

The two most important subjects to occupy the Chief Censor's office were sedition and naval secrets. It was obligatory for advance notice to be given in respect of gatherings, plays, football matches, meetings etc., and local members of the Royal Irish Constabulary closely monitored those that were given permission to proceed.

The censor possessed, through the wide-ranging powers granted to him under the Defence of the Realm Act, the power to alter the text of an article, or to forbid its publication entirely. And if an article was altered by the censor's office, it reserved the right to precede it with insertion of the phrase 'As passed by the censor.' The insertion appeared quite regularly. Its absence could be ambiguous.

It was also forbidden to export newspapers, magazines, pamphlets, photographs and other such material without going through a licensed publishing agent, such as Messrs Eason. These, as with all mails, were intercepted by the Chief Censor's office for England at Liverpool, where everything was scrutinised. The army and navy had their own methods of censorship, and were supplemented by assistance from the office of the Chief Postal Censor.

Reports on naval or military activity of any kind were always to be submitted for approval. The death notice of a soldier might mention his regiment; this was also forbidden without approval. Omissions in this respect, which almost always came to the notice of the censor, would then result in a stern warning. Reports on any kind of naval activity were particularly sensitive, and when they appeared without approval, these often gave rise to an urgent and terse telegram from the Admiralty, who did not seem to miss much.

Lord Decies had no discretional authority concerning naval censorship, and when articles on the subject were submitted to his office for permission to print, the Admiralty had to be consulted. Occasionally, exceptions were made for the 'special reporting' of particular naval engagements and their casualties.

Considered to be much more sensitive, attacks on American vessels prior to that country's entry into the war warranted distinctly separate consideration. Such incidences presented an opportunity which, if presented cleverly, helped demonstrate to American citizens just how indiscriminate German attacks on its shipping could be. Any unsolicited reference to submarines was particularly disconcerting to the Admiralty, and the following unambiguous instruction was given to editors in this regard: 'Operations by or against submarines are a prohibited subject.'

In addition, and quite understandably, photography was absolutely forbidden in most areas without a special permit. It is for this reason, and the lure of more 'glamorous' far-off battlefields, that so few photographers came to Ireland during World War I. The result has been a serious deficit of photographic record, depicting strategic military or naval scenes in Ireland from this period. There is almost nothing in the public archival domain, which includes photographs containing even a glimpse of a discernible Irish coastline, particularly of southern Ireland, from this period. Following requests by the widely acclaimed Irish photographer William Lawrence, he, too, was unfortunately refused permission to take any photographs in Dublin port during the war.

The following instance is a good example of how the office of the Chief Censor carried out its function in such cases.

On 20 April 1918, an unauthorised report of a U-boat attack on the schooner *Wilson* of Arklow appeared in the weekly edition of the *Wicklow Newsletter*. The only copies of the *Wicklow Newsletter* available in Ireland today are held at the National Library. Unfortunately however, this particular issue happens to be missing from a large bound volume of the paper. Details of the report provided below are courtesy of the Newspaper Library at Colindale, London:

"MORE GERMAN CALLOUSNESS ARKLOW VESSEL SUNK"

Widespread indignation was felt in the district when it became known that the schooner *Wilson*, the property of Mr Peter Tyrell, Arklow, had been sunk on Friday evening last about 8 o'clock. The crew comprised the captain, Robert Tyrell, son of the owner, and the three other Arklow men. When the German submarine appeared on the scene the crew were questioned as to whether the schooner was armed. They were subsequently taken aboard the submarine and lined in front of the pirate's gun, being threatened at the same time that if their story was found to be incorrect, they would shoot them. Having placed a couple of bombs in the hold, which sank the ship, the helpless crew were left at the mercy of the waves in a small open boat. The victims of the outrage were given the compass from their lost ship and told to steer a certain course. They did so hoisting a small sail, but the sea was choppy and the men suffered a good deal from exposure all during the night until they were eventually picked up by a cargo steamer at three o'clock on Saturday afternoon. They arrived back in Arklow on Monday.'

The article would seem to be harmless enough, giving nothing away but the loss of a sailing vessel, probably somewhere in the Irish Sea (in the south Bristol Channel, off the Smalls), as a result of a U-boat attack. It was well known by then that U-boats were stopping, searching and sinking vessels in this way, and on occasions, leaving merchant sailors adrift far from shore in desperate conditions. But there are certain references in the article worth commenting on.

The gun fitted on a merchant-ship was ordinarily intended for defence purposes, and having such a weapon aboard the Arklow vessel would not have been a reason for the execution of the crew. It would appear that there were no recorded incidences of German sailors executing British ones for having a gun aboard their vessel in self-defence. But if the weapon had been concealed, and the ship was some kind of decoy, the matter might have been considered quite differently.

The dangers associated with being mistaken for a Q-ship were nothing new to Arklow schooners. Schooner-owners, and crews from Arklow, experienced the full repercussions of the war at sea. They had ships seized by the enemy and sunk by them, sometimes with no warning. Some of their schooners were requisitioned by the Admiralty and used as Q-ships. But just as it was with the 'mystery steamers' that carried concealed guns, and the fishing vessels that were not fishing, Arklow crews were all too aware of the ramifications of being mistaken for a Q-ship. In other words, a U-boat commander might just as easily fire first and approach later.

Lastly, in the case of the *Wilson*, it is obvious that the U-boat commander intended the crew of Arklow boat to have some chance of survival, otherwise, he would not have previously removed the schooner's compass before sinking it, and given it to the men in the lifeboat.

Leaving aside the rights or wrongs of actions by some U-boat commanders, the appearance of such an article in a newspaper without prior consultation with the censor would amount to a violation of the Defence of the Realm Act. When such a violation was spotted, the editor was sent a telegram by the censor's office and asked to explain himself. On this occasion, the editor Samuel Bothwell, of the County Printing Company Ltd. (Owner of the *Wicklow Newsletter*), replied to such a request on 26 April as follows:

'I beg to state that my only object in publishing the paragraph was to give publicity to the inhuman treatment of the crew of the schooner by the enemy submarine, in sending the men adrift in an open boat in the darkness of the night. I was not aware . . . I very much regret . . . an unreserved apology . . . not occur again . . . etc., etc.'

Seemingly satisfied with the addition to his growing mountain of similar apologies, Lord Decies replied:

'the Defence of the Realm Regulations are very clear on the point. No mention of the sinking of any ships by German Agency may be published until officially released by the Press Bureau, London, and it is not in my jurisdiction to allow publication of losses of ships without first receiving sanction from the Admiralty.

In addition to this, the sinking of vessels trading from Ireland to England has had the effect of making it extremely difficult to obtain crews to carry on the work absolutely necessary for the working of these ships, and on these grounds it is not desirable to mention any ships being sunk.

I realise the point you bring forward, but in future I must ask you to take the greatest care in reporting the losses of any ships sunk by German Agency.'

Not unlike many other transgressions of the regulations, the matter ended at that. However, Lord Decies' letter raises some interesting and surprising issues, firstly the reference to being able to publish after the Press Bureau in had released certain information.

After the sinking of the *Leinster* on 11 October 1918, the *Evening Herald* attempted to get out a rushed 'special edition' on the catastrophe. The production was stopped and the paper's offices were closed for several days by the authorities when it was accused of not passing copy through the proper censorship procedures, even though the paper claimed that the offending text had been released by the Press Bureau in London. It was said that the paper's works only just escaped being dismantled. Making little sense, the alleged offending text was printed soon after by its sister paper, the *Independent*.

Secondly, and more surprisingly, Lord Decies unnecessarily highlighted the problems shipping merchants were having with the number of U-boat attacks against their vessels in the Irish Sea.

The final issue in regard to the *Wilson*, concerns the accounts of U-boat crews that were accused of mistreating merchant-seamen, which must have been exactly the type of story that Lord Decies had sought only three months earlier. On 25 January 1918, Lord Decies petitioned Sir Charles Brownrigg, the Chief Naval Censor at Whitehall, with the following request:

'You may remember when I called on you in London you very kindly said you would send me some stories over about submarine attacks on ships, suitable for the *Irish Press*. I think these would be most useful at present if you have any you would send. Harrowing details, particularly if they concern this country, are what is required.'

This was followed shortly by the delivery of a box of pamphlets and a list of 'German Atrocities' from the Intelligence Division of the Admiralty to the censor's office in Grafton Street. (The actual pamphlets were not on file.)

The censor's office did not always get it right. The *Evening Herald* seems to have had a particular knack of printing offending articles, which were sometimes missed by the censor. Some of these oversights even brought reprimand on Lord Decies' head from higher quarters.

The following was a case in point, and it occurred during a period when so much concern was being shown about the security of food and livestock shipments from Ireland to Britain. Mr Burgess, who was Director of Cross Channel Transportation, addressed a letter of reprimand to Lord Decies from his office in Westmoreland Street on 7 March 1918. It read in part:

'I pointed out to you that alarming notices of such occurrences in the Press [reported incident on the torpedoing of *SS Kenmare* with the loss of 29 lives] deters other seamen employed in the city of Cork, Liverpool and Fishguard from performing their ordinary duties, and that this would be a serious hindrance to the transit of traffic, including large quantities of foodstuffs between Ireland and Great Britain. My anticipations in this respect prove correct because the crews of other steamers have since declined to sail and in one case I was able to obtain sufficient Naval Ratings to take the place of the men who left off work, and at the moment I am endeavouring to obtain another crew of Naval Ratings to replace the men on another steamer who will not sail.'

Lord Decies later passed this slap on the wrist on to the editor of the offending newspaper, the *Wicklow Newsletter*, by way of the letter already mentioned, with these additional few sentences:

'I think it right to draw your special attention to the whole matter with the hope that

such notices may be kept out of the papers in future. As you will appreciate the difficulties in working Irish steamers at the present time are great enough without having them accentuated by alarming newspaper reports which can really do no good, even to the general public.'

There is another interesting point worth making in relation to censorship in Ireland, which might not have attracted previous comment. The seas to the north, south, and east of Ireland showed remarkably high levels of U-boat activity during World War I. The Western Approaches were the critical juncture for shipping to and from the north-west of Europe. The large number of U-boat attacks that took place off the Irish coast were evident all too often by the numbers of bodies, large amounts of debris, and the survivors from the stricken vessels that came ashore. And from news of them that reached the public through 'intelligence leaks' at ports and other places. There were numerous sailors rescued by fishing vessels, badly-damaged vessels which limped or were towed into ports, and explosions which were heard at night in coastal villages. Local newspapers often risked the wrath of the censor by printing some details of these, a practice they knew was expressly forbidden. Enlightening the enemy as to his successes, or otherwise upsetting the population of Ireland, was bad enough, but more importantly; Ireland was a neighbour of Britain.

A licence was needed to import foreign or Irish newspapers into Britain, and these all had to pass the scrutiny of the censor. Newspaper reports and newspaper owners in Britain could generally be relied upon, and indeed they often gained more latitude in their reporting. But refusing a British newspaper permission to print sensitive material after it had already appeared in an Irish paper was stretching the understanding.

The prospect posed by an English-speaking neighbour by word of mouth, pamphlet paper or otherwise, had a tremendous potential for propaganda in Britain. Given the large number of registered publications in Ireland during the war, many with nationalist leanings, and the risks some editors were prepared to take, Lord Decies was presented with an uphill task.

Without reading for oneself the rejected and amended proofs that survive in the censor's files, it might be difficult to understand exactly what words the Admiralty did not want to see appearing in newspapers, or for that matter, what words it wanted seen. So it is only prudent to be suspicious of newspaper reports from this period.

Despite growing disaffection amongst Irish skippers and shipping companies, the accounts of the atrocities that were desirable in January 1918 were also used to exploit the deaths of many Irish sailors and civilians during the following months. The reasons for printing such stories was not only an attempt to offset support for Sinn Féin, or to sow uncertainty into the minds of those who were nervous about that organisation's relationship with Germany, but also to instil fervour and incentive into potential recruits.

TEDCASTLE, McCORMICK & Co. Ltd

Regular Steam communication between
DUBLIN & LIVERPOOL.

TEDCASTLE LINE

TEDCASTLE   LINE.

DUBLIN and LIVERPOOL.
Regular Steam Communication.
Reduced Freights and Fares.

R. TEDCASTLE and CO'S First-class Screw Steamers, ADELA (New Steamer), MAGNET, and DUBLIN, Or other suitable Steamers, are intended to sail as under (unless prevented by stress of weather, or other unforeseen circumstances), with Passengers, Live Stock, and Goods.

Proposed Sailings for FEBRUARY, 1879.
Additional Sailings according as the Trade may require.

FROM DUBLIN.	FROM LIVERPOOL.
Cargo Shed, Sir John Rogerson's-quay.	Cargo Shed, West Side, Collingwood Dock.
Saturday, 8th, 12 noon	Saturday, 8th, 9 p m
Wednesday, 12th, 1 p m	Wednesday, 12th, 2 p m
Saturday, 15th, 3 p m	Saturday, 15th, 5 p m
Wednesday, 19th, 6 p m	Wednesday, 19th, 8 p m
Saturday, 22nd, 12 noon	Saturday, 22nd, 9 p m
Wednesday, 26th, 1 p m	Wednesday, 26th, 1 p m
Saturday, Mar. 1st, 3 p m	Saturday, Mar. 1st, 3 p m

Goods for shipment will be received up to One Hour before the advertised time of sailing, after which, if sent down, their shipment cannot be insured.

All descriptions of Goods, also Cattle, Sheep, Pigs, Poultry, Fish, Vegetables, &c., carried at Moderate Rates of Freight.

No Landing Charges by this Line.

Goods are received from, and forwarded by, the English and Irish Railways and Canals as directed.

Steerage Fare, 3s.; Cabin Fare, 8s. (including Steward's Fee).

THOMPSON, TEDCASTLE, and CO.,
Irwell Chambers, Union-street, Liverpool.
R. TEDCASTLE and CO.,
21 GREAT BRUNSWICK-STREET,
And 17 and 18 Sir John Rogerson's-quay,
DUBLIN.

A contemporary advertisement for the Tedcastle shipping line, showing the company flag.

A censored Tedcastle poster advertisement from 1917. The 'X' marks indicate the exception taken by the censor to the inclusion of any printed reference to times of sailings.

The result in either case remained in some doubt, and the introduction of conscription in Ireland continued to be a threat for the remainder of the war.

To bolster the numbers of enlisted men, an opportunity to enlist in the services was soon to be made available to boys in England aged fifteen and a half years, and for men up to the age of fifty and fifty-five years, 'if necessary'. The broadening of the age limits was an indication of the urgency that was associated with the impending battles in France.

The most important land engagement of the war was imminent, and its importance could be measured by the inclusion of Britain's reserve troops in the anticipated battle against Germany in 'Operation Michael' or the 'Spring Offensive', which became a series of offences. 'Operation Michael' began on 21 March, and is described by the military historian Malcolm Brown as having been 'the greatest concerted utterance of modern industrialised warfare to date'. It promised much but ended on 5 April at Amiens with exhaustion and enormous devastation of lives on both sides. The German onslaught prompted Churchill to say: 'We stood for some days within an ace of destruction'.

The Yanks were on their way, but would enough of them arrive in time?

Robert Tedcastle, a Scot from Dumfrieshire, began his career in coal when he joined his uncle's business in Dublin. Their enterprise grew and they moved into cross-channel shipping in the 1840s. Born in Scotland in 1825, Robert left for Ireland while in his teens, and survived until one year after World War I ended. His life spanned the coming of steam, the Great Famine in Ireland, practically all of the major wars of the 19th century, and World War I. He had witnessed the end of the prominence of sailing ships, and the introduction of motorised carriages in the city's thoroughfares, and he must surely have marvelled at the appearance of electric light and the first aeroplane.

Robert's uncle returned to Scotland, leaving the young man to manage a growing fleet of sailing and steam ships that carried coal to Ireland. He also operated an early depot for its distribution at Kingstown (Dun Laoghaire), where a Tedcastle office remains to this day. Tedcastle's ships eventually entered the passenger and general cargo service on the Dublin–Liverpool route in 1872.

In 1885 they absorbed the Whitehaven Steam Navigation Co., and his company became known as Robert Tedcastle & Co. That was, until it entered into partnership with the Dublin coal merchants McCormick & Co. in 1897. The name was then changed to Tedcastle McCormick & Co. Ltd. With the famous City of Dublin Steam Packet Company (C.D.S.P. Co.), this company was also amalgamated after the war with the Coast Line's, British And Irish Steam Packet company (B&I), in 1919.

Robert Tedcastle and his nephew, John Tedcastle, both owned a number of ships, which they later brought to the amalgamation with McCormick's. Some of these were: *SS Dublin, SS Magnet* (1869)*, *Toiler* (a paddle tug) (1875), *SS Adela* (1878), *SS Eblana* (1882), *SS Blackwater* (1883) and *SS Marlay* (1890). *(Here only, do the numbers in brackets denote the year the ship was built.)*

His first steamer, the *SS Dublin*, was supplied in 1866 by the Dublin yard of Walpole Webb & Co, which was established in 1862, and was joined soon after by a new partner, Thomas Bewley. Both companies and persons together became known as Bewley & Webb.

The vessels mentioned above, are ones that Robert Tedcastle would have directly influenced the naming of, and these names may indicate something of the man. Others, such as *SS Blackrock* and *SS Thistle,* were already named when the company acquired them from McCormick and the Whitehaven Steam Navigating Companies.

Robert Tedcastle operated his ships from their berths opposite the entrance to his premises on Sir John Rogerson's Quay. The properties adjoining his on the quayside were occupied by some of the best-known shipping companies of the day, including B&I, Burns, and Dublin General. In addition to owning and renting the adjoining houses on Lime Street and Brady's Court, the highly successful Robert Tedcastle acquired extensive farmlands in Australia. In 1918, Tedcastle McCormick put its last steamer, the *SS Killiney,* into service.

The funnel markings on Tedcastle's ships consisted of two white bands on a black funnel. Their red house flag was swallow-tailed, with the letter 'T', in white, set in the centre of a black diamond. (The company's flag can be seen on the jacket of this book.) '*Sallinia*', '*Emerald*' and '*Diamond*' were names given to earlier Tedcastle sailing vessels; 'Black Diamond' is a type of coal that has been sold by Tedcastle's for many years. It is very unlikely that Robert Tedcastle would have approved, but it is said that there was some smuggling of arms by nationalists aboard Tedcastle's vessels while their steamers *Eblana* and *Cumbria* were operating from City and Sir John Rogerson's Quay. The *Cumbria* is reported to have smuggled the escapee Éamon de Valera from Lincoln Jail to Dublin in 1919, and at a later date, back out again to raise funds in America.

A number of steamship companies began to benefit from the large increase in cross-channel traffic brought about by the advent of World War I, and both the City of Dublin Steam Packet Company and Tedcastles put on extra sailings from 3 October 1917. Tedcastle's *SS Adela* was kept busy by this increase in traffic, and was a popular ship with both passengers and crew. The details of her last voyage are not to be found in the newspapers but in the proof articles that were submitted to the censor's office for approval before printing. Permission to print was refused but the proofs have remained on file, and were subsequently left behind when the threads of the British administration in Ireland unravelled in 1922. These fascinating records have survived within dusty boxes in the National Archives, and have greatly helped in piecing together the last journey of the ship *Adela*.

After the *Adela* was lost off Holyhead, an inquest into the deaths of four of those who died was convened. Not unlike many similar cases, publishing reports of these proceedings was also censored.

Tedcastle steamers alongside Sir John Rogerson's Quay, where its offices were also situated c1920.

The information gleaned from the reports that were later passed by the censor, the remaining prohibited proofs in the censor's files, the surviving log of *U-100,* and recollections of Shay Wolfe, a grandson of one of the crew, form the basis of the following account of the U-boat attack which sunk the *Adela.*

Shay's grandfather, Christy, a ship's stoker who lived in one of the small terraced cottages adjacent to the North Wall, boarded the *Adela* well before the last of the livestock and cargo had been loaded, and apart from the drovers who occupied the steerage, only one other passenger boarded. Although steam had been up for over an hour, her departure was delayed until nearly 5 o'clock, when she slipped her ropes from the wall at City Quay. The delay may have been caused by 'awaiting Admiralty instructions', without which most vessels could not sail. Given the all-clear, Dublin's lights faded behind her as she steamed down the Liffey on what was to be her final journey across the Irish Sea.

Strategy was under constant review at the Admiralty, and at the time of the *Adela's* final journey, recent misgivings concerning activity by U-boats in the Irish channel and elsewhere had been reaching a climax. Unfortunately, the outcome and the resulting changes would not alter the steamer's ultimate fate.

Intelligence gathering by the Admiralty at Room 40 was excellent, but the distribution and prompt use of it left much to be desired. Confidence and morale were at a low ebb within the navy during 1917, and men were not in the best of spirits. A mood of frustration and helplessness was rife, resulting from the widespread belief that the U-boats were bringing the war nearer to home waters, where, by contrast, little success had been achieved in reversing the trend. Confidence in older admirals was eroding, creating a considerable degree of friction at the top. The growing threat in the Irish Sea, the increased losses of Admiralty vessels, and the German successes with surface craft in the North Sea were all becoming significant.

The loss of the large cruiser *HMS Drake* at Rathlin Island, and the battleship *HMS Vanguard* (19,250 tons), with 1,000 sailors, while berthed at Scapa on 9 July 1917, did nothing to inspire confidence. The loss of *HMS Vanguard* was said to have occurred as a result of a massive internal explosion, the cause of which presented something of a mystery at the time. After subsequent investigations into similar explosions in the same class of vessel, the cause was later attributed to failures in the design of their magazines. An earlier explosion on the cruiser *HMS Natal* (13,550 tons), narrowly missed killing Admiral Jellicoe's wife and children, but it was responsible for the deaths of 405 servicemen, and a number of civilians in the Cromarty Firth area. This explosion was suspected to have been the result of the same design fault. There were, however, more than a few high-ranking naval officers who remained convinced that the explosions were the work of German spies.

The pressure mounted on the First Sea Lord, Admiral Jellicoe, and on his boss, the First Lord of the Admiralty, Sir Eric Geddes, who finally sacked Jellicoe on 24 December. After an Admiralty conference on 2 January 1918, Sir Rosslyn Wemyss

replaced Admiral Jellicoe. The changes led to the introduction of a plethora of improved measures for Admiral Beatty's Grand Fleet, and a new anti-submarine division.

After a time, things improved considerably throughout the Admiralty, as did its relationship with the merchant-marine. The crews of the insignificant little steamers that had faced the growing dangers in the channel were unaware of events in high places and remained at the mercy of the U-boats. They carried the much-needed cargoes of beef and coal, and the improvements that followed were too late for those aboard the *Adela*.

It was an aspect of the war which Admiral Bayly himself addressed much later, in his book 'Pull Together', when he said.

'So much has been written of the heroism of the Navy during the War - and rightly so - but how little has been written of the ordinary merchantmen going on their way carrying our trade and facing grave dangers every day! We were brought very close together during the War. Many misunderstandings were forgotten then, and I know that the Navy were very proud of the part played by their brother seamen in the Merchant Navy.'

J. Murray of Glasgow built the *SS Adela* for Robert Tedacstle in 1878. Nearly two hundred feet long, she grossed 684 tons, and was intended for the cross-channel passenger and cargo trade. She was constructed with some modern innovations for the handling of livestock, and with improved cabin space for a number of fare-paying passengers and twenty-one crew. The reader will observe from the accompanying advertisements in the illustrations, that she plied the Dublin and Liverpool route until the day she was sunk.

The majority of those who crewed the *Adela* resided in Dublin's inner city, and her captain, Michael Tyrell, who was said to have had connections with the notable sea-faring town of Arklow, resided at No.5 Oxford Road, Ranelagh. He was forty-four years of age when he became the only survivor after the loss of his ship and all her crew in 1917. A study of the *Adela's* crew lists shows that the majority of her crew were Irish, with several exceptions being those listed as coming from Liverpool. Although born in Britain, many sailors who resided in places like Liverpool, were directly descended from Irish families, and in some cases were known to have kept two families, one on either side of the channel.

As was mentioned earlier, the choice of name given to a ship can occasionally tell something of its owner. The name 'Adela' is German in origin, and was brought to England during the Norman Conquest. Unfortunately, in this case we cannot be certain why Robert Tedcastle chose this particular name for his vessel. In the 1850's, Robert purchased Marlay House and Grange, in the parish of Whitechurch, Rathfarnham, from the De La Touche family, and resided there until 1919. The house, 'Marlay', was named after the maiden name of De La Touche's wife, Elizabeth Marlay, who was a daughter of the Rt. Rev. G. Marlay, Bishop of Dromore.

Becoming owner of the home that had once belonged to one of Ireland's wealthiest businessmen bestowed additional prestige on Robert. It did nothing, however, to enhance his reputation during the 1913 lockout; nor of the niggardly attitude he displayed towards his ship's crews and apprentices. After Robert Tedcastle had a new iron collier built for him in Belfast in 1890, he named her after his stately home in the foothills of Dublin. The sentiment disappeared with the vessel when she foundered off Howth Head during a storm in 1902.

On a stormy night, the only survivor from the sixteen crewmen of the SS *Marlay* was a sixteen-year-old boy from Sutton, Michael McGlue. (From the same townland, and said to have been part of the same but wider McGlue family, as Thomas McGlue of the *W. M. Barkley*). Young McGlue was rescued by a steam trawler from Dublin the following day.

Robert Tedcastle's apparent fondness for naming his vessels after his surroundings might seem to indicate a growing affinity with his adopted Dublin. The *Eblana* derived its name from a reference by the notable historian Ptlolemy to an early settlement at the mouth of the Liffey, known as Eblana Civitas. An apparent Irishness began to run through the naming of Tedcastle's ships until the firm was amalgamated with the B&I in 1919.

Those men below in their U-boats were also Christians, and they too had families. Germany's population was predominantly Catholic at the time, and they celebrated Christmas in just the same way as other Catholics the world over. In December of 1917, however, they came to Dublin, Holyhead and the Irish Sea in order to sink ships, kill sailors and close ports. Their activities were accomplished with skill and daring, and on several occasions, their actions were also tempered with a measure of compassion.

Details from *U-100's* war diary, courtesy of the Military Archives at Freiburg, give no indication of any festive celebrations held aboard this submarine on Christmas Day. This is not altogether surprising, as German submarine officers would not normally have recorded such events in the boat's official documents, and it was generally not a matter of record in the Royal Navy either. These men were no different from their enemy however, and it is probable that at the time of departure, a 'little something' was stowed aboard with which to celebrate the religious and festive occasion during their time at sea.

Approximately three hours prior to the *Adela's* departure from the River Liffey, Commander Loe of *U-100* was already counting the cost of a lean patrol. Of the two torpedoes fired for the duration of his patrol hitherto, the first had just missed one of two steamers in 'Quadrant 37' in the Irish Sea. The reason he gave for this failure was that he was too close, and the torpedo passed under the target. This was almost certainly the ship which *UB-123* sent to the bottom ten months later on 10 October, with such a dreadful loss of life. The packed mail boat, *RMS Leinster*, recorded this near-miss after leaving Holyhead on the 27th. Commander Loe fired only one more torpedo for the remainder of his cruise but the second one did not miss its target.

Despite success in this instance, his return journey to Germany must have been a somewhat reluctant one, carrying nine unused torpedoes.

U-100 was completed at the Weser yard in 1917. She was 220 feet long and displaced 1200 tons. She had two forward and two stern torpedo tubes, and carried eleven 20 inch torpedoes. (Some sources quote nine.) She was also armed with a 4.1 inch and one 22 pound gun, and one machine-gun. This class of submarine was powered by twin 900HP MAN diesel engines that could give the boat a surface speed of between 14-17 knots and a maximum surface range in excess of 10,000 miles. The maximum speed submerged was 8-9 knots and she could travel for a 100 miles at 3 knots submerged on her twin 600HP battery powered electric motors.

Loe had set out in *U-100* from Wilmshaven in northern Germany on 8 December 1917, and reached the north of Ireland on the 18th. The ten-day journey had begun disappointingly when the boat failed to make passage through the English Channel and was forced to re-route north about through the Fair Isle Channel. Here, Loe's first possible target was a sailing ship of approximately 1,000 tons, but it was in the vicinity of a torpedo boat. Although he attempted to torpedo the sailing vessel, this was abandoned because of rough seas, and a 'late sighting'. On the following day he spotted the same sailing ship, but by then he considered it to be 'suspicious', and soon dived to avoid another torpedo boat. This was probably one of the Q- or 'mystery' ships playing the innocent in this area. Commander Loe spotted the sailing vessel once more on the 20th, but by this time, two patrol boats were accompanying her. Suspecting a tightening net, *U-100* made tracks in the direction of the North Channel. During the night of the 20th, Commander Loe guided his submarine past several trawlers and guard ships, and south through the North Channel into the Irish Sea. As chance would have it, he probably passed within shouting distance of *U-62,* which was reportedly passing north through the North Channel on the 19th, having left a trail of destruction behind her in the Alley.

The following day, Commander Loe headed towards the Irish coast, where he observed some small steamers but continued to find it impossible to make an attack. After avoiding a destroyer during daylight hours of the 22nd, Commander Loe surfaced off Holyhead during the night. He soon spotted a steamer of between 6,000 and 8,000 tons, and began to set up an attack as it approached. He suddenly broke off this attack, however, when he discovered that the outer doors of his stern torpedo tubes were jammed in the open position. These had to be shut as soon as possible. The submarine was manoeuvred astern, and with the aid of the 'servo motors' the outer doors were closed.

From 23 to 26 December, *U-100* continued to draw a blank, and spent most of the time avoiding fishing boats and patrols, or rejecting 'small' targets. Whatever Commander Loe's difficulties were, not unlike Commander Hashagen, he had no difficulty finding his way around the Alley, as he later reported in his cruise summary:

'Navigation was easy because of good lighting. Along the Irish Sea and in the North Channel lights were lit, marked as in peace.'

About this time, two unconnected but significant events were taking place, and Commander Loe seemed to have been unaware of both. Firstly, given his criss-crossing of the Irish Sea at the time, he was extremely unlucky not to have made contact with the historic *Leviathan* convoy making north for Liverpool.

The second lay with the movements of the very determined Commander Lohs in *UC-75,* who had set out from Zeebrugge on the 22nd to patrol the Irish Sea, and had reached the Skerries at about the same time that *U-100* was off Liverpool Bay on Christmas Day. It remains uncertain whether these submarines were aware of one another, and there is no evidence at this point to suggest that they were about to co-operate in any co-ordinated plan of attack. If they had, it is no exaggeration to state that they might have changed the course of the war.

Commander Loe's ill luck of being in the wrong place at the wrong time by only a few hours meant that he had missed seeing the screen of US destroyers escorting the largest ship in the world up the Irish Sea on the 23rd. Although this convoy was of considerable importance, there was only one ship being escorted. The *Leviathan* and her 9,000 American servicemen was no ordinary vessel but one that had already provoked considerable controversy. (See also chapter 5: The Hunters and the Hunted)

With seemingly no knowledge of the events that had unfolded in Liverpool Bay, Commander Loe headed for Anglesey on 26 December, where he missed the mail boat *Leinster* with his first torpedo on the 27th. Shortly after this failed attack, he surfaced and carried out some overdue repairs. These comprised of trimming the boat by the head, thus raising the stern, in order to remove an assortment of flotsam that had jammed the stern torpedo tubes' outer doors. These repairs lasted several hours, in daylight. At this point, Commander Loe's log contains an interesting reference to the lack of Admiralty patrols in the area.

While the submarine was on the surface, Commander Loe noticed an oil leak from the starboard bunker which was situated between the outer casing and inner pressure hull. After making some calculations, he estimated that there had been a loss of approximately 'six tons' of fuel. The loss of the fuel was worrying but the discovery of the leak had nevertheless cleared up the nagging problem he was having with the increasing weight of his submarine.

Faced with his new fuel problem, Loe altered his earlier decision to return to Germany via the North Channel; he decided to use the much longer route via the south and west of Ireland. Although the distance was considerably greater, he felt this necessary for the following reasons.

If he had proceeded north through the North Channel, and was subsequently detected, patrols might force him back. He would then have been compelled to backtrack over the same ground, and make his return to Germany via the west of Ireland in any event, thus compounding his fuel problems. Unfortunately for the *Adela,* this meant that *U-100* delayed a while longer in the Alley.

No suitable targets had presented themselves off the *Kish light vessel*, and Commander Loe chose to steer once more for the Skerries off Anglesey; it was there that the fate of the small steamer from Dublin was decided.

It was evident from the increased number of reported sightings and contacts with U-boats towards the end of December 1917 that things were beginning to hot up in the Alley. At 11.40 PM on the 27th, Commandeer Loe positioned his submarine on the surface a few miles northeast of the Skerries. The steamer *Adela* was on a course only 350 metres to the south of him, heading for Liverpool. At 11.50 PM, *U-100* submerged and fired one torpedo from tube IV, hitting the approaching vessel amidships on the starboard side. Commander Loe later reported that the vessel was 'heavily loaded', and was about 4,000 tons.

The light often played tricks with the apparent size and interpretation of targets at sea, but U-boat commanders were also well known for a tendency to exaggerate the size of their 'hits' in order to impress their superiors.

Commander Loe observed the final moments of the *Adela* through the submarine's periscope and recorded this brief epitaph:

'Steamer breaks in front of bridge and sinks immediately. According to her shape she must have been a tanker with three masts, tall bridge in middle, no guards noticed.'

The description given of Loe's victim does not seem to fit the *Adela*, but there were no other losses recorded in that area on that night, and it is to *U-100* that the sinking of the *Adela* is accredited.

Not unaware of, but removed from, the struggles for survival that were being acted out on the surface by the surviving crewmembers from the *Adela*, *U-100* and her crew stole silently away into the night, leaving behind a scene of total carnage. Before she finally disappeared, however, Captain Tyrell caught site of the retreating submarine. The next day, Commander Loe was still in the vicinity of 'the sunken steamer' but fled when a destroyer came into view.

The remaining journey by *U-100* around Ireland, and north about to Wilmshaven, almost passed without further incident. On 1 January 1918, Commander Loe was compelled to disobey radio instructions when he was ordered to 'stay out' for a further twenty four hours. As a result of Loe's earlier fuel leakage and the submarine's dangerous fuel level, he ignored the orders, and proceeded into port.

His decision not to attempt a passage through the North Channel, where *UC-75* had been active, and where patrols might surely have been alerted, proved fortuitous for Commander Loe and his crew.

The patrol covered 5,274 nautical miles on the surface, and 397 submerged. *U-100* and crew survived the war.

Many vessels and their crews perished and disappeared without trace, but from the mangled wreckage of the *Adela,* a lone sailor managed to live and tell the tale of the ship's final moments. Captain Tyrell was the only survivor, and he was badly affected by the experience, and spoke very little of it again.

It is extremely difficult to picture the scene, or to understand what went on in the minds of survivors as they struggled for life in the middle of a dark, cold sea. The story unfolds, however, with the help of censored articles and the available reports on the inquest of crewmen J. Burrows, J. McCalum, Patrick Mackay and A. Donaldson. Theirs were the only bodies recovered.

Several days later, there was an unusual display of grief by the coroner, who 'burst into tears' during his summing up of the inquest. He described the incident as 'the enemy's treachery'. Captain Tyrell was also overcome during the proceeding at Holyhead, when he testified that the crew had 'all discharged their duties faithfully and well'.

The night was described as 'moonlit', and the sea as 'choppy but not rough'. As soon as the *Adela* had cleared the Dublin Channel buoys, she would probably have increased her speed to the normal maximum, which might have been as much as nine or ten knots. This meant that she would have cleared the *Kish Light Vessel* a little later than 6 o'clock. Not all masters followed their instructions to steer a zigzag course and to keep lights extinguished, or to sail with their lifeboats slung out. And it is not clear what instructions were given to the crew in this respect on the night.

Little is known about shipboard activity on the *Adela* during that night, other than what would have been the crew's ordinary duties. Together with tea and chat, gunner and sailor customarily found friendship in the galley. The crossing would normally have lasted about eight to ten hours, during which time some of the crew would have taken the opportunity to retire to their bunk for some sleep, and others might just have chatted for the duration of their free time.

As the ship approached the Skerries, one might expect the crew to have considered the sight of land to be a godsend, heralding the imminent escape from the dangers of open water. This was not the case, and in fact, this particular area was probably considered to be the most dangerous part of the whole journey. The U-boats were well known to regularly lie in wait off Anglesey, and the number of shipwreck symbols speckled on the Admiralty chart for this area is testimony to the slaughter of merchantmen that took place there during World War I.

The attack began at 11.50, and pandemonium erupted on the ship. The loud explosion caused by the torpedo hitting the ship was immediately recognised by the crew for what it was. The little steamer suddenly became a sinking mass of twisted metal and strewn animal carcasses. The *Adela* snapped in two just forward of the bridge, and she began to sink immediately. The lifeboats had not been slung out, and those that were not damaged in the violent explosion crashed onto the deck. There was only one lifeboat reported to have survived the explosion; the captain and four others scrambled into it. It had landed on the deck, and floated off when the ship began to sink.

The *Adela* had just disappeared when *U-100* approached the scene of devastation, and it was at this time that Captain Tyrell later recalled that he had got 'a momentary glimpse of the enemy craft stealing away in the gloom of the night.'

The members of the crew who survived the explosion, and managed to reach the lifeboat, were soaked, battered, and soon freezing cold. Lethargy and a mood of hopelessness, brought about by the condition of hypothermia, soon swept over them. It was only two days after the Christmas celebrations when *Adela*'s only survivors found themselves helplessly adrift in a small lifeboat, bobbing about in the dark amongst the remainder of the struggling livestock. The wretched animals lasted only a short time, and the occupants of the small lifeboat bravely struggled to rescue two more crew from the freezing water.

The lifeboat had been damaged when it was wrenched from its davits, and needed exhaustive baling in order for it to remain afloat.

Three of the men were utterly helpless but not quite dead when they were washed out of the lifeboat 'in their senses' before a destroyer arrived on the scene at 2 PM the following day. The crew of the destroyer located the three who had died, and a fourth succumbed soon after. This was the steward Donaldson, from Liverpool.

Captain Tyrell's long years of experience at sea, and his strong build, probably saved him, as he was later described by an *Irish Independent* reporter as being a 'typical master mariner, a man of powerful physique'.

A study of U-boat activity in the Alley for the latter half of World War I shows a surprising amount of success by the U-boats. This was due to the determination shown by the U-boat crews, who successfully but only temporarily disrupted the movement of ships across the channel. Although shipments of supplies and livestock were sometimes forced to remain in port or were diverted to other less threatened ones, such as Belfast, they were often resumed from Dublin after only short periods of time.

The navies of the Allied forces remembered this period in the Alley for the narrow escapes that so many of them had. For the grieving relatives of the victims on both sides of the Alley, it will always remain a Christmas to remember, for quite the opposite reason. It was a period of terror for both sailors and passengers travelling in the Alley.

The shipping casualties rose sharply in December, and after they continued to escalate into January, the censor's office released some articles for publication. These were typified by an article, which appeared in the *Evening Herald* on 12 January 1918, and is reproduced in the illustrations. The proofs of additional articles that were submitted to the censor and later issued with a 'D notice', preventing publication, are also reproduced in the illustrations. In addition, there are copies of telegrams, relating to these proofs, which passed between the Admiralty and the Censor's office. These reproductions help to inform us of the procedures that the Censor's Office followed during this sensitive period of escalating losses.

As was mentioned earlier, it was only three weeks after the *Adela* incident when Lord Decies appealed to the Admiralty for some more gruesome tales of U-boat victims. Winning the war meant not only fighting with guns and bullets but also with the effective weapon of propaganda.

In an effort to exploit this weapon, news of the events that had occurred in December and early January were seized upon almost immediately. Mr Hooper, editor of *the Freeman's Journal,* thought there was a distinct opportunity to be had by publishing accounts of the U-boat attacks and the tragedies that had befallen the victims and their relatives.

Opinions expressed by Mr Hooper during a visit to the censor's office were relayed by its staff in this message to Lord Decies, while he was in London on 9 January 1918:

'As many Dublin families are now suffering so much by the loss of their bread-winners as a result of the submarine activities in the Channel. He (Mr Hooper) considers a little easing of the restrictions, with regard to the publication of such matters, might have good effect on the Irish people, and would create not only a general anti-German but anti-Sinn Féin atmosphere. He desires permission to publish at least names of the victims as soon as possible after the disaster, and then perhaps names of the ships a few weeks after they are sunk.'

He could have added that paper's sales might also improve as a result.

Somehow, Mr Hooper's relationship with the censor's office was perceived by some of his rival papers as being somewhat special. On the occasion of the funeral of Thomas Ashe, the first hunger striker to die in Ireland from being force-fed, an anti-government article by Dr Fogarty, the Bishop of Killaloe, was prevented from being published in most newspapers, but it did appear in the *Freeman's Journal,* on 28 September 1917. This incident gave rise to other newspapers reportedly stating that this could only have occurred because of that newspaper's 'well-known influence with Dublin Castle.'

Concern escalated in respect of the mounting losses of Irish vessels in the Alley. Representations were made to the Admiralty with a view to obtaining better protection, and a number of questions were tabled by Irish MPs in the House of Commons. But somehow, the question of providing additional protection for Irish vessels frequently appeared to become attached to petitions made by those seeking more favourable consideration for bids on lucrative contract tenders to the Admiralty and various ministries. The replies to queries about the protection given to cross-channel shipping were standard enough, i.e. 'doing all in their power', which, in fairness, seemed to have been the case most of the time. The power of the Royal Navy was limited, but it did promise that there would be a review of the procedures in awarding contracts.

The first days of January saw confusion and anxiety spread through many ports on both sides of the Alley. Vessels were overdue, and questions as to their whereabouts went unanswered. Shortly afterwards, small announcements began to disseminate the news slowly, and in a way that would not alert the enemy as to the extent of its successes. By the end of January, the full impact of what had taken place in the Alley since before Christmas had still not been made known, and the details would not emerge until well after the war was over. The carnage amounted to the loss of at least thirty vessels. There had been attacks on numerous others, causing the deaths of a considerable number of seamen and civilians.

The ferocity of the attacks continued, but the first few days of January were the worst of that period. As they began to subside, the shipping firm of Lamport and Holt suffered the loss of another of their steamers, the *Spenser* (4,186 tons). She was arriving from Buenos Aires with a general cargo when she was torpedoed in the George's Channel by *U-61* on the 6th. There is no record of attacks in the Alley between the 7th and the 23rd, when a torpedo was fired, which luckily just missed the liner *Justicia* (32,234 tons). (Attacks by *U-61* ended during her next patrol in the Alley when she was rammed, depth-charged and sunk in the George's Channel on 16 March. Commander Dieckmann and 35 crew were killed.) The attack on the *Justicia* may have come from the submarine *U-103*, which was in the area at the time.

Luck did not remain with the *Justicia,* however. Her fate was finally sealed when she was sunk in July, off Rathlin Island, in a battle that was joined by several U-boats, as described earlier. Three days later, on the 26th, another shipping company badly affected by attacks from U-boats in the channel, the C.D.S.P.Co., lost its passenger and cargo vessel *SS Cork* (1,232 tons) when it was torpedoed by *U-103* off the north coast of Wales while travelling from Dublin to Liverpool. Twelve lives were lost in the attack.

The lull in the latter half of January proved to be only a temporary reprieve, as the U-boats soon began a new wave of attacks in February, with an even greater ferocity. The attacks seemed to concentrate against the larger supply ships and troop-carriers (as described in chapter 5) which were considered so crucial to the success of oncoming 'big push' in France.

The number of sinkings and attacks rose in February to thirty-five, and continued to escalate until they reached fifty-two in March. The level of carnage began to decline after April but many more Irish vessels were either sunk or attacked in the Alley before the war finally came to an end.

It has already been said that some U-boat commanders remained defiant until the war's end, and considered their submarines to be undefeated. In what was probably the last demonstration of this arrogance, two weeks prior to the end of World War I – during a time when peace was actually being negotiated – *UB-116* attempted to gain entrance to Scapa Flow in order to attack elements of the Grand Fleet. (The last British vessel sunk by a torpedo from a U-boat in the north Sea or Atlantic occurred on the 2/11/1918.)

In a last bid to alter the balance of naval power, this submarine made a suicidal attack in what was described in the *Daily Telegraph* many years later, as a 'Desperate German Gamble'. The submarine was detected by listening devices, and all on board were lost when it was blown up by remotely detonated underwater mines. With the exception of *U-34,* which was destroyed two days prior to the Armistice while attempting to flee the Mediterranean in a bid to reach Germany, *UB-116* was the last submarine to be lost on aggressive patrol during World War I.

The U-boats had failed to stem the flow of troops, supplies and food into and out of Britain and Europe once America had entered the war. Without the possibility of significant successes in other spheres of the war, it was a mistake for Germany to continue to use their submarines to slaughter people by sinking merchant ships after early April. There was no possibility of producing enough submarines, or being able to man them with competent crews, in order to achieve any realistic hope of forestalling her impending defeat. Germany's belligerent miscalculation in this respect may have been one of the reasons why she was forced to accept such humiliating treatment after the Armistice.

I have attempted throughout the book to demonstrate how equally important Ireland's geography, her capacity to produce food, and her industries, were to both Britain and Germany during a critical period in World War I. More so, the book is meant to honour the memory of thousands of ordinary merchant sailors who died maintaining this lifeline, and in particular, those who died on small ships which plied the waters between Ireland and England. Accounts of their passing, and those of the sailors who manned the outmatched converted fishing boats, have not been well recorded; the large number of sailing ships and sailors lost by the Scandinavian countries is another example of this. Norway lost well over 2,000 merchant sailors and 915 vessels during the war years.

The following is a list of the sailors who died on the *Adela* when she was torpedoed during a cross-channel voyage in the Irish Sea on 27 December 1917:

SS Adela.
Barry, W. *Fireman.* No.31 Leland Place, Dublin.
Burrows, Samuel J. *Chief engineer.* No.84 Palmerstown Road, Ranelagh, Dublin.
Byrne, P. *Winchman.* No.11 Pigeon House Road, Dublin.
Caldwell, H. *2nd. Engineer.* Liverpool.
Connolly, P. *Carpenter.* Liverpool. (Said to be cousin to the patriot James Connolly)
Corcoran, Patrick. *Cattleman.* No.77, Townsend St., Dublin.
Daly, T. ? Davey, Fred. *Gunner RNR.* No.3 Crofton Avenue, Kingstown, Co. Dublin.
Donaldson, A. *Steward.* Saint Andrews, Liverpool.
Dumbell, Mr. *Engineer.* Liverpool.
Farrell, James. *Cattleman.* ?
Fisher, John. *Seaman.* Lime Street, Dublin.
Fortune, James. *Cattleman.* No.8 Hastings Road, Ringsend, Dublin-.
(Courtown Co. Wexford.)
Halpin, Patrick. *Seaman.* No.52 York Road, Kingstown, County Dublin.
Jones, George. *Lamp trimmer.* Clontarf, Dublin.
(George Jones and W. Barry above were related, and also lost another member of the family when the *Memphian* was torpedoed in the Irish Sea three months earlier.)
Jones, T. *Fireman.* No.100 Lower Gardiner St., Dublin.

Keegan, L. *Cattleman.* Coolock, Dublin.
Mackey, J.P. *Fireman.* No.17 Lr.(Upper.?) Oriel Street, Dublin.
Mangan, F. *Fireman.* Guild Street, Dublin.
Manning, J. *Fireman.(Seaman)* No.64 Dock Street (Townsend Street), Dublin.
McCalum, J. *Seaman.* Mount Street, Dublin.
Murray. *Cattledrover.*
Pitt, M. ?
Prescott, Charles P. *Mate.* Liverpool.
Walsh, A. *Donkeyman.* No.8 Tigh Cottages, Newfoundland St., Dublin.
Wolfe, Christy. *Winchman.* No.22 Leland Place, Dublin.

There was one only one person on board whose status was a little unclear. She was the passenger Christina Kavanagh (Miss). She was twenty-four years of age, and lived at No.25 Queen's Square, Great Brunswick Street (now Pearse Street), Dublin. Miss Kavanagh was reported to have been visiting her sister in England, and was in the care of a crewman and friend of the family, crane-man, Peter Byrne.

All of those who died in the Alley deserve to be mentioned in this book. Unfortunately, far too many were killed to make the task of recording their names practical. Meriting a special exception, are those who died in the incident which took place in the mouth of the Mersey, during the early hours of 28 December. This incident had a drastic impact on one particular group of Liverpool sailors and their families. These sailors were going about their routine duties in a place so close to their harbour that they might never have expected such a disaster to occur.

Designed to sink large ships, the exploding mine laid by *UC-75* had a devastating effect on the 500-ton pilot cutter *Alfred H. Read* and its crew.

There were forty-one men aboard the pilot cutter when the explosion obliterated the vessel at the entrance to the Mersey. Two were lucky to survive; of the other thirty-nine killed, nineteen were pilots.

Listed on page *269* are the names of those pilots and other crewmen.

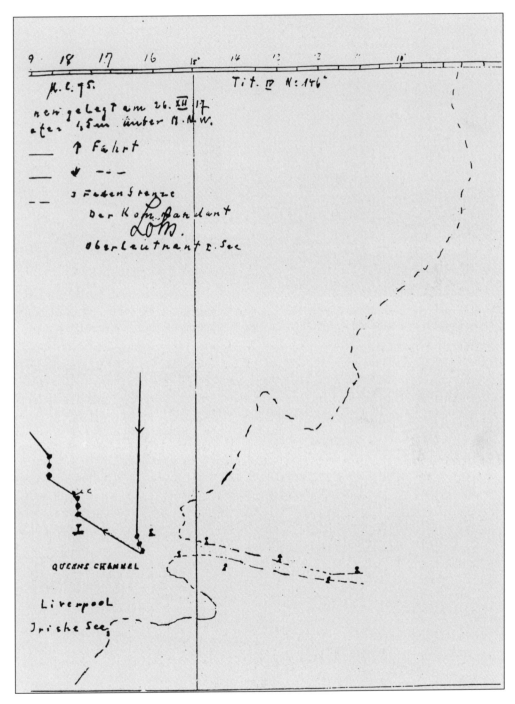

A sketch by Commander Lohs of *UC-75* showing the pattern of mines he laid across the Queen's Channel at the entrance to the Mersey on December 26th. The largest vessel afloat in the world, the troopship *Leviathan*, narrowly missed being sunk by these mines but one did sink the pilot boat *Alfred H. Read* and resulted in a terrible loss of personnel.

The Liverpool pilot boat *Alfred H. Read*. She was sunk on December 28th 1917 at the mouth of the Mersey, probably by a mine laid by *UC-75* on the 26th. Thirty-nine pilots and crew were killed.

The *AMC Leviathan* (*Ex. Vaterland*) built in Germany. Confined in New York after the outbreak of WW1, she was seized by the U.S. Government in April 1917.
She is seen here embarking troops in New York for Europe.
She narrowly escaped being sunk by the minelayer *UC-75* in the Irish Sea on December 26th, 1917, while on her first troop-convoy duty to Liverpool.

Pilot Cutter *Alfred H. Read*

The following are the names of those pilots who ended their lives guiding others.

John Lewis *(Pilot Boat Master)*. Frederick Rogers *(Pilot Boat Master)*. And *pilots,* Charles H. Barnard, James Wookey, Frederick E.T. Penny, James F. Jones, Robert J. Durrant, Robert Taggart, Albert E. Ankers, Alfred A.M. Knowler, Henry Rawson, Henry M. Tibbles, Albert J. Lever, James Birchall, Norman W. Climo, James H. Cross, John F. Cameron, Edgar S. Freeman, William Broadie.

Also lost were 8 apprentices, 2 engineers, 3 fireman, 1 cook, 2 examination officers, 2 signalmen, and 2 Marconi operators.

Conclusion

There are many fine memorials in Ireland erected in honour of those who fell in the Great War, including the Garden of Remembrance, Islandbridge and the Military cemetery on Blackhorse Avenue. There are even a fair share of memorials in churches and towns throughout the country, but sadly, many of these are not in prominent places, and are seldom recognised. There are probably none so fine as those in Saint Patrick's Cathedral, Dublin, which were erected in memory of Irish Regiments and individual officers of prominent lineage. However, they are far away from the eyes and consciousness of the general public.

Honour rolls and ceremonies commemorating those who died during World War I usually represent only broad groupings. Casualties lumped together in this way do not proportionally represent the inordinate suffering that has been experienced by some communities as a result of the war. The small coastal town of Rush, for example, with long seafaring traditions, lost nineteen seamen during World War I. The figures often exclude civilians, who are normally accounted for under the official figures for deaths held in civic records. In the case of merchant-mariners, the statistic is quite separate, and put at approximately 15,000 from vessels that were sunk by enemy action; I cannot say whether every single merchant sailor who died in World War I is included in these statistics. Even so, the figure gives no indication as to the disproportionate number of these that hailed from the same small coastal and maritime communities on both sides of the Alley. In Ireland's case, the death toll exceeds 1,000, and most of these hailed from ports on the east coast and from Cork.

At the beginning of World War I many ships on both sides were seized by the enemy in foreign ports, and many of the merchant sailors were made prisoner for the duration of the war. The following list *(on page 275)* appeared in the *Irish Times* on 8 October 1917, and gives the names of Irish merchant-sailors who were taken prisoner. It was extracted from a more comprehensive list, which had been released by the Press Bureau and published in the *London Times*. It makes quite clear, how certain family names and places that are commonly associated with strong traditions of seafaring activity, were affected by the war. It was promised that further lists would follow:

Photos of victims from torpedoed ships in the 'Alley' prior to Xmas 1917.
Published in the *Saturday Herald* on January 12th, 1918.

Commander Loe and SM *U-100* with crowd and crew duting unknown celebraions at Kiel.
U-100 was not the most successful of U-boats but her crew all survived the war.
Almost 5,000 other German submariners didn't.

Christopher Wolfe (WW1) who died when the *SS Adela* was torpedoed by *U-100*, in December , 1917.
Shown here with his wife Elizabeth.

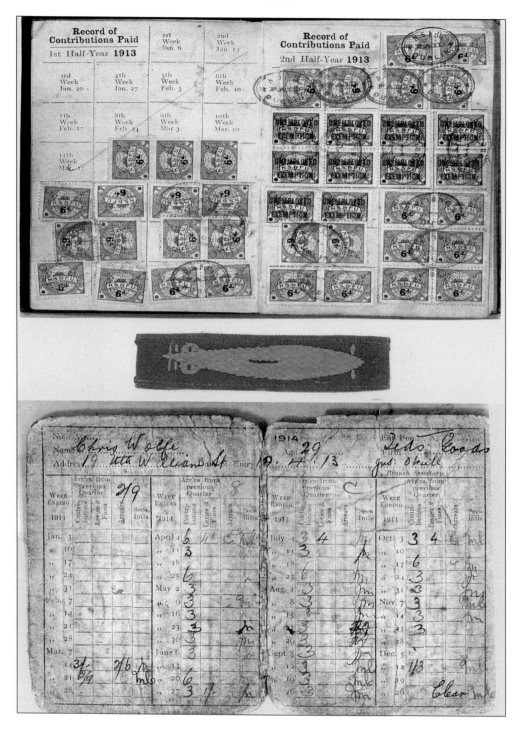

Kit Wolfe's Irish Transport, and Seaman's Union cards with torpedo badge.
Note the unemployment stamps for the period during the labour troubles in 1913.

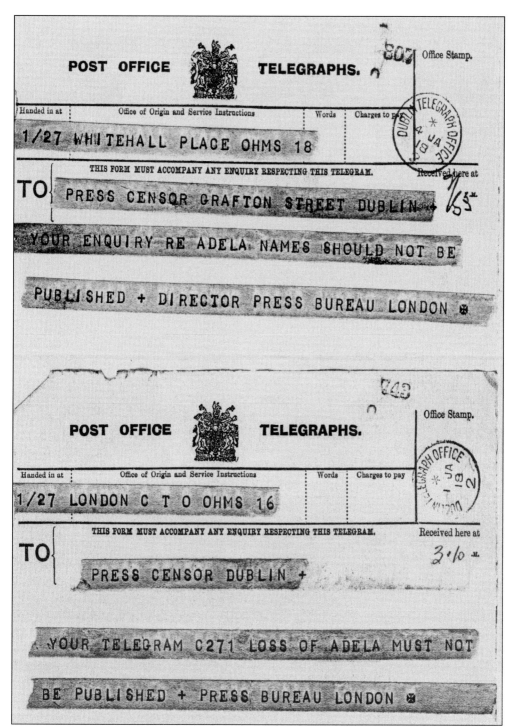

Urgent telegrams from Admiralty to the censor's office at Grafton Street, Dublin, refusing permission for any publication to contain mention of the 'loss' of *Adela* or the 'names' of those aboard her.

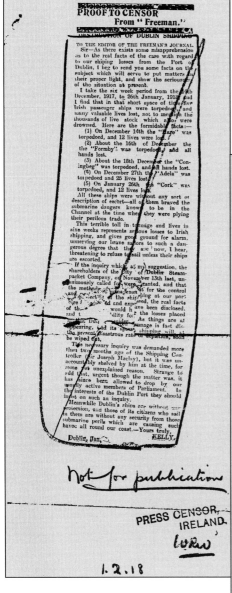

Censored article by *Freeman's Journal* on the sinking of Irish steamers before Christmas 1917.

Censored article on the sinking of the *Adela* by the *Irish Times*.

The Irish Times on 8 October 1917

Anthoney, J. 2nd Engineer, Dublin. *City of Cadiz.*

Farrell, L. Fireman, Dublin. *City of Cadiz.*

Bent, W. 2nd Officer, Dublin. *City of Berlin.*

Carroll, J. Carpenter, Kildare. *City of Berlin.*

Clarke, P. Seaman, Dublin. *City of Berlin.*

Caffey, M. Seaman, Dublin. *City of Berlin.*

Campbell, T. Steward, Drogheda, *City of Berlin.*

Blacklock, J. Steward, Dublin. *City of Munich.*

Cavanagh, J. Chief officer, Belfast. *City of Munich.*

Byrne, P. Chief officer, Dundalk. *City of Belfast.*

Caffrey, C. Ist Engineer, Dublin. *City of Belfast.*

Donnelly, J. Seaman, Dublin. *City of Belfast.*

Green, W. Fireman, Dublin. *City of Belfast.*

Dnoa, L. (uncertain spelling.) Seaman, Dublin. *City of Hamburg.*

Ford, W. Fireman. Dublin. *City of Hamburg.*

Fortune, J. Seaman, Gorey, Wexford. *City of Hamburg.*

E….,(?) J. 2nd Officer, Dublin. *City of Hamburg.*

Daly, T. Fireman, Kinsale. *Rubens.*

Doyle, W. 2nd Mate, Arklow. *Sprightly.*

Drammery, P. Seaman, Cork. *Victorian Transport.*

Duffin, J. Steward, Wexford. *Dacre Hills.*

These simple merchant sailors sought no glory nor honour but only wages to feed their families. In contrast, there are men who were fortunate to have found themselves in positions to make significant achievements during their lifetime, and many of these have long since and continue to be remembered.

The remains of Arthur Guinness, for example, lie with those of his ancestors in the ancient but beautiful church ruin and graveyard, designated a 'national monument', at the little-known parish of Oughterard in County Kildare. Perched on top of a hill, overlooking the rich 'Plains of Kildare', this is a very private and little-frequented place. To the general public, Arthur Guinness's name is recalled with no difficulty, and is toasted by the thousands of tourists that pass through his brewery and salute his effigy in Saint Patrick's Cathedral.

Probably remembered by anyone in Dublin who has ever burned coal in their fireplace, Robert Tedcastle was laid to rest in the well-tended family crypt in his old parish church of Whitechurch, Rathfarnham, not long after the war ended. The church is adjacent to what was once his large stately home, set in the beautiful sprawling parklands of Marlay Grange. Both of these men were laid to rest in fine style, and their place in history has been secured. In contrast, the one-time employees of these well-known gentlemen, who died aboard their masters' ships, the *W. M. Barkley* and the *Adela,* retired from this life in a less dignified and most violent way. They sailed the Alley for wages, when it was known to harbour a deadly enemy that was attacking and sinking ships at alarming rates.

Their ships exploded beneath them, and their bodies were never recovered. Their employers suffered no loss but the sailors' families were deprived of the full and comforting mourning ritual, and their spirits still roam the waters deep.

As it says on the fine memorial on Liverpool's dockside, albeit a dedication to distinguished officers, lost at sea: 'They have no grave but the sea.'

It is to be regretted that the descendants of such brave and innocent victims are unable to visit a simple carving on a stone in a quiet place, which marks their passing. Or why there should not be a more fitting and prominent tribute to their sacrifice for our freedoms? Other than a tiny granite plaque on the Seamen's Mission on Eden Quay in Dublin, there is no other public monument in Dublin City, which recalls the large number of Irish merchant seamen that were lost during World War I.

He wasn't orphaned but he did become the son of a war widow. Christy Wolfe's son, also called Christy, and known as Kit, followed like many others in the salty tradition of their forefathers, and served on merchant vessels. Another world war arrived in 1939, and Christy Junior must have broken his mother's heart when he followed in his father's footsteps and left home to sail in the dreaded North Atlantic convoys. Unlike his father's bad luck, he made fourteen crossings and survived against all the odds. His son, Shay Wolfe, for medical reasons, was never able to follow in this tradition, but he is responsible for inspiring this book, and has supplied many details of his grandfather's history. He has added this final but unusual little reminiscence from his family history.

Shay Wolfe's mother, Brigid Murphy, married his grandfather's son, Christy Wolfe Junior. His mother's sister, Nancy Murphy, married Jimmy Farrell Junior, the son of cattleman Jimmy Farrell. Both of their husbands' fathers were lost together on the *Adela*.

To my knowledge, the remains of the *Adela* have never been visited by scuba divers. She lies in relatively deep water off Anglesey, and is unlikely to attract the attentions of these inquisitive sportsmen. She has remained, after all, an insignificant little cross-channel steamer, which has almost been forgotten.

Like Shay, there are many who relish the huge wealth of our maritime heritage, and we are steeled by the few unflagging and dedicated maritime historians who continue with their efforts to highlight the rich tapestry of our maritime past. We find it our duty to recall, and to celebrate the memory of those who were sacrificed in one of nature's most wondrous elements, but one which man can turn so violent.

Also lost in the broad statistical groupings, the scale of losses has grown even hazier with the passage of time. Many families lost several of their loved ones, sons and bread-winners, and many were left to brood over those who were never seen again and never buried, during the difficult years that followed. Many of those who survived the sicknesses, maiming from bullets and bombs, poison gas, inhuman living conditions in stinking trenches, rotten food, tuberculosis, and the explosion of their ships without

warning in the cold seas returned broken men. Many returned to Ireland only to face forced emigration after the serious economic decline that followed the country's new found independence from Britain. Many were afflicted with incapacitating injuries for the remainder of their lives.

After demobilisation, many of those that had come from the farming communities could not bring themselves to leave the cities to return home. The newspapers soon forgot the atrocities of war, and once more striking workers were being battened in the streets. The new enemy was the lack of work, and a shortage of food. Ireland's economic difficulties lasted until it was time to fight the same battles all over again. Irishmen once more took up arms in foreign armies, and 'went away' again. The memory of the pain and the sacrifices made during the previous Great War faded into the mists of time, when the world began to experience the new horrors of yet another emergency.

When some of the bitterness had subsided, many men from both sides were spurred on to speak out against the evils of World War I, and the terrible toll of death and destruction it had claimed. In 1932, Commander Hashagen published some memories of his escapades in *U-62*. The book's final pages contained the following address he made to his fellow Germans, and his words also befits the dreadfull toll of suffering and death that occurred in the Alley:

'Can you hear it still . . . how do know what you have lost. How much of your being and your hopes lie sunk . . . overgrown by barnacles and seaweed enveloped in the silent depths of the Sea?'

Appendix

I expressed certain views in *Death in the Irish Sea* which further research can now clarify. The *RMS Leinster*, originally built by Lairds of Birkenhead for the City of Dublin Steam Packet Company at a cost £95,905, was insured at the time of her loss for £250,000. This was the amount that the company finally received in compensation for her loss.

Relatives of servicemen, crew and 'some passengers' who were lost in the tragedy received 'servicemen's pensions', and pensions due to them under the War Risk Insurance Scheme. No record of any compensation for the loss of property or life that might have been paid to relatives of the 'civilians' lost in the disaster has been uncovered. In respect of the huge charitable collection, 'The Leinster Fund', which was mounted and organised by prominent citizens from the Mansion House, Dublin for this purpose, no records appear to have survived. The method of distributing the considerable sum collected also remains unclear.

The *RMS Leinster* did not come under the normal operations of harbours, where the Admiralty could order vessels to sail when it considered it safe to do so, or prevent them from sailing when it was not. Rather, the mail boats were always compelled to sail. Refusal to do so resulted in financial penalties that were applied under the terms of their contract with the Post Office. Failure to sail did occur, but very seldom. The penalties were financial but the crews remained safe, until their luck ran out on 10 October 1918.

The antagonistic relationship that existed between the Admiralty, the Shipping Controller, the L.N.W.R.Co., the B.I.S.P.Co. and the C.D.S.P.Co. lasted for the duration of the war. The exact parameters under which the C.D.S.P.Co.'s vessels operated during that period remain somewhat difficult to comprehend fully, but the broad outline of the government's implementation of the War Risk Insurance Scheme was as follows.

Ships were insured by their owners or by groups of owners through brokers. They in turn would spread the risk through several insurers. This was not an uncommon practice, where there was a requirement to cover a large risk, and remains a common practise to this day. In the event of a vessel being lost as a result of enemy action, these insurers paid out and then sought recompense from the government under the War Risk Insurance Scheme. However, if a company sailed its vessels in direct contravention of the Shipping Director's recommendations or Admiralty instructions, the War Risk recompense scheme could be deemed inapplicable.

Difficulties with the administration of the scheme were not uncommon. For instance, with the case of the Waterford steamer *Formby,* the Maritime Company War Risk Underwriters contested that she was not lost because of the war but as a result of bad weather. Compensation was not forthcoming until the insurers lost the case in the courts in June 1919.

A modern-day comparison might be made with the initial reactions by governments after terrorists attacked the Twin Towers in New York, on 11 September 2001 with hijacked aeroplanes. After these losses, and the president of the United States' declaration of 'war against terrorists', insurers withdrew cover for aeroplanes in certain circumstances. Governments then moved to protect the commercial interests of their national carriers and underwrote any loss by the insurers. But where this left non-national and smaller carriers, or others who might suffer financially from the outbreak of 'war', wasn't made clear.

The value and moral justification for censorship during war is not disputed, but unless certain issues are subsequently redressed during a more peaceful period, at a time when freedom has been restored to the press, the record of historical events can remain distorted.

A simple example of this was the case of the *Leinster*, when so many people still ask why such a terrible tragedy was almost forgotten. Obviously, the horrors of World War I were overshadowed by those of World War II, but little balance was ever restored between the persistent portrayals of German servicemen in a cruel and often sadistic light, and the actual events. It would also appear that events in Ireland and the significance of the German U-boat attacks in its waters were deliberately and continually underplayed for reasons other than ordinary wartime security.

Much of World War I's history was written before World War II – and by many who took part in it. Many British histories, which include an account of this tragic episode, record the casualty figure from the *Leinster* disaster as being in the low hundreds. This figure only reflected the civilian casualties and omitted the major portion of the overall number, who were servicemen of various nationalities. Mention of them was prohibited at the time of the incident and for long afterwards. The official toll for those killed as a result of the attack on the *Leinster* in the Irish Sea on 10 October 1918 is 501. This figure is put as high as 527 by John Terraine in *Business in Great Waters*. Despite what is written today, many history books will always contain the much lower and less dramatic, civilians-only, figure, thus helping to ease this event down the pecking order of 'atrocities' and into obscurity.

The fact, that in some publications the lower toll is sometimes qualified by the phrase 'this figure does not include military personnel' strikes me as being a little disingenuous. The true figure sometimes appearing in an often-unread part of a book, resulting in the reader being misled. Although many war crimes were listed when World War I ended, and their perpetrators pursued, the attack on the *RMS Leinster* was not amongst them.

The credit for sinking the *RMS Leinster* has officially been attributed to *UB-123*. As she did not return from her mission, this was only deduced from her operational instructions, and subsequent assessment of her 'coming in' communications with *UB-125*, off the northeast coast of Scotland. *UB-123* was later reported to have been lost in that area while returning to Germany, presumably after striking a mine in the northern barrage.

The credit given to *UB-123* for this sinking has been questioned on several occasions since. In more recent times, the credit for sinking the *Leinster,* and the *SS Dundalk* four days later, has alternatively been given to *U-90*. This submarine was certainly in the general area at the appropriate time, but similarly, the action is again unconfirmed. The confusion is not helped when one considers the fact that between the beginning of October 1918 and the end of the war six weeks later, five known U-boats operated in the Alley. These sank ships between 2 and 21 October. In order of ships sunk, these were as follows:

10/10/1918. *RMS Leinster* sunk by *UB-123* in the Irish Sea.
10/10/1918. *SS Maja* sunk by *UB-126* off county Down.
12/12/1918. *SS Laila* sunk by *UB-126* in the Irish Sea. (Began return voyage to Germany on this day through the North Channel.)
14/10/1918. *SS Dundalk* sunk by *UB-123* in the Irish Sea.
16/10/1918. *SS Pentwyn* sunk by *U-90* in the north end of George's Channel.
17/10/1918. *SS Bonvilston* sunk by *UB-92* in the North Channel.
18/10/1918. *SS Hunsdon* sunk *by UB-92* south east of county Down.
18/10/1918 *RFA Industry* sunk by torpedo in the same area as the *Hunsdon*.
     (This sinking and her twenty fatalities was not made public until twelve
     months after the event. The British submarine *R8* was operating in this area,
     and some believe the *Industry* to have been a Q-ship.)
21/10/1918. *SS Saint Barchan* sunk by *U-105* off county Down. (This U-boat did not
     enter the Alley until the 18/10/1918. This was also the last sinking by a U-boat
     in Irish waters.)

In respect of which U-boat was responsible for the sinking of the *Leinster,* no confirmation can be gleaned from the above, except to say that two or maybe three of the above U-boats were present in an area, during a time frame that would have made it possible for either of them to attack her. As *U-105* and *UB-126* were not in the Irish Sea at the time, they are definitely ruled out.

It would appear that some of these submarines were going off patrol, and being replaced by others coming in, but the full details of these movements cannot be confirmed without further in-depth study of the operational details of each of the submarines.

A report was received from the Admiralty by the commodore at Larne, which stated that two submarines were passing through the North Channel, and were expected to be in the Irish Sea on the evening of 14 October. According to *British Vessels Lost at Sea,* there were two failed attacks off north Wales during this period. The first was against the *SS Sheerness,* on 10 October 1918, and the second was against the *SS Dara.*

According to U-boat archives, both of these attacks were carried out by the very successful submarine *U-90*, which might have made carrying out the fatal attack on the *Leinster* fifty miles to the east seem a little unlikely, but certainly not impossible.

We might therefore conclude that *U-90, UB-123* and *UB126* were equally capable of being in the right place at the right time in order to sink the *Leinster.* As there was no claim by *UB-126* in this regard, we are down to the remaining two.

In September and October, the Alley had a large volume of convoys and solitary vessels passing through it. Many vessels were lost, and there was some criticism as to the effectiveness of the patrol vessels, and their apparent delay in coming to the rescue of the *Leinster*'s victims in particular. It was probably unfortunate that this was at a time when the effectiveness of patrol vessels was being badly affected by an outbreak of the 'flu'. A report from Larne relating to this matter read:

'Influenza continues to seriously affect the patrols. 9 or 10 ships are out of action with no crews. 138 cases in bed in hospital and in various extemporised sick quarters, while several cases are sick in their houses.'

German shipyard figures for this period show that UB coastal-class submarines were being completed more quickly and in greater numbers, and that they were becoming more daring - but they still lacked sufficient numbers of experienced officers and crew. It was reported that some German commanders had complained that these were superior vessels, and that they had greater potential than the longer-to-complete and more-expensive U-class ones.

In a bid for superiority or perfection, there had been too many design changes and improvements made, where a single type should have been settled upon early, and mass-produced in line with American 'Liberty' methods. These were being honed in respect of the latest UB-type programme in 1918 but by then it was too late.

Using the sinking of the *Leinster* as a benchmark of a type, in his book, *Indiscretions of the Naval Censor,* published in 1920, none other than the Chief Naval Censor, Rear-Admiral Sir Douglas Brownrigg, catalogued another inaccuracy that might have twisted the mater of record.

In an explanation given for the value of the understandable restrictions placed on the publication of trains' and ships' timetables during the war, he stated:

'The convenience of the public was borne in mind, but still more so the safety of the ships, and it says much for the care taken by all and sundry that no cross-channel craft was lost until late in 1918, when the *Leinster* was sunk in daylight in the Irish Channel.'

I don't know exactly what meaning Admiral Brownrigg intended to be taken from his words 'cross-channel craft'. But considering all of the craft that crossed the Channel, all the craft that were sunk, and all of the lives that were lost on them, before and after the *Leinster* incident, one cannot help wondering, just how long limiting the truth must continue after events.

Omissions, untruths and bias have twisted the details and influenced the memory and record of important historic events forever. The extent and importance of the U-boat war in the Alley during World War I has not been made known. The result has been a lack of understanding an even misinterpretation of the actual events that took place there. This situation may ultimately be very difficult, and take prolonged effort, to rectify.

Bibliography.

A History Of The Port Of Dublin.- H.A. Gilligan. Gill&McMillan, 1988.

America's Forgotten Pandemic.- Alfred W. Crosby. Cambridge University Press, 1989.

An Cosantoir. (Issues of 1983, 1988, 1989, 1990.) Defence Forces of Eire in-house magazine.

Beam (Vol.10,1978. Vol.13, 1982. Vol.7, 1975.)- Journal of the Irish Lighthouse service.

Bright Light, White Water.- Bill Long, New Island Books, 1993.

British Vessels Lost At Sea.- Patrick Stephens Limited, 1976.

Business In Great Waters.- John Terraine. Leo Cooper, London, 1989.

Clyde And Other Coastal Steamers.- Duckworth & Langmuir. T. Stephenson & Son Ltd., Mersyside, 1977.

Danger Zone. - E.K. Chatterton. Rich & Cowan Ltd. London, 1934.

David Beatty.- Rear-Admiral W.S. Chambers. Hodder and Stoughton, London, 1951.

Donegal Shipwrecks.- Ian Wilson. Impact Printing, Colraine, 1998.

Endless Story.– Captain T.D. Taffrail R.N. Hodder & Stoughton, London, 1931.

Fifty Ships That Saved The World. - Philip Goodhart. Heinman, London, 1965.

Gallant Gentlemen - E.K. Chatterton. Hurst & Blackett, Limited, 1934.

German Warships of World War I. - British Library Cataloguing in Publication Data, Greenhill Books, London, 1992

Guinness Time.- Internal company publication, 1950.

In Time Of War.- Robert Fisk. Andre Deutsche Ltd., London, 1983.

Indiscretions of The Naval Censor.– Rear-Admiral, Sir Douglas Brownrigg. Cashel & Co., 1920.

Ireland- Atlantic Gateway.- Tim Phelan. John Lane The Bodley Head, London, 1941.

Ireland in the Great War– Charles James O'Donnell. Athol Books, Belfast, 1992.

Ireland's War Industries, 1361-1987. – John Kelleher. Cork, 1992.

John Kelly Ltd. & History.- Ian Wilson.

Journal of the Upper Ards Historical Society. - Jim Blaney. No.6, 1982.

Lion of the Fold. - Donal Nevin, Gill & McMillan Ltd., 1998.

Maritime Arklow. - Frank Forde. The Glendale Press, 1988.

Merchantmen at Arms.- David W. Bone. Ctto & Windus, 1936.

Michael Collins.– Tim Pat Coogan. Arrow Books, London, 1990.

Modern Irish Trade And Industry. – E.J.Riordan. Methuen & Co. Ltd., London, 1920.

Pull Together. The Memoirs of Admiral Sir Lewis Bayly. – George G. Harrap & Co Ltd., London, 1939.

Room 40.- Patrick Beezley. Hamish Hamilton Ltd., London, 1982.

Sea Breezes (Magazine) July, 1982.

Sea Killers In Disguise. – Tony Bridgeland. Leo Cooper, Barnsley, 1999.

Seas Of Adventure.- E.K. Chatterton.- Hurst and Blackett Ltd., London, 1936.

Ships Monthly.- A periodical magazine.

The B&I Line.- Hazel Smyth. Gill & McMillan, 1984.

The Dark Invader.- Captain von Rintelen. Peter Davies Ltd., London, 1933.

The Enemy Within.- Captain Henry Landau. G.P. Putnam's Sons, 1937.

The Eyes Of The Navy.- Admiral Sir William James. Methuen & Co. Ltd, London, 1955.

The Germans In Cork.- Lady Mary Carbery. The Talbot Press, Dublin, 1917.

The Grand Fleet.- Admiral Viscount Jellicoe. Cassell & Co. Ltd., London, 1919.

The Hay Plan.– Jerome Aan de Wiel. The Irish Sword Vol. XXI. No.86, 1999.

The Imperial War Museum Book of 1918. Year of Victory.-Malcolm Brown, Sidgwick & Jackson, 1998.

The Kynoch Era in Arklow. - Hilary Murphy.

The Last Days of Dublin Castle. – Diaries of Mark Sturgis. Produced by Michael Hopkinson. Irish Academic Press, 1999.

The Last Voyages Of The Waterford Steamers.- Richard McElwee, The Book Centre, (Waterford Ltd.) 1993.

The Life And Letters Of Walter H. Page.- B.J.Hendrick. London, 1924.

The Log of a U-BOAT Commander. - Ernst Hashagen. Germany 1931.

The Queenstown Patrol, 1917. The Diary of Commander Joseph Knefler Taussig, US Navy. – Edited by William N. Still, Jr. Naval War College Press, Rhode Island.,1996.

The Storm Passed By.- Trevor Allen, Irish Academic Press, 1996.

The Zimmermann, Telegram.- Barbara W.Tuchman. MacMillan Publishing Co., New York,1958.

Three Wars With Germany.- A.J. Peaslee and Admiral Sir Reginald Hall. New York,1944.

Too Proud To Fight. – Patrick Devlin. Oxford University Press, London, 1974.

US Naval Air Station Wexford 1918.– An Irish times historian award winning paper by Breda Carthy & Veronica Keeling.

U-Boat Intelligence 1914-1918.- Robert M.Grant. Archon Books, Conneticut, 1969.

When The U-boats Came To America.- William Bell Clark. Little, Brown, & Co., Boston, 1929.

U-Boats Destroyed.- Paul Kemp. Arms and Armour Press, London. 1997.